VISUAL QUICKSTART GUIDE

WORDPRESS 2

Maria Langer
Miraz Jordan

 Peachpit Press

Visual QuickStart Guide
WordPress 2
Maria Langer & Miraz Jordan

Peachpit Press
1249 Eighth Street
Berkeley, CA 94710
510-524-2178 • 800-283-9444
510-524-2221 (fax)

Find us on the Web at: www.peachpit.com

Peachpit Press is a division of Pearson Education

Editors: Nancy Davis, Tracy O'Connell
Indexer: Julie Bess
Cover Design: Peachpit Press
Production: Maria Langer, David Van Ness

Colophon

This book was produced with Adobe InDesign CS and Adobe Photoshop 7.0 on a dual-processor Power Macintosh G5. The fonts used were Utopia, Meta Plus, and PIXymbols Command.

Notice of Rights

Notice of Liability

Trademarks

ISBN 0-321-45019-1

9 8 7 6 5 4

Printed and bound in the United States of America.

Dedications

To Mike,
my husband of 22 years
(or something like that).

With love,

Maria

To Deb.

With love,

Miraz

Thanks from Maria

To Miraz, for bringing her vast knowledge of WordPress to this project and answering the seemingly stupid questions I managed to come up with regularly.

To Nancy Davis and Tracy O'Connell, for putting up with lengthy delays and uncertain futures, not to mention the usual wait, wait, *hurry* situations that have characterized many of my projects these days. (I'm getting old, but am determined to reach my goal of 100 books before burnout causes brain death.)

To David Van Ness, for his usual upbeat, can-do attitude and production assistance.

To Julie Bess for another index, quickly and expertly prepared.

To the Camden Lady, for allowing us to show off her blog as a sample in the Introduction of this book.

To the WordPress development team, the plugin authors, the support volunteers, and open source programmers everywhere, for making WordPress and other free software available and easy to use.

And to Mike, for the usual reasons.

Visit Maria on the Web at

Maria Langer, the Official Web Site* and WebLog**:
www.marialanger.com

Thanks from Miraz

To Maria, for inviting me to join her in this exciting project, and freely sharing her expertise and experience.

To Rachel McAlpine, for bounteous support and encouragement.

To Virginia DeBolt, for sending me some stats to look at when I needed them, and the members of the Wise Women mailing list for asking great questions at just the right time.

To the WordPress team for making such great software, and the plugin authors, theme designers, Codex writers, forum contributors and bloggers for helping to make it such a versatile platform for self-expression, communication and community.

To my friends Carol and Lise, and my partner Deb, just for being themselves.

Visit Miraz on the Web at

TiKouka:
mactips.info

Table of Contents

Introduction

Introduction to WordPress

WordPress 2 is the latest version of the powerful and flexible Open Source project that puts blogging within reach of millions. With WordPress, you can set up a weblog on the WordPress.com service, on your ISP's server, or on your own server for complete control over your blog, its appearance, and its content. WordPress is customizable through the use of template tags and extendible through the use of hundreds of plugins. Best of all, WordPress is free.

This Visual QuickStart Guide will help you learn WordPress by providing step-by-step instructions, plenty of illustrations, and a generous helping of tips. On these pages, you'll find everything you need to know to get up and running quickly with WordPress—and a lot more!

This book was designed for page flipping. Use the thumb tabs, index, or table of contents to find the topics for which you need help. If you're brand new to WordPress, however, I recommend that you begin by reading at least the first three chapters and this Introduction. In them, you'll find the information you need to understand how WordPress works, install and configure WordPress, and add content to your blog.

This introduction explains what blogging is, takes you on a tour of a typical WordPress blog, explains how WordPress works, and discusses options for setting up WordPress.

Introduction to Blogging

Blog is short for *weblog*, which is a compound word formed from *Web* and *log*.

The first weblogs appeared in the late 1990s as a way to share links and commentary with Web site visitors. The earliest bloggers would read an article on the Web and create a weblog entry or *post* with a link to that article, often with some personal comments about the article. Since then, the number of blogs available on the Internet has soared to an estimated 20 million.

Most blogs focus on specific topics, making them especially appealing to readers interested in those topics. For example, blogs can be used to express political opinions (**Figures 1** and **2**), share tips for using computers (**Figure 3**), provide community information (**Figure 4**), or publish a personal online journal (**Figure 5**).

Some blogs have become quite popular and are quoted in the press. Others, written by influential bloggers, may change public opinion about controversial topics. But most blogs appeal to a smaller group of readers, some of whom read the blog regularly and share their comments with other readers.

Most weblogs offer the following features:

◆ Automatic creation of Web pages based on the contents of posts. The most recent post appears at the top of the home page or the category page for the post's assigned category.

◆ Automatic formatting of Web pages based on a predefined template or *theme*. Change the blog's theme and the entire site's appearance changes automatically.

◆ The ability to include links and images, like any other Web page.

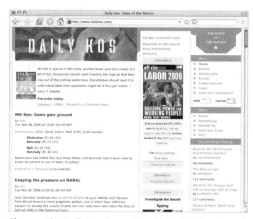

Figure 1 The Daily Kos is a political blog leaning toward the left.

Figure 2 Captain's Quarters is a political blog that leans toward the right.

Figure 3 Miraz's TiKouka offers news and tips for Macintosh users.

Figure 4 Maria runs a blog-powered site with information about the town of Wickenburg, AZ.

Figure 5 Maria's Web site includes her blog, with lots of stories and opinions.

Figure 6 If you're a new blogger, read the "Introduction to Blogging" on the WordPress.org Web site.

◆ Automatic archiving of old posts by category and date.

◆ The ability of readers to enter comments about a post, thus starting an online discussion of its contents.

◆ RSS feeds, which allow readers to have blog posts delivered to them in their newsreader software. This makes it easy for readers to monitor dozens of blogs and to refer to your posts in their own blogs.

◆ Links to related sites or blogs, offering blog readers similar content.

WordPress offers all of these features and more, making it a powerful and flexible blogging tool.

It's easy to understand the appeal of blogging. What easier way is there to get your thoughts and opinions out on the Web?

✔ Tip

■ WordPress.org's article, "Introduction to Blogging" (codex.wordpress.org/ Introduction_to_Blogging; **Figure 6**) provides a wealth of information of interest to new bloggers.

BLOGGING

Anatomy of a WordPress Blog Page

Although the appearance and features in a WordPress blog can vary depending on the theme file that determines its appearance and any plugins that might be installed, there are several basic features that can be found in most WordPress blogs. On these pages, we show you some pages from a sample blog, Camden Lady (`camdenlady.wordpress.com`; **Figures 7** and **8**) and explain the commonly found blog components they include.

1. Header

The header, as you might imagine, appears at the top of each page. It normally contains the name of the blog and a brief description.

2. Links to static pages

WordPress enables you to include static pages in your blog. Most bloggers use them to provide information about the blog or themselves, but they can be used for any content. Links to static pages can appear in the header, as shown here, in the sidebar, or elsewhere.

3. Posts

Posts are individual entries in the blog. Each post normally includes the post title, the post date (and time), and the post author (if the blog has more than one poster). Posts can be as long or as short as you like. In some blogs, long entries are truncated and a Read More link appears so readers can read the entire article. This makes it possible to keep the home page short. As you can see here, posts can also include images and links to other pages. Comment links offer access to comments by readers, along with a comment entry form (**Figure 8**).

Figure 7 The home page for a typical WordPress.com blog.

Figure 8 Clicking the title of a post or a Comments link displays the post and its comments in a page with a comments form.

4. Footer

A footer appears at the bottom of each page. It normally includes copyright information and may include details about the blog's theme. In some blog themes, you can find the RSS feed links in the footer.

5. Sidebar

The sidebar, which also appears on every page, usually includes a variety of navigation links and other features:

◆ **Search form** makes it possible to search the entire blog for entries that match a search word or phrase.

◆ **Calendar** displays links for dates with posts. Click a link to view that day's posts. You can also use links in the calendar to view previous or next months.

◆ **Recent posts** lists recent posts. This is especially useful if you only display a few posts on the home page.

◆ **Category** list displays a list of all categories in the blog. Categories are used to group entries by topic. Click a category name to view a page with recent entries in that category.

◆ **Archive** is a list of months for which entries exist. Click a month name to view entries for that month.

◆ **Links** lists favorite blogs and other Web sites. Links are usually organized by link category. In this example, you can see Blogroll and Interesting sites.

◆ **Feeds** are links or buttons for accessing post and comment RSS feeds.

◆ **Meta**, when present, lets users log in or register and commonly includes links to check XHTML and CSS coding.

Understanding WordPress

WordPress isn't your typical computer computer program. For example, it doesn't run on your computer, like Microsoft Word. It isn't a plugin for your Web browser, like QuickTime or Adobe Reader. Instead, it's a Web publishing system built on PHP and MySQL, both of which run on Unix.

Although that may sound scary, it shouldn't. As you'll see in this book, you can create and maintain a WordPress blog without knowing a single Unix, PHP, or MySQL command. But, as you'll see in the book's later chapters, knowing these languages can give you more power when going beyond the basics to customize WordPress.

How WordPress works

WordPress uses PHP commands on a PHP-compatible Web server to communicate with a MySQL database. On installation, WordPress creates the required tables in the database and fills them with sample and default information.

When you use your Web browser to administer your blog, your browser sends commands to add and modify entries in the MySQL database. In fact, the content for your entire blog is stored in a single MySQL database file.

When readers visit your blog, their Web browsers send PHP commands to your MySQL database. The database contents are returned to their Web browsers for them to read.

To display blog contents and administration screens properly, WordPress uses *theme* files which include templates for displaying various kinds of information and pages. These plain text files combine PHP, XHTML, and CSS codes to control how content is presented on your site.

WordPress offers many theme files to choose from, so you don't have to create them from scratch. As you learn more about WordPress and how it works, you may be able to modify your site's theme to customize its appearance and add features. We explain how in **Chapters 6** through **8**.

WordPress client requirements

The software you use to administer Word-Press is referred to as *client* software.

If you access the World Wide Web—and who doesn't these days?—you probably already have the software you need to administer your WordPress blog: a Web browser.

Although just about any Web browser will work with WordPress, some browsers are better suited than others for administering a blog. One of the browsers we recommend is Firefox because it properly displays all Java-Script tools for editing entries. If you don't have FireFox, you can download it for free from www.getfirefox.com. Firefox is available for Windows, Macintosh, and Linux in an impressive variety of languages.

In addition to a Web browser, you also need access to the Internet or a network connection to the server on which WordPress is running.

WordPress server requirements

As we discuss a little later in this introduction, you can either create and maintain a WordPress blog on the free WordPress.com service or on your server or an ISP's server.

If you set up your blog on WordPress.com, you can skip this section; you don't have any server requirements. But if you plan on using WordPress on a server, read on.

Continued on next page...

CLIENT & SERVER REQUIREMENTS

Continued from previous page.

To run WordPress on a server, the server must have the following:

◆ **PHP version 4.2 or greater.** You can get PHP from www.php.net.

◆ **MySQL version 3.23.23 or greater.** You can get MySQL from www.mysql.com.

◆ **Web server software that supports PHP and MySQL.** The WordPress programming folks recommend Apache (httpd.apache.org) or Litespeed (litespeedtech.com). The Web server should support the mod_rewrite Apache module for full WordPress functionality.

If you're using your ISP's server and you're not sure if the server meets these requirements, contact your ISP's technical support and ask them. Be sure to mention that you need all this to install and run a WordPress blog.

✔ Tips

■ You can learn more about WordPress server requirements at wordpress.org/about/requirements/.

■ You don't need the latest and greatest versions of PHP, MySQL, or your Web server to work with WordPress. In fact, it might be better to have an older version installed. Maria runs WordPress 2.0.1 very successfully on a Mac OS X 10.4 Server with PHP v4.3.11, MySQL v4.0.20, and Apache 1.3.

WORDPRESS SERVER REQUIREMENTS

Using WordPress

There are three ways you can use WordPress to build and maintain a blog:

◆ **Create a blog on the WordPress.com server.** This is the easiest way to get your blog up and running quickly, and it's absolutely free. Although your blog will have full functionality, you won't be able to take advantage of many customization features or install WordPress plugins.

◆ **Install WordPress on your ISP's server.** This is an excellent way to have your own blog with its own unique domain name. Many ISPs offer Web hosting with the features you need to install WordPress.

◆ **Install WordPress on your own server.** This gives you complete control over the blog and the software it runs on. It does require, however, that you have a computer with a dedicated connection to the Internet and a fixed IP address. For best results, you should also have access to a DNS server that points a domain name to your IP address.

We explain how to complete each type of installation in **Chapter 1**.

✔ Tips

■ We discuss customizing WordPress and installing plugins in **Chapters 6** and **7**.

■ You can get a partial list of WordPress compatible Web hosts at wordpress.org/ hosting/.

■ If you want to run WordPress on your own server but you don't know anything about IP addresses, DNS, or configuring Web server software, you're probably not ready to set up your own server. Get started with one of the other two methods of using WordPress. You can always move your WordPress blog to your own server one day in the future.

Getting Started

Setting Up WordPress

As discussed in the Introduction, there are two ways you can set up WordPress:

- ◆ **Create a free account on WordPress.com.** This sets up a basic version of WordPress that has most—but not all—features of a full installation. This is both easy and free.

- ◆ **Install WordPress on a server.** This enables you to use just about all of Word-Press's features and to customize WordPress by installing new themes, modifying theme files, and installing and activating plugins. You have two choices for the server:

  - ▲ **Set up on an ISP's server.** Keep in mind that your ISP may impose restrictions on access, installation, or running PHP scripts.

  - ▲ **Set up on your own server.** This requires that you maintain your own server and Internet connection if you want your blog accessible on the Internet. But if you're a Web designer interested in running a WordPress blog for internal development, the Internet connection is not required.

This chapter explains how to set up Word-Press on WordPress.com and a server.

Setting Up a WordPress.com Account

WordPress.com is a free service that enables you to set up your own WordPress blog without relying on your ISP's server or setting up your own server. Setup is quick and easy.

To enter basic account information

1. Use your Web browser to access wordpress.com (**Figure 1**).

2. Click the Get a WordPress Blog now link.

3. Fill in the form on the WordPress.com Blog page (**Figure 2**):

   ▲ **Username** is the name you want to use to access your blog. This name becomes the first part of the URL for your blog, so you might want to make it something that helps identify what your blog is all about.

   ▲ **Blog Title** is the name of your blog.

   ▲ **Email Address** is your e-mail address. This address is used for your Word-Press account setup, so make sure it's correct.

   ▲ **Language** is the language in which you'll be composing most of your blog entries. Choose an option from the menu.

   ▲ **Privacy** enables you to specify whether you want your blog to appear in search engines and public listings. Leaving this check box turned on makes it easier for potential readers to find your blog.

4. Click Sign Up. A confirmation screen with information about your blog appears (**Figure 3**).

Figure 1 The WordPress.com home page.

Figure 2 Use this form to enter basic information about your blog.

Figure 3 Information about your account appears in a window like this one.

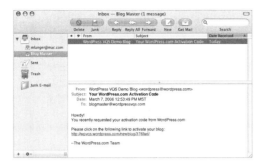

Figure 4 You'll get an e-mail message from your blog with a link to complete the signup process.

Figure 5 Clicking the link displays your new blog in a Web browser window.

To complete the signup process

1. Check your e-mail. You should find a message from your blog (**Figure 4**).

2. Click the link that appears in the message. Your Web browser displays the home page of your new blog (**Figure 5**).

✔ Tip

- When you first create a blog, a sample post and comment are automatically created. We explain how to delete these items in **Chapter 3**.

Installing WordPress on a Server

You can also set up WordPress on your ISP's server or on your own server. This is a multi-step process:

- ◆ Create a MySQL database for the Word-Press installation.

- ◆ Download WordPress from the wordpress.org Web site and extract its files.

- ◆ Create the WordPress configuration file.

- ◆ Copy the WordPress files to a directory on the server.

- ◆ Run the WordPress installer.

The following pages provide instructions for each of these steps.

✔ Tips

- ■ These instructions assume that the server is already running MySQL and PHP, as well as a compatible Web browser.

- ■ You can learn more about the minimum software requirements for installing and running WordPress in the **Introduction**.

- ■ You can also install WordPress on a computer running Mac OS X 10.4 Tiger or later. Remember, you must have an always-on Internet connection and fixed IP address (or dynamic DNS setup) if you want your blog accessible over the Internet.

- ■ How you create a MySQL database depends on the tools and access available on your server. The following pages offer several examples; choose the one that's best for you.

- ■ If you are unable to connect to MySQL or create a new database as discussed here, you may need to ask your system administrator to create the database for you or try one of the other techniques covered in this section to create the database.

- ■ Be sure to write down the exact name of the MySQL database you create; you'll need this information later in the Word-Press installation process.

- ■ A complete discussion of MySQL is far beyond the scope of this book. To learn more about MySQL, pick up a copy of *MySQL: Visual QuickStart Guide* by Larry Ullman.

INSTALLING WORDPRESS ON A SERVER

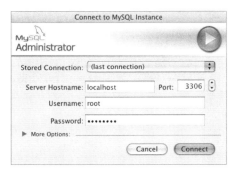

Figure 6 Use this dialog to connect to MySQL on the server.

Figure 7 The Catalog window lists all Schemata (or databases) you have access to.

Figure 8 Enter a name for the new database in the Create Schema dialog.

Figure 9
The database you created is added to the Schemata list.

To create a MySQL database with MySQL Administrator

1. Launch MySQL Administrator.

2. In the Connect to MySQL Instance dialog that appears (**Figure 6**), enter the information needed to connect to the server and click Connect.

3. The Information window for the server appears. Click the Catalogs button to display existing catalogs (**Figure 7**).

4. Click the + button beneath the Schemata list.

5. Enter a name for the database in the Create Schema dialog that appears (**Figure 8**) and click OK. The new database is added to the Schemata list (**Figure 9**).

6. Exit or Quit MySQL Administrator.

✔ Tips

- MySQL Administrator is a graphic user interface tool for working with MySQL. Windows and Macintosh versions are available. You can download it from the MySQL Web site at www.mysql.com.

- If you're not sure what to enter in step 2, consult your system administrator.

CREATING A MYSQL DATABASE

To create a MySQL database using your ISP's tools

1. Login to your account maintenance pages on your ISP's server and navigate to the page you can use to create or maintain MySQL databases. **Figure 10** shows an example of the page on Maria's ISP, GoDaddy.com.

2. Follow the instructions that appear onscreen to create a new MySQL database.

✔ Tip

- Each ISP has its own system for allowing users to create or maintain MySQL databases. It's impossible for us to provide details for every ISP. Consult the online help or technical support department for your ISP if you need specific instruction.

To create a MySQL database from the command line

1. Use a command line interface application, such as a DOS prompt in a Console window on Windows or Terminal on Unix or Mac OS, to connect to MySQL.

2. Type CREATE DATABASE *databasename*; (where *databasename* is the name of the database you want to create) and press Return. MySQL should confirm that the query was OK (**Figure 11**).

3. Type quit and press Return.

✔ Tip

- The exact instructions for connecting to MySQL with a command line vary depending on your operating system and the MySQL installation. Consult your system administrator if you need assistance.

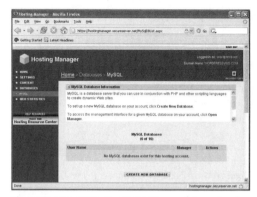

Figure 10 Many ISPs, like GoDaddy.com (shown here), offer Web-based tools for creating and maintaining MySQL databases.

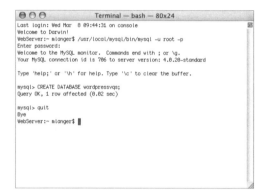

Figure 11 If you have physical access to the server, you can use a command line interface to create a MySQL database. In this example, I'm using the Terminal application on a Mac OS X 10.4 server.

Figure 12 The WordPress.org home page.

Figure 13 The Download WordPress 2 page offers links for downloading WordPress files.

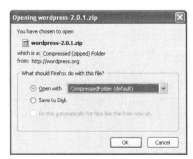

Figure 14 A dialog like this may appear when you click a download link.

To download and extract WordPress

1. Use your Web browser to visit wordpress.org (**Figure 12**).

2. Click the Download link near the top of the page.

3. On the Download WordPress 2 page (**Figure 13**), click the DOWNLOAD.ZIP link.

4. If a dialog like the one in **Figure 14** appears, select the Open with option and choose an application to open the file. In most instances the correct application will already be selected for you.

5. Wait while WordPress is downloaded.

6. Exit or Quit your Web browser program.

7. If necessary, locate and double-click the wordpress-2.x.x.zip file you just downloaded to extract its contents. You should end up with a folder named *wordpress* that's full of PHP files and folders (**Figure 15**).

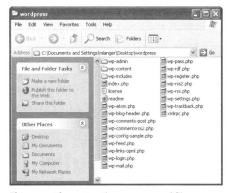

Figure 15 After extracting compressed files, you should wind up with a wordpress folder that contains PHP files and folders.

To create the wp-config.php file

1. Open the file named *wp-config-sample. php* in the wordpress folder with your favorite text editor. **Figure 16** shows the file opened with Maria's favorite, Text-Wrangler.

2. Locate the line that says
define('DB_NAME', 'wordpress');
and replace wordpress with the name of the MySQL database you created for your blog.

3. Locate the line that says
define('DB_USER', 'username');
and replace username with a MySQL user name that has full access to the database file.

4. Locate the line that says
define('DB_PASSWORD', 'password');
and replace password with the password for the user name you entered in step 3.

5. If your database host is not *localhost,* locate the line that says
define('DB_host', 'localhost');
and replace localhost with the domain name or IP address of the database host. If you're not sure what this is, ask your system administrator or consult the settings screen for your MySQL database on your ISP's server.

6. When you're finished making changes, it might look like **Figure 17**. Check your typing carefully! Be sure you entered the database name, user name, and password correctly and did not remove any single quote characters, punctuation, or parentheses characters or make any other changes in the file.

7. Save the file as *wp-config.php* in the wordpress folder.

8. Exit or Quit your text editor.

Figure 16 The wp-config-sample.php file is a template for creating a WordPress configuration file.

Figure 17 When you're finished, your configuration file should have your database information in it.

✔ Tips

■ It's *vital* that you use a text editor that saves files in plain text format. Word processors like Microsoft Word often introduce additional characters to documents and should not be used for editing PHP files such as those used by WordPress.

■ You can find more information about using text editors in **Appendix C.**

Figure 18 Here's the root directory for a Web site opened with Fetch, a Mac OS FTP client.

Figure 19 In this example, we're putting the individual WordPress files right into the Web site's root directory.

Figure 20 The Web site's root directory with the individual WordPress files copied into it.

To copy WordPress files to your server

1. Use your favorite FTP client program to open your Web directory on the server. **Figure 18** shows Fetch on Mac OS opening a Web directory on a GoDaddy.com server.

2. Copy (or put) the wordpress folder or its contents in the Web directory:

   ▲ To access your blog by entering *www.example.com*/wordpress/, put the wordpress *folder* into the Web directory. This installs the WordPress files in the wordpress folder in your root Web directory.

   ▲ To access your blog by entering *www.example.com* put the *contents* of the wordpress folder into the Web directory (**Figure 19**). This installs the WordPress files in your root Web directory (**Figure 20**). Keep in mind that this will overwrite any files in that directory that have the same name, such as index.php.

3. Exit or Quit your FTP client.

✔ Tips

- You can learn more about FTP tools and how to use them in **Appendix B**.

- If you want your blog to be your Web site, copy the contents of the wordpress folder to your Web site's root directory. That's what's shown in **Figures 19** and **20**.

- To access your blog by entering something like *www.example.com*/myblog, change the name of the wordpress folder to myblog *before* copying the *folder* to your root Web directory. You can name your blog folder anything you like, as long as the name does not contain spaces or special characters.

To run the WordPress installer

1. If WordPress is installed in its own folder in your Web site's root directory, use your Web browser to open *www.example.com/wordpress/wp-admin/install.php*.

   or

   If the individual WordPress files are installed in your Web site's root directory (**Figure 20**), use your browser to open *www.example.com/wp-admin/install.php*.

2. The first WordPress installation screen should appear (**Figure 21**). Click the First Step link.

3. In the First Step window (**Figure 22**), fill in the form:
   - ▲ **Weblog title** is the name of your blog or site.
   - ▲ **Your e-mail** is your e-mail address.

4. Click the Continue to Second Step button.

5. The Second Step window appears (**Figure 23**). The installation is complete. Write down your login information.

6. You have three choices to continue:
   - ▲ Follow the instructions on the next page to view your blog.
   - ▲ Follow the instructions later in this chapter to log in to your blog.
   - ▲ Exit or quit your browser and do something else.

✔ Tip

- ■ If something is going to go wrong, it'll usually go wrong right after step 1 of these instructions. Read the error message that appears onscreen; it usually has all the information you need to troubleshoot the problem.

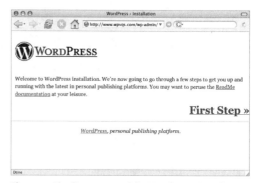

Figure 21 The first screen of the WordPress installer.

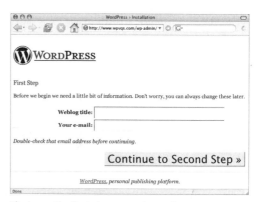

Figure 22 The first step prompts you for some very basic information about your blog.

Figure 23 The second step just tells you that installation is done. Can't be much easier than that!

Figure 24 Here's a WordPress blog, freshly installed on an ISP's server.

To view your blog

Use your Web browser to view the URL for your blog:

◆ If you installed the wordpress folder inside your Web site's root directory, view *www.example.com*/wordpress.

◆ If you installed the contents of the wordpress folder inside your Web site's root directory, view *www.example.com*.

Your blog's home page appears in your Web browser window, with a sample post and comment formatted with the default Word-Press theme (**Figure 24**).

✔ Tip

■ We explain how to change the blog's theme later in this chapter, how to add and remove posts in **Chapter 3**, and how to work with comments in **Chapter 4**.

Logging in to a Blog

To make changes to a blog, you must log in. This applies whether you're the blog's administrator or just another user.

✔ Tips

- To log in to a blog, you need your username and password. This information was e-mailed to you when you created your WordPress.com account or installed WordPress on a server.

- If you turn on the Remember me check box when you log in (**Figure 25**), you'll be automatically logged in each time you visit your blog.

- When you are logged into your blog, the Login link on a blog page appears as a Site Admin link.

- If you can't find your blog password, click the Lost your password? link in the login window (**Figure 25**) and follow the instructions to have your password e-mailed to you.

To log in to a WordPress.com blog

1. Click the Login link on your Blog's home page (**Figure 5**).

   or

   Use your Web browser to open *username*.wordpress.com/wp-login.php.

2. The WordPress login screen appears (**Figure 25**).

3. Enter your username and password in the boxes.

4. Click Login. The Dashboard administration panel appears (**Figure 26**).

Figure 25 Use this screen to log into a WordPress blog.

Figure 26 The Dashboard for a WordPress.com blog offers basic administration buttons and links as well as WordPress.com community news.

LOGGING INTO A BLOG

Figure 27 The Dashboard for a server-installed WordPress blog offers a few more buttons and links for administration, plus links to WordPress developer information and news.

To log in to a server-installed WordPress blog

1. Click the Login link on your Blog's home page (**Figure 24**).

   or

   If WordPress is installed in its own folder in your Web site's root directory, use your Web browser to open *www.example.com/wordpress/wp-login.php*.

   or

   If the individual WordPress files are installed in your Web site's root directory, use your browser to open *www.example.com/wp-login.php*.

2. The WordPress login screen appears (**Figure 25**).

3. Enter your username and password in the boxes.

4. Click Login. The Dashboard administration panel appears (**Figure 27**).

WordPress Administration Panels & the Dashboard

You administer your WordPress blog using its administration panels, each of which includes buttons and links for performing tasks.

The Dashboard (**Figures 26** and **27**) is the main administration panel—the one that appears when you log in to your WordPress blog. It offers buttons and links for performing a wide variety of tasks and for learning more about how to use WordPress.

To view the Dashboard

There are several ways to view the Dashboard for your blog:

◆ Follow the instructions on the previous pages to log in to your blog. The Dashboard appears automatically.

◆ Click the Admin link in a WordPress blog window. If you are not already logged in, this link will appear as a Login link.

◆ Click the Dashboard button at the top of a WordPress.com blog. This button only appears if you are already logged in.

◆ Enter the URL for the blog's home page followed by /wp-admin/. So, in our example, we could go to our server-hosted WordPress VQS demo blog's Dashboard by entering www.wpvqs.com/wp-admin/ in a Web browser. If you're not already logged in, the log in screen (**Figure 25**) will appear first.

✔ Tip

■ You might want to bookmark the Dashboard administration panel for your blog. This will make it quick and easy to access in the future.

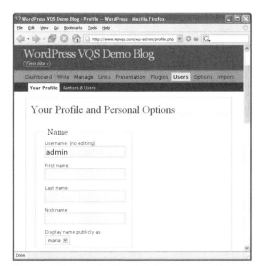

Figure 28 The Your Profile administration panel is where you set your personal account preferences.

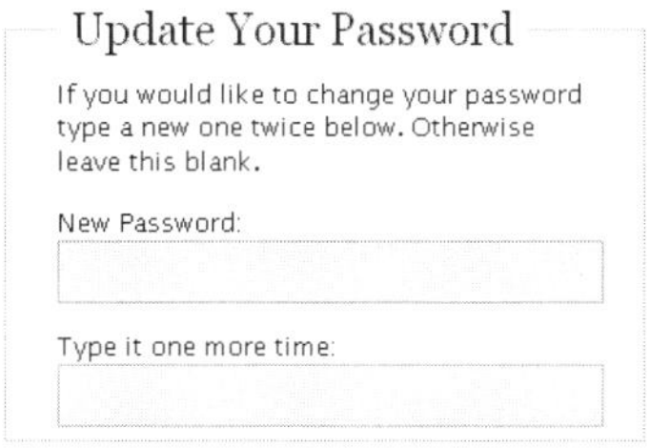

Figure 29 Enter the same new password in each box.

Changing Your Password

One of the first things you might want to do after setting up your blog is to change your password. Although the WordPress-generated password is secure, it isn't very easy to remember. You may want to change it to a password that's easier to remember.

To change your password

1. On the Dashboard, click the Users button. The Your Profile administration panel appears (**Figure 28**).

2. Scroll down to the Update Your Password section (**Figure 29**).

3. Enter the same new password in each box.

4. Click the Update Profile button at the bottom of the page.

   After a moment, a note near the top of the page confirms that your profile has been updated.

✔ Tips

- We tell you more about Users options, including the Your Profile administration panel, in **Chapter 5**.

- On a WordPress.com blog, a note near the top of the Your Profile administration panel may provide an API key. This string of characters, which should be kept secret, is used for additional WordPress-compatible services, such as the Akismet anti-spam service. We explain how to use Akismet in **Chapter 4**.

Choosing a Theme

The last thing you might want to do as part of the setup process is to choose a theme for your blog.

As we explain in detail in **Chapter 6**, your WordPress theme controls the appearance of your blog's pages. **Figures** 5 and 24 show the default theme WordPress applies to all new blogs. Although there's nothing wrong with this theme, you may want to choose one that better reflects the personality of your blog.

WordPress.com account users are lucky in that many themes are preinstalled and ready to apply to their blogs. That's the good news. The bad news is that these themes cannot be customized nearly as much as the ones available to WordPress users with a server-installed blog. In fact, I cover all of the customization options for WordPress.com blog users on the following few pages.

If you have a server-installed blog, you can choose from one of the hundreds of Word-Press themes developed by WordPress devotees over the years. But first, you must download and install the theme; we explain how to do that in **Chapter 6**. For now, you can choose from two preinstalled themes: Word-Press Default and WordPress Classic.

No matter how your blog is installed or accessed, you choose a theme the same way: with the Themes administration panel (**Figures** 30 and 31).

✔ Tips

- The currently selected theme always appears at the top of the Themes panel (**Figures** 30 and 31).

- You can change your blog's theme any time you like and as often as you like.

- **Chapter 6** is your source of information for installing and customizing themes.

Figure 30 The Themes administration panel in a Word-Press.com blog offers dozens of themes to choose from.

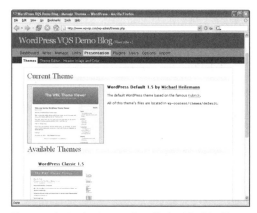

Figure 31 A standard server installation of a WordPress blog includes just two relatively plain themes.

Figure 32 When you choose a new theme, you'll see confirmation that it has been activated at the top of the Themes panel.

To choose a theme

1. On the Dashboard, click the Presentation button. The Themes panel appears (**Figures 30** and **31**).

2. Click the link or preview icon for the theme you want to apply. After a moment, a message near the top of the screen confirms that a new theme has been activated and the preview for that theme appears at the top of the page (**Figure 32**).

3. Click the View site link at the top of the page. The site is reformatted with the theme you selected (**Figure 33**).

Figure 33 Your blog automatically takes on the formatting of the new theme.

To use Sidebar Widgets

1. On the Dashboard, click the Presentation button. The Themes panel appears (**Figures** 30 and **32**).

2. Click the Sidebar Widgets button to display its panel of options (**Figure 34**).

3. Drag the widget icons for the sidebar components you want to include from the Available Widgets list to the Sidebar 1 list in the order you want them to appear (**Figure 35**).

4. To configure a widget, click the configure button on its right side. A dialog appears (**Figure 36**). Set options as desired and click the dialog's close button to save them.

5. To rearrange items in the Sidebar 1 list, drag them up or down in the list. When you release the mouse button, they move (**Figure 37**).

6. To remove an item from the Sidebar 1 list, drag it from that list into the Available Widgets list.

Figure 34 The Sidebar Arrangement options in the Sidebar Editor panel.

Figure 35 Drag sidebar components called widgets from one list to the other.

Figure 36 You use a dialog like this one to set configuration options for various widgets.

Figure 37
Here's an example of how a sidebar's components might be arranged in the Sidebar 1 list.

USING THE SIDEBAR EDITOR

Figure 38a & 38b Here's what the sidebar set up in **Figure 37** might look like in the Default WordPress theme (left) and the Rubric theme applied in **Figure 33** (right).

Table 1

Sidebar Widget Configuration Options	
Widget Name	**Configuration Options**
Archives	Title
Categories	Title, show post counts, show hierarchy
Links	none
Meta	Title
Pages	Title
RSS 1	RSS Feed URL, number of items to display
Recent Comments	Title
Recent Posts	none
Search	none
Text 1	Title, text
del.icio.us	Title, del.icio.us login, number of links, tags to show

7. When you're finished setting options, click the Save changes button near the bottom of the page. A message at the top of the page confirms that the sidebar has been updated.

8. Click the View Site link near the top of the page. Your blog's home page appears with the newly configured sidebar (**Figures 38a** and **38b**).

✔ Tips

- **Table 1** lists the available widgets and their configuration options.

- If you remove all widgets from the Sidebar 1 list, the default sidebar will be displayed.

- This feature is only available for certain themes, such as the WordPress Default 1.5 theme.

USING THE SIDEBAR EDITOR

To set the header image & color

1. On the Dashboard, click the Presentation button. The Themes panel appears (**Figure 30**).

2. Click the Header Image and Color button to display its panel of options (**Figure 39**).

3. Beneath the sample image, click the button for the color you want to change: Font Color, Upper Color, or Lower Color.

4. A color picker appears (**Figure 40**). Click the color you want to apply. The sample image changes immediately.

5. Repeat steps 3 and 4 for each color you want to change.

6. Click Save. After a moment, an onscreen message confirms that your changes have been saved.

✔ Tips

- This feature is only available for certain themes, such as the WordPress Default 1.5 theme.

- If you don't like your changes, you can revert to the default settings by clicking the Revert button beneath the sample image.

- You can also manually enter hexadecimal codes for the colors you want to use. Instead of following steps 3 and 4, click the Advanced button to display text boxes (**Figure 41**) and enter the codes. You can find an online list of color codes at www.december.com/html/spec/colorhslhex.html.

Figure 39 Some themes include options for customizing the header.

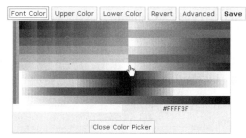

Figure 40 Click a button, then use the Color picker to choose the color you want.

Figure 41 You can also manually enter hexadecimal codes for the colors you want.

Setting Blog Options

Blog Options

Whether your blog is hosted on WordPress.com, on an ISP's server, or on your own server, there are certain options you can set to control the way it looks and works. You may want to set some or all of these options before you begin adding content to your WordPress blog.

You can find blog options in various administration panels:

- ◆ **General Options** include things like the blog title and tagline, language, search engine compatibility, membership requirements, e-mail address, and date and time formatting.

- ◆ **Writing Options** include the size of the post box, formatting options, default post category, writing by e-mail options, and update services.

- ◆ **Reading Options** include the number of posts to display on a page or in an RSS feed, encoding, and compression options.

- ◆ **Discussion Options** are settings for WordPress's comments feature. We tell you more about these options and about working with comments in **Chapter 4**.

- ◆ **Permalink Options** enable you to set up the formatting of permanent links. This set of options is only available for Word-Press server installations.

Continued on next page...

Continued from previous page.

◆ **Miscellaneous Options** include upload folder location and other options. This set of options is only available for WordPress server installations.

◆ **Delete Blog** enables you to permanently delete your blog. This option is only available for WordPress.com accounts.

In this chapter, we tell you more about these options and how to set them for your blog.

✔ Tip

■ As you'll see throughout this chapter, there are slight differences between options in a WordPress.com account and a WordPress server installation. Be sure to consult the correct instructions and screenshots for your kind of Word-Press installation.

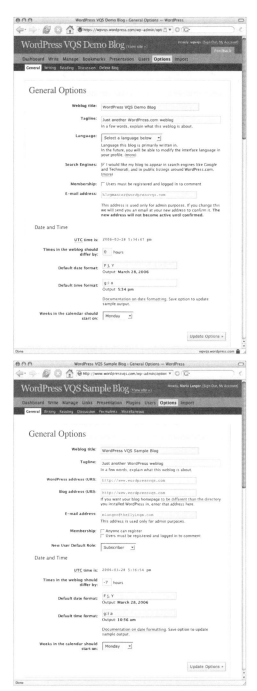

Figures 1a & 1b The General Options administration panel for a WordPress.com account (top) and a Word-Press server installation (bottom).

To set General Options

1. If necessary, log in to your WordPress blog and navigate to the Dashboard administration panel.

2. Click the Options button.

3. If necessary, click the General button in the second row of buttons. The General Options administration panel appears (**Figure 1a** or **1b**).

4. Set general options in the top half of the window:

   ▲ **Weblog title** is the name of your blog, which normally appears in the blog page header (**Figure 2**).

   ▲ **Tagline** is a short description of your blog that appears with your blog's name in the header (**Figure 2**).

   ▲ **WordPress address** (URI) is the Web address of your blog. This address depends on whether you installed WordPress in its own directory or in your Web site's root directory. This option is only available for WordPress server installations.

   ▲ **Blog address** (URI) is the Web address of your blog's home page, if you want it to be different from the directory in which you installed WordPress. This type of installation is a more advanced feature of WordPress; you can click the link beneath this option to learn more. This option is only available for WordPress server installations.

   ▲ **Language** is the primary language for your blog. This option is only available for WordPress.com accounts.

Continued on next page...

Continued from previous page.

- ◆ **Search Engines** tells WordPress that you want your blog searchable by search engines like Google, Yahoo!, and Technorati. This option is only available for WordPress.com accounts.

- ▲ **Membership** offers one or two options, depending on how Word-Press is installed. **Anyone can register** makes it possible for any blog visitor to register for access to your blog. This option is only available for WordPress server installations. **Users must be registered and logged in to comment** requires users to be registered and logged in to your blog (for a server-installed blog) or WordPress.com (for a WordPress.com blog) to enter comments about blog posts.

- ▲ **E-mail address** is the e-mail address for the blog administrator. This address is used for administrative purposes only. If you change your e-mail address for a WordPress.com account, you'll get an e-mail message to confirm it before the change is finalized.

- ▲ **New User Default Role** is the default access level for newly registered users. This option is only available for WordPress server installations. We tell you more about user accounts and roles in **Chapter 5**.

5. Set Date and Time options near the bottom of the window:

- ▲ **Times in the weblog should differ by** enables you to enter the number of hours your time zone varies from Greenwich Mean time (also known as UTC time). This value should be set for your time zone.

Figure 2 The blog name and tagline normally appear in the header. This example also shows a calendar in the page sidebar.

▲ **Default date format** enables you to set date formatting using PHP date format codes. The Output area below the entry box shows how the date appears with the format codes applied. We tell you more about date formatting codes in **Chapter 6**.

▲ **Default time format** enables you to set time formatting using PHP time format codes. The Output area below the entry box shows how the time appears with the format codes applied. We tell you more about time formatting codes in **Chapter 6**.

▲ **Weeks in the calendar should start on** is the day of the week that should appear in the first column of the calendar. The calendar is displayed in the sidebar of some themes (**Figure 2**).

6. Click the Update Options button at the bottom of the page. A message appears at the top of the page, confirming that the options have been saved.

✔ Tips

■ Don't change the settings in the Word-Press address and Blog address boxes unless you know what you're doing. Making incorrect changes to these options can make your blog inaccessible.

■ Search engine access is enabled by default in a WordPress server installation. To disable it, you need to set options in a robots.txt file; you can learn more about that at www.searchtools.com/robots/robots-txt.html.

■ Additional comment-related options for WordPress server installations appear in the Discussion Options administration panel. We tell you about them in **Chapter 4**.

■ Make your blog more user-friendly by spelling out the month as a word and the year with 4 digits. Remember, blogs are viewed by people from all over the world. Some will understand 7/5/06 to be the fifth day of July while others will read it as the seventh day of May.

To set Writing Options

1. If necessary, log in to your WordPress blog and navigate to the Dashboard administration panel.

2. Click the Options button.

3. If necessary, click the Writing button in the second row of buttons. The Writing Options administration panel appears (**Figure 3a** or **3b**).

4. Set writing options as desired:

   ▲ **Size of the post box** is the size of the edit box you use to compose posts. The default size is 10 lines (**Figure 4a**), but you can make it bigger (**Figure 4b**) or smaller.

   ▲ **Formatting** offers two or three options, depending on your installation. **Users should use the visual rich text editor by default** displays the WYSIWYG text editor for writing posts (**Figure 4a**). This option only appears for WordPress server installations. **Convert emoticons like :-) and :-P to graphics on display** converts emoticon character strings (which are often referred to as "smilies") to corresponding graphic characters in posts in which they appear (**Figure 5**). **WordPress should correct invalidly nested XHTML automatically** tells WordPress to correct tag nesting errors in HTML code included in posts.

   ▲ **Default post category** is the category that should automatically be applied to new posts. This category can be changed when the post is created and saved. The drop-down list includes all defined categories.

Figures 3a & 3b The Writing Options administration panels on a WordPress.com account (top) and a WordPress server installation (bottom).

Figures 4a & 4b The standard 10-line post box with visual rich text editor (top) and a custom 20-line post box with the standard HTML text editor.

Figure 5 Emoticons or smilies can appear as graphics in posts. This is the resulting post from **Figure 4a**.

5. If you're using WordPress with a server installation, you can set options for submitting posts by e-mail:

   ▲ **Mail server** is the server name or IP address and port for the server on which the e-mail address resides.

   ▲ **Login name** is the login name or e-mail address for the e-mail account the posts will be sent to.

   ▲ **Password** is the access password for the e-mail account the posts will be sent to.

   ▲ **Default post by mail category** is the category that will be applied to posts entered by e-mail.

6. To automatically inform update services each time there is a new entry on your blog, enter the URLs for the services in the **Update Services** box at the bottom of the page. Be sure to start each service on a new line.

   or

   To stop notifying update services about new content in your blog, remove the contents of the **Update Services** box at the bottom of the page.

   This option is only available for Word-Press server installations.

7. Click the Update Options button at the bottom of the page. A message appears at the top of the page, confirming that the options have been saved.

Continued on next page...

Continued from previous page.

✔ Tips

- We tell you more about writing posts—including how to submit posts by e-mail for WordPress server installations—in **Chapter 3**.

- The visual rich text editor does not work properly in all browsers. For example, as of this writing, it does not work in Safari for Macintosh. If the visual text editor in your installation does not look like the one in **Figure 4a**, try another browser. We recommend FireFox, which is available for Windows, Mac OS, and Linux.

- Users can change their text editor preference in their account settings. We tell you more about user account options in **Chapter 5**.

- We explain how to create, edit, and delete categories in **Chapter 3**.

- Ping-o-Matic is a single service that automatically "pings" or notifies other services about your new blog posts. You can learn more about this and other services at codex.wordpress.org/ Update_Services.

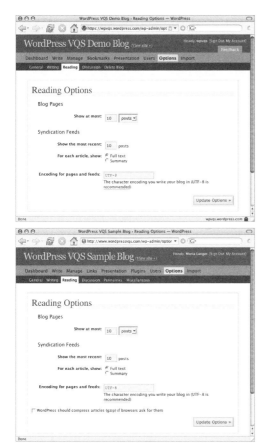

Figures 6a & 6b The Reading Options administration panels on a WordPress.com account (top) and a WordPress server installation (bottom).

✔ Tip

■ Don't change the character encoding in step 6 unless you know what you're doing. Setting this option incorrectly could make your blog unreadable.

To set Reading Options

1. If necessary, log in to your WordPress blog and navigate to the Dashboard administration panel.

2. Click the Options button.

3. If necessary, click the Reading button in the second row of buttons. The Reading Options administration panel appears (**Figure 6a** or **6b**).

4. In the Blog Pages area, indicate the maximum number of posts that should appear on a page by entering a value in the **Show at most** box and then choosing days or posts from the drop-down list beside it. If you choose days, WordPress counts only the days that have posts.

5. Set Syndication Feeds options as desired:

   ▲ **Show the most recent** enables you to set how many posts appear in feeds.

   ▲ **For each article, show** enables you to specify whether feeds should show the full text or a summary of each post. A summary is just the first 100 or so words of the post, with text to indicate that there's more.

6. To change the character encoding for your blog, enter a different encoding in the **Encoding for pages and feeds** box.

7. To enable gzip compression, turn on the **WordPress should compress articles (gzip) if browsers ask for them** check box. This option is only available on a WordPress server installation.

8. Click the Update Options button at the bottom of the page. A message appears at the top of the page, confirming that the options have been saved.

To customize the Permalink Structure (server installation only)

1. If necessary, log in to your WordPress blog and navigate to the Dashboard administration panel.

2. Click the Options button.

3. If necessary, click the Permalinks button in the second row of buttons. The Customize Permalink Structure administration panel appears (**Figure 7**).

4. To set the permalink format using a common option, select the radio button for the option you want. Each option displays a sample of the format it uses.

   or

   To create a custom permalink format, enter the tags you want to use in the Custom Structure box. For example, if you wanted a post's permanent link to look like:
   http://www.example.com/archives/2006/03/my-post
   you'd enter:
   /archives/%year%/%monthnum%/%postname% in the Custom structure box. **Table 1** lists the available tags.

5. To use a custom prefix for category URLs, enter the prefix you want to use in the Category base box. So, for example, if you wanted the word hello to appear in all category links, you'd enter /hello in the Category base box. The resulting URLs would look like http://www.example.com/hello/categoryname/.

6. Click the Update Permalink Structure button at the bottom of the page. A message appears at the top of the page, confirming that the options have been saved.

Figure 7 The Customize Permalink Structure administration panel for a WordPress server installation blog.

Table 1

Permalink Structure Tags	
Tag	**Purpose**
%year%	The year of the date.
%monthnum%	The month number of the date.
%day%	The day number of the date.
%hour%	The hour number of the time.
%minute%	The minute number of the time.
%second%	The second number of the time.
%postname%	An Internet-friendly version of the post title.
%post_id%	The post ID.
%category%	An Internet-friendly version of the category name.
%author%	An Internet-friendly version of the author name.

✔ Tip

- For permalinks to work properly, the Apache mod_rewrite module must be properly configured on your server. For more information, consult your ISP or system administrator.

Figure 8 The Miscellaneous Options administration panel for a WordPress server installation.

To set Miscellaneous Options (server installation only)

1. If necessary, log in to your WordPress blog and navigate to the Dashboard administration panel.

2. Click the Options button.

3. If necessary, click the Miscellaneous button in the second row of buttons. The Miscellaneous Options administration panel appears (**Figure 8**).

4. Set uploading options as desired:
   ▲ **Store uploads in this folder** enables you to specify a path within your WordPress root directory for files uploaded from the Write Post page.

   ▲ **Organize my uploads into month- and year-based folders** creates year and month folders to organize all uploads. For example, a file uploaded on March 28, 2006 would be saved in wp-content/uploads/2006/03 relative to your WordPress root directory.

5. To include link updates in site update notifications, turn on the **Track Links' Update Times** check box. This feature works with the update services feature discussed in the section titled "To set Writing Options" earlier in this chapter.

6. To utilize the my-hacks.php file for small WordPress hacks, turn on the **Use legacy my-hacks.php file support** check box. The my-hacks.php file has been replaced by WordPress plugins and, as a result, is beyond the scope of this book.

7. Click the Update Options button at the bottom of the page. A message appears at the top of the page, confirming that the options have been saved.

✔ Tip

■ The folder you specify in step 4 must be writable. We explain how to set permissions for a folder in **Chapter 6**.

Deleting a WordPress Blog

If you decide you no longer want to maintain a blog, you can delete it. How you delete it depends on how the blog is installed.

◆ If you have a WordPress.com blog, you can delete it from the Delete Blog administration panel.

◆ If you have a WordPress server installation blog, you can delete it by removing it from your Web server.

✔ Tip

■ If you delete your blog, its contents will be lost forever. Make sure you really want to delete your blog before you do.

To delete a WordPress.com blog

1. If necessary, log in to your WordPress blog and navigate to the Dashboard administration panel.

2. Click the Options button.

3. If necessary, click the Delete Blog button in the second row of buttons. The Delete Blog administration panel appears (**Figure 9**).

4. Read what's on the page carefully.

5. Turn on the check box near the bottom of the page.

6. Click Delete My Account Permanently. A confirmation window like the one in **Figure 10** appears.

7. Check your e-mail. You should receive a message from your blog (**Figure 11**).

8. Click the link in the e-mail message. Your blog is deleted.

Figure 9 The Delete Blog administration panel on a WordPress.com blog.

Figure 10 WordPress confirms that you've asked to delete your blog.

Figure 11 You must click the link in the confirmation e-mail you receive to delete the blog.

DELETING A BLOG

To delete a WordPress server installation blog

1. Delete all WordPress files.

2. Delete the WordPress MySQL database you created for the blog.

✔ Tips

- How you delete the WordPress files and MySQL database depends on your access to the server. In most instances, you'll use the same tools you used to install the WordPress files and create the database. See **Chapter 1** for additional information.

- If your WordPress blog had its own domain name, you should replace it with other Web content or modify settings on your DNS server to point that domain name to another Web site. If necessary, consult your ISP or system administrator for details. A discussion of DNS is beyond the scope of this book.

DELETING A BLOG

Adding Content

Blog Content

One of the best things about creating and maintaining a blog is that you have complete control over its content. Write about anything—things you do, things you think, things you like, things you don't like. That's what Maria does in Maria's WebLog. Or share information about a specific topic that interests you—sports, current events, politics, cooking, books, or computer news and tips. That's what Miraz does in her MacTips.info blog. Your blog is your way to share information with the world.

In addition to text, a blog entry can include the following:

- ◆ **HTML formatting**, to make content easier to read. For example, you can include headings, bulleted or numbered lists, and text formatting.

- ◆ **Links** to other content on the Web. In fact, this is how blogging started—as a way to highlight and analyze other content.

- ◆ **Images**, including photographs, to illustrate your posts.

In this chapter, we explain how to add content to your blog, including blog categories, posts and pages, and links.

✔ Tip

- ■ Update your blog frequently, so it always has fresh content. If a visitor likes your blog but doesn't see something new each time he visits, he'll probably stop coming. Although there's no rule for how often you should update your blog, we recommend at least once a week. We usually update our blogs several times *a day*—when time permits, of course—but certainly no less often than several times a week.

Working with Categories

Blog posts are normally organized by *category*. This enables readers to find content by topic. A post's categories usually appear at the beginning or end of the post and most Word-Press themes include a category list in the blog's navigation sidebar (**Figure 1**).

WordPress enables you to create as many categories as you like. Categories can have long or short names and can even have subcategories (**Figure 2**).

In this part of the chapter, we explain how to create, modify, and remove categories and subcategories for your WordPress blog. You do all this with the Categories administration panel (**Figure 3**).

✔ Tips

■ In most themes, a category will only appear in the sidebar's category list if there is at least one post in it.

■ WordPress.com accounts use post categories to organize links or bookmarks. This is a relatively recent change to WordPress.com and marks a departure from how links are organized on Word-Press server installations.

Figure 1 Our sample blog, which uses the Default theme in this illustration, includes the category name at the end of the post and a list of categories in the sidebar.

Figure 2 One of Maria's projects, wickenburg-az.com, has a complex system of categories and subcategories.

To display the Categories administration panel

1. If necessary, log into your blog and display the Dashboard.

2. Click the Manage button.

3. Click the Categories button in the second row of buttons. The Categories administration panel appears (**Figure 3a** or **3b**).

✔ Tips

■ As shown in **Figures 3a** and **3b**, there are minor differences between the way the Categories administration panel appears for a WordPress.com blog (**Figure 3a**) and a WordPress server-installed blog (**Figure 3b**). The administration panel has the same basic functionality for either setup.

■ A WordPress.com blog has two default categories: Feeds and Uncategorized. Feeds is the default category for bookmarks; Uncategorized is the default category for posts.

Figures 3a & 3b The Categories administration panel lists all defined categories and includes a form for creating new ones. On a WordPress.com blog (top), categories are used for both posts and bookmarks, while on a WordPress server-installed blog (bottom), categories are just used for posts.

To add a category or subcategory

1. Open the Categories administration panel (**Figure 3**).

2. Click the add new link or scroll down to the Add New Category area.

3. Enter the following information for the category:

   ▲ **Name** is the name of the category.

   ▲ **Category parent** is a higher-level category for the category. To create a subcategory, choose another category from this drop-down list. The list will include all categories and subcategories already defined (**Figure 4**). You can leave this option set to None if you don't want the category to be a subcategory.

   ▲ **Description** is an optional description for the category. The text you enter here appears in most Web browsers when the visitor points to a category link (**Figure 5**). It's a good idea to keep this description short, even though WordPress gives you a big text box.

4. Click Add Category. The category is added to the list near the top of the window (**Figure 6**).

✔ Tips

■ On a server installation of WordPress, categories are assigned unique numeric IDs in the order in which they were created. On a WordPress.com blog, category IDs are assigned based on existing categories in other WordPress.com blogs, so the numbers will be out of sequence.

■ When you create a subcategory, it appears indented under its parent category in the Categories list (**Figure 6**).

Figure 4
To create a subcategory, choose a category from the Category parent drop-down list. This example shows the category/subcategory structure on the site illustrated in **Figure 2**.

Figure 5
Pointing to a category link in your blog displays the category's description.

Figure 6 The category list after adding four categories and two subcategories.

Figure 7 The Edit Category administration panel enables you to change options for a category.

To edit a category

1. Open the Categories administration panel (**Figure 6**).

2. Click the Edit link beside the category you want to edit. The Edit Category administration panel appears (**Figure 7**).

3. Change settings as desired:

   ▲ **Category name** is the name of the category.

   ▲ **Category slug** is a short name for the category that is used in permalinks. This option does not appear in the Edit Category administration panel for a WordPress.com blog.

   ▲ **Category parent** is a subcategory's parent category.

   ▲ **Description** is a brief description of the category.

4. Click Edit category to save your changes.

✔ Tips

- We tell you about permalinks in **Chapter 2**.

- To change a category into a subcategory, choose another category from the Category parent drop-down list (**Figure 4**).

- To change a subcategory into a category, choose None from the Category parent drop-down list (**Figure 4**).

To remove a category

1. Open the Categories administration panel (**Figure 6**).

2. Click the Delete link beside the category you want to remove.

3. If the category contains posts or bookmarks, a warning dialog like the one in **Figure 8** appears. To delete the category, click OK.

   The category is removed from the category list.

✔ Tips

- You cannot delete the default categories. The default post category is normally named *Uncategorized* (**Figure 6**), unless you change it as shown in **Figure 9**. The default bookmarks category for WordPress.com blogs is *Feeds* (**Figure 3a**).

- Deleting a category does not delete any post or bookmark assigned to that category.

- When you delete a category, any post or bookmark with that category assigned is reassigned to the corresponding default category.

- When you delete a parent category, all of its subcategories are "promoted" from subcategory to category.

- In a WordPress server installation, category IDs are not reused. If you delete a category, it's ID is automatically "retired" and won't be used again—even if you create a new category with the same name.

Figure 8 When you delete a category that has posts or bookmarks assigned to it, a confirmation dialog like this appears.

Figure 9 In this example, we changed the Uncategorized category to Unfiled and gave it a description.

Creating a Post or Page

WordPress offers two ways to display content:

◆ **Posts** or blog entries are date-sensitive content that are displayed in reverse chronological order on blog pages. They can be assigned categories and they become part of the site's archives when created.

◆ **Pages** are content that are not part of the blog itself. Instead, they are accessed through page links that can be displayed in the header, sidebar, or elsewhere in the blog.

This terminology can be confusing, since both posts and Pages appear on Web "pages." In an attempt to keep things straight in everyone's mind the WordPress Codex and this book use title case to indicate content using the Page feature.

Most of the content you create for your blog will be created by writing posts. You're likely to use Pages for content that you want immediately accessible from blog pages, such as information about yourself or the blog, a contact form, or an archive index page.

In this part of the chapter, we explain how to create both types of content. As you'll see, they're very similar.

✔ Tip

■ The instructions in this part of the chapter assume you are using the visual rich editor to create and edit posts and Pages. We explain how to use the HTML editor near the end of this section.

Important note about Web browsers and editing toolbars

The visual rich editor and editing toolbars that appear in WordPress's Write Post or Write Page administration panels are created with JavaScript. While most Web browsers are capable of displaying these toolbars properly (**Figures 10a**, **10b**, and **10c**), not all can (**Figure 10d**).

Your choice of Web browser will determine how well you can follow the instructions presented throughout this chapter. If your Web browser cannot properly display the editing toolbar, we recommend that you download and install a compatible browser, such as Firefox.

✔ Tips

■ You can download a free copy of the Windows, Macintosh, or Linux version of Firefox from www.getfirefox.com.

■ We use Firefox for most browser screenshots throughout this book.

Figure 10a, 10b, 10c, and 10d Not all Web browsers are equal. Although the editing toolbar appears to function properly in Explorer for Windows (top), Firefox for Windows (middle), and Firefox for Macintosh (bottom-left), it doesn't appear at all in Safari for Macintosh (bottom-right). Shame on Apple!

To create a post or Page

1. If necessary, log into your blog and display the Dashboard.

2. Click the Write button.

3. To create a post, click the Write Post button to display the Write Post administration panel (**Figure 11**).

   or

   To create a Page, click the Write Page button to display the Write Page administration panel (**Figure 12**).

4. Enter a title for the post or Page in the Title or Page Title box.

5. Enter the text of the post or Page in the Post or Page Content box. The text can be as long or as short as you like. Be sure to press [Enter] or [Return] each time you want to start a new paragraph.

6. Format the text, insert links, split the text, or check the spelling as instructed in the next section titled, "To use the visual rich editor's toolbar."

7. Insert images as instructed in the section titled "To insert an image."

8. Set post or page options as instructed in the section titled "To set post options" or "To set Page options."

9. Click Publish. The post or Page is added to your site.

✔ Tip

- Newly added posts with the current date and time appear at the top of your site's home page, as well as at the top of the appropriate category page(s) and current month's archive page. Newly added Pages appear in the sidebar if the sidebar is configured to include a list of Pages.

Figure 11 The Write Post administration panel, with some options displayed.

Figure 12 The Write Page administration panel, with most options displayed.

To use the visual rich editor's toolbar

1. To apply text formatting, select the text you want to format and click the appropriate button (**Figure 13**):

   ▲ **Bold** applies bold formatting (**Figure 14**).

   ▲ **Italic** applies italic formatting (**Figure 14**).

   ▲ **Strikethrough** applies strikethrough formatting (**Figure 14**).

   ▲ **Unordered list** applies bulleted list formatting. Use this option on multiple paragraphs of selected text (**Figure 15**) to make each paragraph a bulleted item (**Figure 16**).

   ▲ **Ordered list** applies numbered list formatting. Use this option on multiple paragraphs of selected text (**Figure 15**) to make each paragraph a numbered item (**Figure 17**).

   ▲ **Outdent** shifts indentation to the left or removes blockquote formatting. This button is only available if you have used the Indent List/Blockquote button on the selected text.

   ▲ **Indent list/Blockquote** either increases the indentation of a bulleted or numbered list or formats the selected text as a block quote.

   ▲ **Align left**, **Align center**, and **Align right** changes the paragraph alignment of the selected text.

2. To insert a link, select the text you want to turn into a link and click the Insert/edit link button. Enter the following information in the dialog that appears (**Figure 18**) and click Insert:

Figure 13 The visual rich editor's toolbar. Standard buttons include: Bold, Italic, Strikethrough, Unordered list, Ordered list, Outdent, Indent list/Blockquote, Align left, Align center, Align right, Insert/edit link, Unlink, Insert/edit image, Split post with More tag, Toggle spellchecker, Edit HTML source, and Help.

> Creating a WordPress post is as easy as typing a document in your favorite word processor. Just type in the text and format it the way you like by applying, **bold**, *italic*, or ~~strikethrough~~ formatting.

Figure 14 You can apply bold, italic, or strikethrough formatting to selected text.

> You can also created bulleted or numbered lists. Just:
>
> Enter the text you want to appear on the list with each item in its own paragraph.
>
> Select the list items.
>
> Apply the formatting.

Figure 15 To create a list, start by selecting the paragraphs that will make up the list.

> You can also created bulleted or numbered lists. Just:
>
> - Enter the text you want to appear on the list with each item in its own paragraph.
> - Select the list items.
> - Apply the formatting.

Figure 16 Then click the Unordered list button...

> You can also created bulleted or numbered lists. Just:
>
> 1. Enter the text you want to appear on the list with each item in its own paragraph.
> 2. Select the list items.
> 3. Apply the formatting.

Figure 17 ...or the Ordered list button.

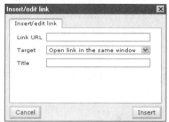

Figure 18 Use a dialog like this one to set options for a link.

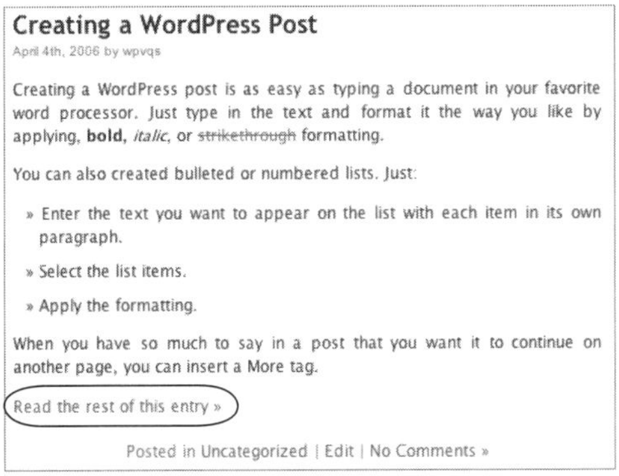

Creating a WordPress Post
April 4th, 2006 by wpvqs

Creating a WordPress post is as easy as typing a document in your favorite word processor. Just type in the text and format it the way you like by applying, **bold**, *italic*, or ~~strikethrough~~ formatting.

You can also created bulleted or numbered lists. Just:

» Enter the text you want to appear on the list with each item in its own paragraph.

» Select the list items.

» Apply the formatting.

When you have so much to say in a post that you want it to continue on another page, you can insert a More tag.

Read the rest of this entry »

Posted in Uncategorized | Edit | No Comments »

Figure 19 A More link—which can display any text you like—gives readers access to the next page of a split post.

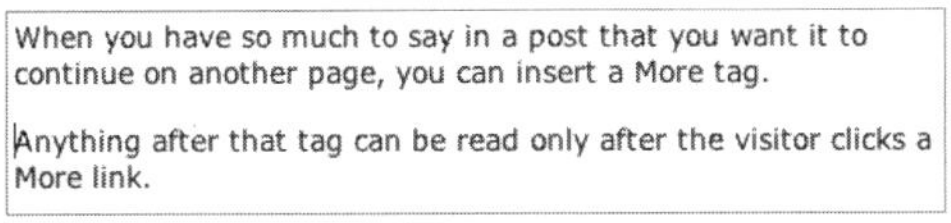

When you have so much to say in a post that you want it to continue on another page, you can insert a More tag.

Anything after that tag can be read only after the visitor clicks a More link.

Figure 20 Position the insertion point where you want to split the post or Page text.

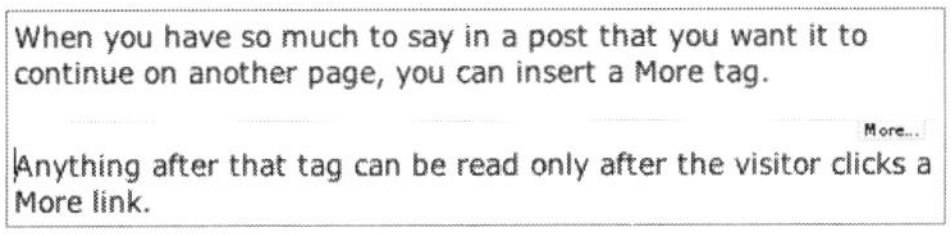

When you have so much to say in a post that you want it to continue on another page, you can insert a More tag.

More...

Anything after that tag can be read only after the visitor clicks a More link.

Figure 21 A More tag appears at the split.

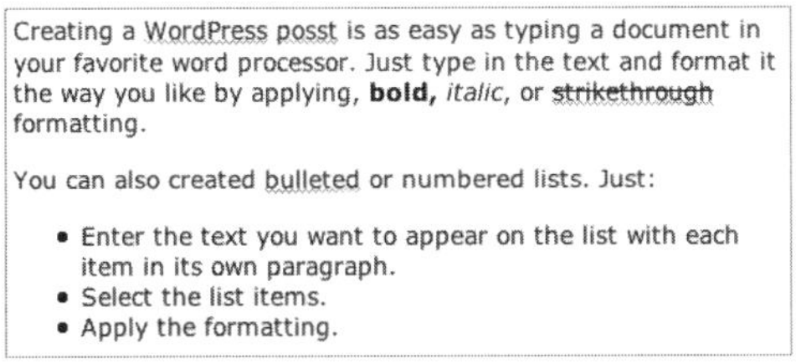

Creating a WordPress posst is as easy as typing a document in your favorite word processor. Just type in the text and format it the way you like by applying, **bold**, *italic*, or ~~strikethrough~~ formatting.

You can also created bulleted or numbered lists. Just:

• Enter the text you want to appear on the list with each item in its own paragraph.
• Select the list items.
• Apply the formatting.

Figure 22 The spellchecker identifies all the words it doesn't know.

▲ **Link URL** is the complete URL for the link. In most cases, this will begin with either http:// or mailto://.

▲ **Target** is where you want the link to open. Choose an option from the drop-down list to specify whether the link should open in the same window or a new window.

▲ **Title** is text that appears in a box when you point to the link.

or

To remove a link, select the link text and click the Unlink button.

3. To split the text so it appears on multiple pages with a More link to access the second page (**Figure 19**), position the insertion point where you want the split to appear (**Figure 20**) and click the Split post with More tag button. A More tag appears (**Figure 21**).

4. To check spelling in a WordPress.com blog, click the Toggle spellchecker button. After a moment, the text is checked and red squiggly underlines appear beneath unknown words (**Figure 22**). To get a suggestion for an unknown word, click it. You can then choose a correction from the list of words that appears (**Figure 23**). When you're finished using the spelling checker, click the Toggle spellchecker button to remove the red lines.

5. To edit the HTML code for a page while still using the visual rich editor, click the Edit HTML Source button. Then use the HTML Source Editor window that appears (**Figure 24**) to modify the code and click Update. Your changes are reflected in the visual rich editor window.

Continued on next page...

USING THE VISUAL RICH EDITOR'S TOOLBAR

Continued from previous page.

✔ Tips

- The visual rich editor is also known as the WYSIWYG editor.

- If you're not sure what a button does, point to it. A box with the name of the button appears to identify it.

- The visual rich editor applies standard XHTML codes such as <strong>, <em>, and <ul> to text. These codes are hidden from view unless you click the Edit HTML Source button on the toolbar.

- How various list and blockquote formatting appears in your blog depends on the associated tag options set in the style.css file for the blog's theme. We tell you more about themes and formatting in **Chapter 6**.

- The exact text of a More link (**Figure 19**) varies depending on settings in your blog's theme. We tell you how to modify this text in **Chapter 6**.

- To remove a More tag, select it (**Figure 25**) and press Backspace or Delete.

- As this book went to press, the spelling checker was not available in the server installation version of WordPress.

- The HTML Source Editor (**Figure 24**) is not the same as the HTML Editor you use when the visual rich editor is disabled. We tell you more about that later in this chapter.

- To get additional information about using the visual rich editor, click the Help button in its toolbar. A window like the one in **Figure 26** appears with more information.

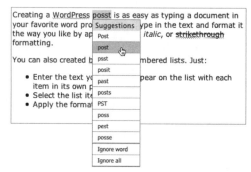

Figure 23 You can use a pop-up menu like this one to select the spelling you want.

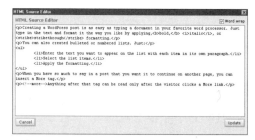

Figure 24 Use the HTML Source Editor to modify HTML code for a post or Page.

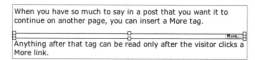

Figure 25 You can select a More tag to delete it.

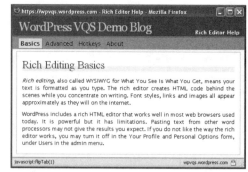

Figure 26 Clicking the Help button displays more information about the visual rich editor.

USING THE VISUAL RICH EDITOR'S TOOLBAR

Figure 27 The Insert/edit image dialog.

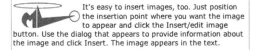

Figure 28 This example shows an inline image positioned at the baseline.

It's easy to insert images, too. Just position the insertion point where you want the image to appear and click the Insert/edit image button. Use the dialog that appears to provide information about the image and click Insert. The image appears in the text.

Figure 29 The same image, with left alignment.

To insert an image

1. If necessary, use your FTP client software to upload the image to your WordPress blog or Web server.

2. In the Post or Page Content box, position the insertion point where you want the image to appear.

3. Click the Insert/edit image button in the toolbar (**Figure 13**).

4. Enter the following information in the Insert/edit image dialog that appears (**Figure 27**) and click Insert:

   ▲ **Image URL** is the complete URL for the image file.

   ▲ **Image description** is the text that appears if the image cannot be found or if browsing images is disabled.

   ▲ **Alignment** allows you to set the alignment for inline images (Baseline (**Figure 28**), Top, Middle, Bottom, TextTop, Absolute Middle, or Absolute Bottom) or text wrapped images (Left (**Figure 29**) or Right).

   ▲ **Dimensions** is the size of the image in pixels. WordPress automatically retrieves this information from the image file, but you can override it to resize the image.

   ▲ **Border** is the thickness, in pixels, of an image border. Leave this box blank or enter 0 for no border.

   ▲ **Vertical space** is the number of pixels between the top and bottom of the image and other content.

   ▲ **Horizontal space** is the number of pixels between the left and right sides of the image and other content.

   The image appears with the text (**Figure 28** or **29**) in the Post or Page content box.

Continued on next page...

INSERTING IMAGES

Continued from previous page.

✔ Tips

■ We explain how to use some popular FTP client software to upload files to a server in **Appendix B**.

■ You can also insert an image uploaded to your WordPress blog using options in the Browse tab of the Upload area on the Write Post or Write Page administration panel (**Figures 11** and **12**). We explain how to upload images and insert them into posts or Pages in the section titled "Uploading Files" later in this chapter.

■ To resize an image proportionally, enter a value in just one of the Dimensions boxes in step 4.

■ To return an image to its original size, clear the values in the Dimensions boxes in step 4.

■ To remove an image, select the image in the Post or Page Content box and press Backspace or Delete.

■ The WordPress Codex has an excellent reference guide for using images in your blog's posts and Pages. Read it at codex.wordpress.org/Using_Images.

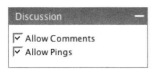

Figure 30 Use Discussion options to allow or disallow comments, pingbacks, and trackbacks.

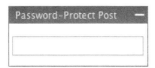

Figure 31 You can password-protect a post by entering a password in this box.

Figure 32 In your blog, visitors are prompted to enter a password to view a password-protected post.

Figure 33
A post slug is used by the permalinks feature.

Figure 34
Toggle check boxes for the categories you want to apply to a post.

To set post options

1. In the Write Post window (**Figure 11**), if necessary, click the + button on the right end of the blue title bar for any category of options you want to set. The section expands to show options.

2. To control comments and pings, set Discussion options (**Figure 30**):

   ▲ **Allow Comments** allows blog visitors to enter comments about the post.

   ▲ **Allow Pings** allows visitors to post pingbacks or trackbacks to the post.

3. To require a password to view the post, enter a password in the Password-Protect Post box (**Figure 31**). With this option enabled, a visitor will be prompted to enter a password (**Figure 32**) before the post or its comments are displayed.

4. To set the name of the post to be used in permalinks, enter a name in the Post Slug box. The name can include only letters, numbers, and hyphens. **Figure 33** shows an example.

5. To assign one or more categories to the post, in the Categories list, turn on the check box beside each category you want to assign (**Figure 34**). You can also use this area to quickly add a category to your blog; enter the new category name in the box and click the Add button; the category immediately appears in the list and is selected.

Continued on next page...

SETTING POST OPTIONS

Continued from previous page.

6. To determine how the post will be saved or published, select one of the Post Status options (**Figure 35**):

   ▲ **Published** publishes the post to the blog. This option is automatically selected when you click the Publish button after composing your post if you have not selected Private.

   ▲ **Draft** enables you to save your post as a draft to be completed at a later time. To use this option, be sure to click the Save button instead of the Publish button when you're finished working with the post.

   ▲ **Private** enables you to publish the post so it only appears when you view the blog. You must be logged into the blog to view your private posts.

7. To assign a specific date and time to a post, in the Post Timestamp area (**Figure 36**) turn on the Edit timestamp check box and set date and time options as desired.

8. To set the post author, in the Post author area (**Figure 37**), choose a user name from the drop-down list. This list will include all blog users who have been assigned a role of author or higher.

9. To create a custom excerpt for the post, enter the text you want to appear in the Optional Excerpt box (**Figure 38**). This excerpt is used for RSS feeds if you chose the Summary option in the Reading Options administration panel and may be used in various archive and category pages, depending on the theme applied to your blog.

Figure 35
You have three options for setting the status of a post.

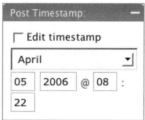

Figure 36
To change a post's timestamp, turn on the check box and set the desired date and time.

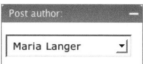

Figure 37
You can choose an author name from the Post author drop-down list.

Figure 38 You can enter an optional excerpt for a post to be used in RSS feed summaries and elsewhere.

SETTING POST OPTIONS

Figure 39 Enter URLs for sites you want to send track-back pings to.

Figure 40 WordPress users with their own WordPress server installation can include custom fields with their posts.

10. To send a trackback ping to another site, In the Trackbacks area, enter the URL for the trackback in the Send trackbacks to box (**Figure 39**). To enter more than one URL, separate each one with a space.

11. To include a custom field in the post, set options in the Custom Fields area (**Figure 40**) and click Add Custom Field. This option, which is discussed in greater detail in **Chapter 10**, is available for WordPress server installations only.

✔ Tips

■ Access to the comments feature is also controlled by settings in the General Options and Discussion Options administration panels, as discussed in **Chapters 2** and **4**.

■ We tell you more about comments, pingbacks, and trackbacks in **Chapter 4**. about permalinks and reading options in **Chapter 2**, and about users and roles in **Chapter 5**.

■ The Draft option in the Post Status area (**Figure 35**) can also be used to "unpublish" a post and save it as a draft.

■ In step 7, if you do not turn on the check box, the date and time you manually set will not be used.

■ You can use the post timestamp feature (**Figure 36**) to schedule a post's publication date and time. For example, suppose you write a post today but don't want it to appear until next week. If you set the timestamp for the date and time you want the post to appear, it will not appear in your blog until on or after that date and time.

To set Page options

1. In the Write Post window (**Figure 12**), if necessary, click the + button on the right end of the blue title bar for any category of options you want to set. The section expands to show options.

2. To control comments and pings, set Discussion options (**Figure 30**):
   - ▲ **Allow Comments** allows blog visitors to enter comments about the Page.
   - ▲ **Allow Pings** allows visitors to post pingbacks or trackbacks to the Page.

3. To require a password to view the Page, enter a password in the Password-Protect Page or Password-Protect Post box (**Figure 31**). With this option enabled, a visitor will be prompted to enter a password (**Figure 41**) when he clicks a link to the Page.

4. To assign a parent Page to the Page you are creating, in the Page Parent area (**Figure 42**) choose a Page name from the drop-down list. The list includes all existing pages. Choosing an option other than Main Page (no parent) creates a *subpage* that appears indented beneath its parent in Page lists (**Figure 43**).

5. To set a specific template for the Page, in the Page Template area (**Figure 44**), choose a template name from the drop-down list.

6. To set the name of the Page to be used in permalinks, enter a name in the Page Slug or Post Slug box. The name can include only letters, numbers, and hyphens. **Figure 33** shows an example.

Figure 41 When a Page is password-protected, the password prompt appears when you click its link.

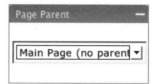

Figure 42 You can use the Page Parent feature to turn a page into a subpage.

Figure 43 A subpage appears indented beneath its parent Page in lists.

Figure 44 You can apply a specific template to a Page.

Figure 45 Use the Page Order option to assign a page number to a Page.

7. To set the Page author, in the Page Author or Post author area (**Figure 37**), choose a user name from the drop-down list. This list will include all blog users who have been assigned a role of author or higher.

8. To specify where the Page will appear in Page lists, in the Page Order box (**Figure 45**), enter a value that sets the Page's order in relation to other Pages. For example, if you wanted this Page to appear last and you have about 10 Pages, enter 10.

9. To include a custom field in the Page, set options in the Custom Fields area (**Figure 40**) and click Add Custom Field. This option, which is discussed in greater detail in **Chapter 10**, is available for WordPress server installations only.

✔ Tips

- Access to the comments feature is also controlled by settings in the General Options and Discussion Options administration panels, as discussed in **Chapters 2** and **4**.

- We tell you more about comments, pingbacks, and trackbacks in **Chapter 4**. about page templates, in **Chapter 6**, about permalinks in **Chapter 2**, and about users and roles in **Chapter 5**.

- To display a list of pages in the sort order you specify with the Page Order option (**Figure 45**), you must use the sort_column=menu_order argument with the wp_list_pages template tag. We tell you more about themes and templates in **Chapter 6**.

SETTING PAGE OPTIONS

To use the WordPress bookmarklet

1. Scroll down to the WordPress book-marklet area near the bottom of the Write Post window (**Figure 11**).

2. In Windows, right-click on the Press-It link.

   or

   In Mac OS, hold down ⎝Control⎠ and click the Press-It link.

   A menu of options should appear (**Figures 46a** and **46b**).

3. Choose the appropriate command to add the link to your bookmarks or favorites. The exact wording of the command varies from browser to browser.

4. Follow any additional steps required by your browser to add the link as a book-mark or favorite item. For simplicity's sake, we'll assume you kept the "Press It" name (**Figure 47**).

5. Use your Web browser to view a Web page you want to write about in your blog.

6. Select the Press It bookmark or favorite item. The Write Post administration panel of your WordPress blog appears. The title is filled in with the name of the page you were viewing and a link to the page is entered in the Post box (**Figure 48**).

7. Modify the post and set options as desired to complete the post.

8. Click Publish.

   The entry is created (**Figure 49**) and you are returned to the page you were viewing when you accessed the bookmarklet.

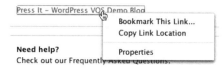

Figures 46a & 46b The shortcut menu for the bookmarklet link on Windows using Internet Explorer (left) and Mac OS using Firefox (below).

Getting Started   Latest Headlines   Press It – WordPress …

Figure 47 You may find it useful to add the bookmark-let to your browser's bookmarks bar.

Figure 48 The bookmarklet does most of the work of creating a new post about a Web page.

Figure 49 An entry created from a slightly edited ver-sion of what's in **Figure 48**.

✔ Tips

- If you have a Macintosh with a two-button mouse, you can follow the Windows instructions in step 2.

- On some browsers, you can create a bookmark bar button for the bookmarklet link (**Figure 47**) by simply dragging it to the bookmark bar and releasing it.

- You only have to complete steps 1 through 4 once for each browser you use. After the bookmarklet is installed in a browser, it can be used at any time.

- If you selected any text in the Web page you browsed in step 5, that selected text also appears in the Post box in step 6.

- In step 7, it isn't necessary to modify the post in any way. You can simply click Publish to publish it to your blog as it is created by the bookmarklet.

- If you are writing a post about a blog entry, you might want to copy the entry's trackback link before accessing the Press It bookmark. You can then paste it into the Trackbacks box for your WordPress post. We tell you more about trackbacks in **Chapter 4**.

USING THE WORDPRESS BOOKMARKLET

To preview a post or Page before publishing it

1. Follow the instructions throughout this part of the chapter to prepare your post or Page in the Write Post or Write Page administration panel (**Figure 11** or **12**).

2. Click the Save and Continue Editing button.

3. Wait for the page to refresh.

4. Scroll down to the bottom of the page. A preview of your post appears in the Post Preview area (**Figure 50**).

✔ Tips

■ The preview area of the window has its own scroll bar. Be sure to use that scroll bar and not the window's main scroll bar to view the entire post preview.

■ Any time you change the contents of the Post or Page Content box, you must click the Save and Continue Editing button to refresh the preview.

■ The date and time in a new post's preview may not be accurate. The time will be corrected when the post is published.

■ To save all your changes and publish the new post, click the Publish button. If you are editing an existing post, click the Save button. We tell you more about editing posts later in this chapter.

Figure 50 A fully-functioning preview of the entry appears in a scrolling window near the bottom of the Write Post or Write Page administration panel.

Figure 51 The HTML Editor has QuickTag buttons instead of a formatting toolbar.

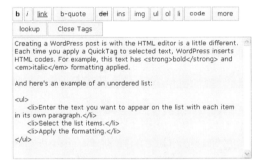

Figure 52 Here's some sample text, formatted with the QuickTags. You need to know HTML to use this feature.

To use the HTML editor instead of the visual rich editor

1. Follow the instructions in **Chapter 5** to disable the visual rich editor for your user profile.

2. Follow the instructions earlier in this section to open the Write Post or Write Page administration panel. The toolbar over the Post or Page Content box is replaced with QuickTag buttons (**Figure 51**).

3. Enter the text of your post in the box.

4. Use QuickTag buttons to apply formatting to selected text. Instead of the text appearing with the formatting applied, HTML tags are inserted around the text to apply formatting (**Figure 52**).

5. Complete the post or Page as instructed earlier in this section and click Publish to publish it to your blog.

✔ Tips

- The HTML editor can automatically recognize and code a single Enter or Return as <br /> and a double Enter or Return as

. This makes it unnecessary to use <p>, </p>, and <br /> tags in the Post or Page Content box when composing your post.

- The HTML editor isn't for everyone. Clearly, you need a solid understanding of how HTML works to use it. It does, however, give you more control over formatting the contents of a post or Page.

- A complete discussion of HTML is beyond the scope of this book. For more information about HTML, check out Liz Castro's *HTML for the World Wide Web with XHTML and CSS: Visual QuickStart Guide.*

USING THE HTML EDITOR

Uploading Files

WordPress makes it easy to upload images and other files to your blog. You can then include the image or a link to the file in a post or on a Page. You do all this with the Upload area of the Write Post or Write Page administration panel (**Figure 11** or **12**).

✔ Tip

■ To upload a file to a WordPress server installation blog, the uploads folder inside the wp-content folder must be writable. We tell you more about making folders and files writable in **Chapter 6**.

To upload a file

1. In the Write Post or Write Page administration panel (**Figure 11** or **12**), scroll down to the Upload area (**Figure 53**).

2. Click the Browse button beside the File box.

3. Use the dialog that appears to locate and select the file you want to upload (**Figures 54a** and **54b**).

4. Click Open. The pathname to the file appears in the File box.

5. Enter a name for the file in the Title box.

6. Enter a brief description for the file in the Description box.

7. Click the Upload button.

8. Wait while the file is uploaded to your blog. The amount of time you have to wait depends on the size of the file and the speed of your Internet connection.

   When it's finished, the Browse tab appears with either a thumbnail image (**Figure 55a**) or the name (**Figure 55b**) of the file you uploaded.

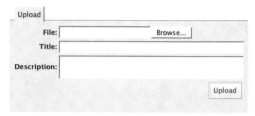

Figure 53 The Upload area of a Write Post or Write Page administration panel before any files have been uploaded to the blog.

Figures 54a & 54b The File Upload dialog on Windows with an image file selected (top) and on Mac OS with a PDF file selected (bottom).

Figures 55a & 55b The Browse pane with an image thumbnail (top) and with a file name (bottom).

Figure 56
Clicking the image thumbnail displays a menu of options.

Figure 57 In this example, I've inserted a thumbnail of the image in the post as a link to a page.

Figure 58 Here's the post from **Figure 57**.

Figure 59 Here's the page that appears when you click the image.

To insert an uploaded image in a post or Page

1. In the Browse or Browse All tab of the Upload area (**Figure 55a**), click the image thumbnail. A menu of options appears over the item (**Figure 56**).

2. To choose which image to use, click the first option to toggle settings:
   - ▲ **Use Thumbnail** uses the thumbnail image that appears in the Browse tab.
   - ▲ **Use Original** uses the uploaded image.

3. To indicate how the image file should be linked, click the second option to toggle settings:
   - ▲ **Not Linked** does not link the image to anything.
   - ▲ **Linked to Image** displays the image in its own Web browser window when you click the image in a post or Page.
   - ▲ **Linked to Page** displays the picture on a page created with the current theme (**Figure 59**) when you click the image in a post or Page.

4. To insert the image (with the settings from steps 2 and 3) at the insertion point in the Post or Page Content box, click Send to editor. The image appears in the editing box (**Figure 57**).

5. Finish composing the post or Page as instructed earlier in this chapter and click Publish. The image appears in the post (**Figure 58**) or Page.

✔ Tip

- ■ If you are using the HTML editor, the image will not appear in the editing box. Instead, the HTML code for the image will appear there.

To insert a link to an uploaded file in a post or Page

1. In the Browse or Browse All tab of the Upload area (**Figure 55b**), click the file name. A menu of options appears over the item (**Figure 60**).

2. To indicate how the file should be linked, click the first option to toggle settings:
   - ▲ **Linked to File** creates a link that, when clicked, downloads the file.
   - ▲ **Linked to Page** creates a link that, when clicked, displays the displays a page that includes the title, description, and file name of the file. Clicking the file's title on that page downloads the file.

3. To indicate what should be used as the text for the link, click the second option to toggle settings:
   - ▲ **Using Title** uses the title you entered for the file when you uploaded it.
   - ▲ **Using Filename** uses the file's name on disk.

4. To insert the file (with the settings from steps 2 and 3) at the insertion point in the Post or Page content box, click Send to editor. The link appears in the editing box (**Figure 61**).

5. Finish composing the post or Page as instructed earlier in this chapter and click Publish. A link to the file appears in the post (**Figure 62**) or Page.

✔ Tip

- You can use this feature to create a basic podcast. Just insert a link to an uploaded MP3 file. Then subscribe to the blog's RSS feed to automatically download MP3 files into your podcatching software. We tell you more about podcasting in **Chapter 10**.

Figure 60
A menu of options like this one appears for uploaded files.

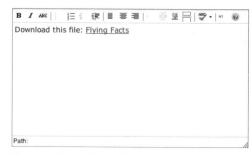

Figure 61 You can insert the link in the Post or Page content box.

Figure 62 Here's a simple blog entry with the link from **Figure 61**.

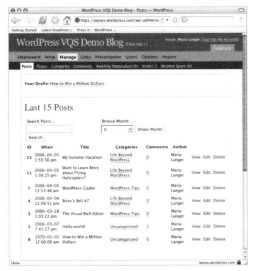

Figure 63 The Manage Posts administration panel.

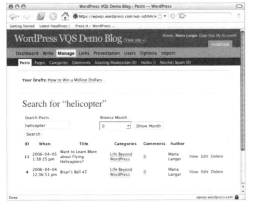

Figure 64 Search results appear in the Manage Posts administration panel.

Figure 65 Choose a month from the Browse Month drop-down list.

Managing Posts

The Manage Posts administration panel (**Figure 63**) offers easy access to all of your posts. From this panel, you can display recent posts, search for specific posts, or display posts by month. You can also view posts and associated comments, edit posts—including draft posts—and delete posts.

In short, the Manage Posts panel enables you to manage every aspect of your posts.

To view the Manage Posts administration panel

1. If necessary, log into your blog and display the Dashboard.

2. Click the Manage button.

3. Click the Posts button in the second row of buttons. The Manage Posts administration panel appears (**Figure 63**).

To search for a post

1. Near the top of the Manage Posts administration panel (**Figure 63**) enter a search word or phrase in the Search Posts box.

2. Click Search.

   WordPress displays the search results in the Manage Posts administration panel (**Figure 64**).

✔ Tips

- WordPress searches both the title and the content of posts to match search criteria.

- Searching for Pages works the same way, but in the Page Management administration panel (**Figure 74**). We discuss managing Pages later in this chapter.

To browse posts by month

1. Near the top of the Manage Posts administration panel (**Figure 63**) choose a month from the Browse Month drop-down list. The list will include all months for which there are posts (**Figure 65**).

2. Click Show Month.

   WordPress displays the posts for the month you chose in the Manage Posts administration panel (**Figure 66**).

To view a post

In the Manage Posts administration panel (**Figure 63**), click the View button for the post you want to view.

The post appears on its own page in your blog.

To edit a post

1. In the Manage Posts administration panel (**Figure 63**), click the Edit button for the post you want to modify.

   or

   In your blog, click the edit link for a post you want to modify.

   The post appears in a Write Post administration panel (**Figure 67**).

2. Make changes as desired to the post's contents or other settings as discussed earlier in this chapter.

3. Click the Save button beneath the Post box.

   Your changes are saved.

✔ Tip

■ If your user profile does not have an administrative role, you can only modify a post you authored.

Figure 66 Only posts from the selected month are displayed.

Figure 67 Edit a post in the Write Post administration panel.

Figure 68 When you edit a draft post, a Publish button appears beneath the Post box.

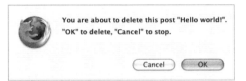

Figure 69 Click OK in this dialog to confirm that you want to delete the post.

To publish a draft post

1. Near the top of the Manage Posts administration panel (**Figure 63**) click the name of a post listed after Your Drafts.

   The post appears in the Write Post administration panel (**Figure 68**).

2. Make changes as desired to the post's contents or other settings as discussed earlier in this chapter.

3. Click the Publish button beneath the Post box.

   The post status is changed to Published and the post appears in your blog.

To delete a post

1. In the Manage Posts administration panel (**Figure 63**), click the Delete button for the post you want to remove.

   or

   In the Write Post administration panel for a post you are editing (**Figure 67**), click the Delete this Post button.

2. In the confirmation dialog that appears (**Figure 69**), click OK.

   The post is removed permanently from your blog.

✔ Tip

■ If you want to remove a post from the blog without actually deleting it, use the Write Post window to change its Post Status to Draft and click Save.

Posting by E-mail

If you're running a server installation of WordPress, you can configure it to accept and publish posts submitted via e-mail. This makes it possible to post entries to your blog without using a Web browser.

Here's how it works. Begin by creating a unique e-mail address. The new address will be used only for receiving blog posts and should not be revealed to anyone not authorized to post to the blog. Next, configure the Writing by e-mail options in the Writing Options administration panel (**Figure 70**) to provide settings for this new e-mail address. Then use your e-mail client software to compose a message containing the text of a post you want to publish and send it to the e-mail address you specified. Finally, tell WordPress to check for new posts—or set it up to check automatically. The message is imported into your blog as a post.

In this part of the chapter, we explain how to compose an e-mail message to be posted to your blog and how to tell WordPress to check for new posts by e-mail.

✔ Tips

- This feature is not available for Word-Press.com blogs.

- If you need help setting up an e-mail address, consult your ISP or system administrator.

- We explain how to configure Writing Options to use this feature in **Chapter 2**. This step must be completed once *before* sending posts by e-mail.

- The e-mail address you set up for posting by e-mail must be unique and used only for posting to your blog. Keep it secret— anyone who has this address will be able to post to your blog!

Figure 70 To post by e-mail, you must set Writing by e-mail options in the Writing Options administration panel.

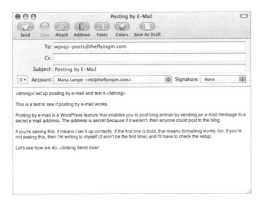

Figure 71 Here's an example of a blog post in an e-mail message.

To submit a post by e-mail

1. Launch your e-mail client software.

2. In the To field of a new message form, enter the e-mail address you specified in the Writing Options administration panel (**Figure 70**).

3. In the Subject field, enter the text you want to appear as the title for the post.

4. In the body of the message, enter the text you want to appear in the post. **Figure 71** shows an example of a completed post.

5. Use the Send button or command to send the message.

✔ Tips

- You can include HTML tags in the body of the message for formatting, links, and other post content.

- Do not use rich text formatting features offered by your e-mail client software. Doing so may render the message unreadable by WordPress.

SUBMITTING POSTS BY E-MAIL

To import e-mailed posts

1. If WordPress is installed in its own folder in your Web site's root directory, use your Web browser to open *www.example.com/* wordpress/wp-mail.php.

   or

   If the individual WordPress files are installed in your Web site's root directory, use your browser to open *www.example.com/*wp-mail.php.

2. Wait while WordPress checks for the message and loads it. When it's finished, you should see something like what's shown in **Figure 72**.

3. Use your Web browser to view your blog. The message should appear as a post (**Figure 73**).

✔ Tips

■ You may see the following error message in step 2: Oops POP3: premature NOOP OK, NOT an RFC 1939 Compliant server. If so, you'll need to use a text editor to modify the contents of the class-pop3.php file in your wp-includes folder for a quick fix. Search the file for if($this->RFC1939) { and replace it with if(!$this->RFC1939) { (note the exclamation point). Save the file and repeat these steps. It should work without errors from that point on.

■ You can automate this process by installing and activating the WP-Cron and WP-Cron-Mail plugins. You can learn more about these plugins at www.skippy. net/blog/category/wordpress/plugins/ wp-cron/. We tell you about plugins in **Chapter 7**.

Figure 72 WordPress shows the text it imported with the text it posted. They should be the same.

Figure 73 Here's how the post might appear in your blog.

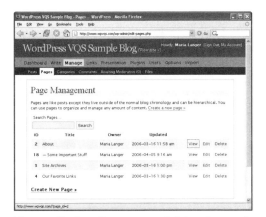

Figure 74 The Page Management administration panel lists all Pages you have created.

Figure 75 The search results appear in the Page Management administration panel.

Managing Pages

The Page Management administration panel (**Figure 74**) offers access to all of your Pages. From this panel, you can search for, view, edit, and delete Pages.

To view the Page Management administration panel

1. If necessary, log into your blog and display the Dashboard.

2. Click the Manage button.

3. Click the Pages button in the second row of buttons. The Page Management administration panel appears (**Figure 74**).

To search for a Page

1. Near the top of the Page Management administration panel (**Figure 74**) enter a search word or phrase in the Search Pages box.

2. Click Search.

   WordPress displays the search results in the Page Management administration panel (**Figure 75**).

✔ Tip

■ WordPress searches both the title and the content of Pages to match search criteria.

To view a Page

In the Page Management administration panel (**Figure 74**), click the View button for the Page you want to view.

The Page appears in your blog.

To edit a Page

1. In the Page Management administration panel (**Figure 74**), click the Edit button for the Page you want to modify.

   or

   In your blog, click the edit link for a Page you want to modify.

   The Page appears in a Write Page administration panel (**Figure 76**).

2. Make changes as desired to the Page's contents or other settings as discussed earlier in this chapter.

3. Click the Save button beneath the Page content box.

   Your changes are saved.

✔ Tips

■ If your user profile does not have an administrative role, you can only modify a Page you own.

■ To publish a draft Page, follow these steps, but in step 3, click the Publish button that appears beneath the Page Content box.

To delete a Page

1. In the Page Management administration panel (**Figure 74**), click the Delete button for the Page you want to remove.

   or

   In the Write Page administration panel for a Page you are editing (**Figure 76**), click the Delete this Page button.

2. In the confirmation dialog that appears (**Figure 77**), click OK.

   The Page is permanently removed from your blog.

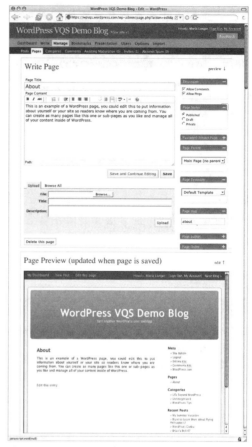

Figure 76 The Write Page administration panel for editing a Page.

Figure 77 Click OK to delete the Page.

Working with Links & Bookmarks

Most blogs include links to other blogs, Web sites, and specific Web pages. WordPress's *links* feature enables you to maintain a database of links, organized by category, that you can display in the sidebar of your blog. You do all this with the Links or Bookmarks administration panels.

The Links feature differs slightly between WordPress.com blogs and WordPress server-installed blogs:

◆ Links are called *links* on a server-installed blog. Links are called *bookmarks* on a WordPress.com blog.

◆ Link categories on server-installed blogs are separate from post categories. Posts and bookmarks share the same categories on WordPress.com blogs.

This part of the chapter explains how you can add, modify, and categorize links and bookmarks in your blog.

✔ Tips

■ The display of links in your blog is controlled by your blog's theme. We tell you more about themes in **Chapter 6**.

■ To keep things simple, throughout this book, we use the word *links* to refer to *links* or *bookmarks*.

To view a list of links

1. From your WordPress Dashboard, click the Links or Bookmarks button.

2. If necessary, click the Manage Links or Manage Bookmarks button in the second row of buttons.

   A list of all existing links appears in the Bookmarks Management (**Figure 78a**) or Manage Links (**Figure 78b**) administration panel .

✔ Tips

- Your WordPress blog will automatically include some links when you install it. The links installed with a WordPress.com account differ from those in a WordPress server installation. You can remove any of the preinstalled links.

- You can customize the view of the links in the Bookmarks Management (**Figure 78a**) or Manage Links (**Figure 78b**) administration panel:

  ▲ To narrow down the list of displayed links to those in a single category, choose that category from the Currently showing (**Figure 78a**) or Show links in category (**Figure 78b**) drop-down list and click Update or Show.

  ▲ To sort links, choose a column from the bookmarks ordered by (**Figure 78a**) or Order by (**Figure 78b**) drop-down list and click Update or Show.

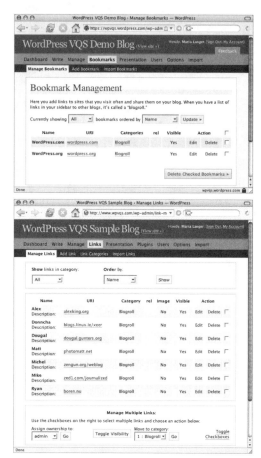

Figures 78a & 78b The Bookmark Management administration panel for a WordPress.com blog (top) and the Manage Links adminsitration panel for a WordPress server-installed blog(bottom).

Figure 79a Use the Create Bookmark administration panel to add links to a WordPress.com blog's bookmarks list.

To add a bookmark or link

1. From your WordPress Dashboard, click the Bookmarks or Links button.

2. Click the Add Bookmark or Add Link button in the second row of buttons. The Create Bookmark (**Figure 79a**) or Add a link (**Figure 79b**) administration panel appears.

3. Enter information for the link in the Basics area:

   ▲ **URI** is the fully-qualified URL to the page or site you're linking to. Be sure to include the http://.

   ▲ **Link Name** is the name of the link as you want it to appear in your Links list.

   ▲ **Short description** is a brief description of the page, site, or blog you're linking to. This may or may not appear beneath the link (depending on the settings in your theme) but it always appears when a visitor points to the link.

   ▲ **Categories** or **Category** is the category you want to group the link in. For WordPress.com sites, turn on one or more check boxes in the Categories area (**Figure 79a**), which includes all defined categories. For WordPress server-installed blogs, choose an option from the drop-down list (**Figure 79b**), which includes all defined link categories.

4. If desired, enter information for the link in the Link Relationship (**XFN**) area by toggling check boxes and selecting radio buttons.

Continued on next page...

Continued from previous page.

5. If desired, enter information for the link in the Advanced area:

   ▲ **Image URI** is the complete URL for an image you want to display with the link. For best results, this image should be 16x16 pixels in size.

   ▲ **RSS URI** is the complete URL for the RSS feed for the linked site.

   ▲ **Notes** is for storing notes about the linked site.

   ▲ **Rating** is your own personal rating for the link. This option is useful if you set up your link display to sort links by rating.

   ▲ **Target** is the target attribute for the link tag: **_blank** opens the link in a new page, **_top** opens the link in the same page after clearing frames, and **none** opens the link in the same page. These options appear in the Target area for WordPress.com blogs (**Figure 79a**) and in the Advanced area for WordPress server-installed blogs (**Figure 79b**).

   ▲ **Visible** determines whether the link will appear in Links lists. The Yes and No options appear in the Visible area for WordPress.com blogs (**Figure 79a**) and in the Advanced area for WordPress server-installed blogs (**Figure 79b**).

6. Click Add Bookmark or Add Link.

   The link is added to your blog's link list.

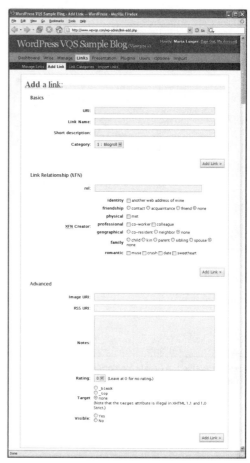

Figure 79b Use the Add a link administration panel to add a link to a WordPress server-installed blog.

ADDING LINKS

Figure 80

This example shows how a links list might appear in the Default theme if an Image URI is provided for one of the links.

Blogroll

ML.
» com
» WordPress.com
» WordPress.org

✔ Tips

■ You may have to click the + button at the right end of a section name (**Figure 79a**) to display options in that section.

■ We tell you more about themes in **Chapter 6** and explain how to add and modify link categories later in this part of the chapter.

■ *XFN* stands for *XHTML Friends Network*. Setting options in the Link Relationship area includes special coding for participation in this program. You can learn more at gmpg.org/xfn/.

■ If you include an Image URI in step 5, the image may appear instead of the text link, depending on your blog's theme and settings for the link's category. **Figure 80** shows an example using the Default theme in a WordPress.com blog. We tell you more about link categories starting on the next page.

■ If the page or site you're linking to has a favicon.ico file, you may want to use that as the Image URI in step 5. You can normally find it in the root directory for the site. So, for example, the URI for the favicon file on Maria's site (**Figure 80**) would be http://www.marialanger.com/favicon.ico.

ADDING LINKS

73

To add a link category (server-installed blogs only)

1. From your WordPress Dashboard, click the Links button.

2. Click the Link Categories button in the second row of buttons to display the Link Categories administration panel (**Figure 81**).

3. If necessary, scroll down to the Add a Link Category area.

4. Set options in the Category Options area:

   ▲ **Name** is the name of the category.

   ▲ **Show** enables you to specify what should show for each link in the category. **Image** is the link's image, **Description** is the link's description, **Rating** is the link's rating, and **Updated** is the date you modified the link. (Most of these options are set when you add a link as discussed on the previous two pages.) You can turn on the check box for any combination of these options.

   ▲ **Sort order** determines how links in the category are sorted: by name, unique ID, URL, rating, update date, or random. Turning on the Descending check box displays them in the reverse order.

   ▲ **Limit** enables you to specify the maximum number of links to display. Leave the box empty for no limit.

   ▲ **Toggle** displays only the newest link in the category by hiding all others when a new link is added.

Figure 81 The Link Categories administration panel.

5. Set options in the Formatting area to specify the HTML tags to be used for formatting the links list:

   ▲ **Before Link** is the tag that should be placed before each link. By default, this is the <li> or *start list item* tag.

   ▲ **Between Link and Description** is the tag that should be placed between the link and its description (if displayed). By default, this is <br /> or *line break*.

   ▲ **After Link** is the tag that should be placed after each link. By default, this is the </li> or *end list item* tag.

6. Click Add Category.

   The link category is added to the list of categories at the top of the Link Categories administration panel.

✔ Tips

- To add categories for bookmarks in a WordPress.com blog, follow the instructions in the section titled "To add a category or subcategory" near the beginning of this chapter.

- If a category has a lot of links but you don't want to display them all, enter the maximum number of links you want to display in the Limit box and set the Sort order option to Random. This way, each time the links list is loaded, a different collection of links will appear for the category.

- In the Before Link box in step 5, if you use a tag that requires a closing tag, you must put the corresponding closing tag in the After Link box.

To work with link categories (server-installed blogs only)

1. From your WordPress Dashboard, click the Links button.

2. Click the Link Categories button in the second row of buttons to display the Link Categories administration panel (**Figure** 81).

3. To modify a link category, click the Edit link on the right end of the category's row. Then set options in the Edit Category administration panel that appears (**Figure** 82) and click the Save Category Settings button.

4. To delete a link category, click the Delete link on the far-right end of the category's row. Click OK in the confirmation dialog that appears (**Figure** 83) to delete the link category.

✔ Tips

■ To modify or delete bookmark categories in a WordPress.com blog, follow the instructions in the sections titled "To edit a category" and "To delete a category" near the beginning of this chapter.

■ Deleting a link category does not delete any links. When you delete a link's category, the default category (Blogroll) is assigned to it.

Figure 82 The Edit Category administration panel is for editing link categories.

Figure 83 You must click OK in a dialog like this one to delete a link category.

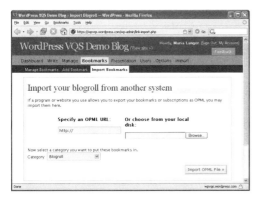

Figure 84 Use this administration panel to import links stored in an OPML file.

Figure 85 WordPress confirms that it has imported the links.

To import links from an OPML file

1. From your WordPress Dashboard, click the Bookmarks or Links button.

2. Click the Import Bookmarks or Import Links button in the second row of buttons to display the Import your blogroll from another system administration panel (**Figure 84**).

3. Enter the URL for an OPML file in the Specify an OMPL URL box.

   or

   Use the Browse button to locate, select, and open an OPML file on your hard disk.

4. Use the Category drop-down list to choose the category into which you want to import the links. This list will include all defined link categories.

5. Click Import OPML File. The links are imported and listed in the window (**Figure 85**).

✔ Tips

- *OPML* stands for *Outline Processor Markup Language*. It's an XML-based standard format for transfering information. You can learn more about OPML format at www.opml.org.

- As you can imagine, this is a quick way to add links to your site. All you need to do is get them in the OPML format!

To manage links

1. From your WordPress Dashboard, click the Bookmarks or Links button.

2. If necessary, click the Manage Bookmarks or Manage Links button in the second row of buttons to display the Bookmarks Management (**Figure 78a**) or Manage Links (**Figure 78b**) administration panel.

3. To modify a link, click the Edit button in the link's row. Then use the Edit Bookmark or Edit a link administration panel that appears to modify link settings. (This panel looks and works just like the Create Bookmark (**Figure 79a**) or Add a link (**Figure 79b**) shown and discussed earlier in this section.) When you're finished making changes, click Save Changes.

4. To delete a link, click the Delete button in the link's row. Click OK in the confirmation dialog that appears to remove the link.

5. To change multiple links at once in a WordPress server-installed blog, turn on the check box beside each link you want to change. Then:

   ▲ To change the owner of the links, choose a user from the Assign ownership to drop-down list and click Go.

   ▲ To toggle the visibility of the links, click Toggle Visibility.

   ▲ To move the links to another link category, choose a category from the Move to category drop-down list and click Go.

✔ Tips

■ In step 4, for a WordPress.com blog, you can turn on the check box beside each link you want to delete and click the Delete Checked Bookmarks button to delete them all at once.

■ In step 5, you can click the Toggle Checkboxes link to toggle the settings for all check boxes. This is a quick way to check or uncheck them all.

MANAGING LINKS

Moderating Comments

Figure 1 An example of a post that includes both a pingback and a comment.

Comments, Trackbacks, & Pingbacks

One blog feature that makes blogs so appealing to readers is the ability to enter *comments* about a post right in the blog. It doesn't matter whether a reader agrees, disagrees, or just wants to share additional information related to a post—the comment feature can handle it all. Then, when a reader views a post with its comments, he can see the original entry as well as all of the comments that are associated with it (**Figure 1**).

Trackbacks are similar to comments but originate in the commenter's blog rather than the post author's blog. Say, for example, that Blogger A reads a post in Blogger B's blog and wants to share it her blog readers. A would write a post in her blog and include a special trackback link that pointed to the original post in B's blog. When the post is published, a trackback comment appears in the comments area for the post on B's blog.

Pingbacks work a lot like trackbacks, but do not require a special trackback link. Instead, using the example above, A would simply include a link to B's site in her post. When the post is published, WordPress informs B's site that A included a link to it. A pingback comment is created on B's site (**Figure 1**).

This chapter explains how to configure, use, and moderate comments, trackbacks, and pingbacks.

Setting Discussion Options

The comments, trackbacks, and pingbacks features are controlled, in part, with settings in the Discussion Options administration panel (**Figure 2**). These settings let you enable or disable specific features, including pingbacks and comment moderation.

✔ Tip

- We tell you more about comment moderation and spam prevention later in this chapter.

To set discussion options

1. If necessary, log into your blog and display the Dashboard.

2. Click the Options button.

3. Click the Discussion button in the second row of buttons to display Discussion Options (**Figure 2**).

4. Set default options for new articles in the Usual settings for an article area as desired:

   ▲ **Attempt to notify any Weblogs linked to from the article** enables the pingback feature. As noted in the option, this may slow down posting of a post because each link must be pinged when the post is published.

   ▲ **Allow link notifications from other Weblogs** enables your posts to accept trackbacks and pingbacks. Turn this check box off if you do not want comments created from posts on other blogs.

   ▲ **Allow people to post comments on the article** enables your posts to accept comments from blog visitors.

Figure 2 Set comment-related options in the Discussion Options administration panel.

5. Set e-mail notification options in the E-mail me whenever area:

   ▲ **Anyone posts a comment** sends you an e-mail message whenever a comment is posted.

   ▲ **A comment is held for moderation** sends you an e-mail message whenever a comment is held for moderation.

6. Set comment options in the Before a comment appears area:

   ▲ **An administrator must approve the comment** enables comment moderation and requires each comment to be approved by an administrator before it appears in the entry.

   ▲ **Comment author must fill out name and e-mail** requires a commenter to include his name and e-mail address to submit a comment.

   ▲ **Comment author must have previously approved comment** can automatically approve comments submitted by commenters who have already had comments approved. For automatic approval to occur, the first option in this section must be turned off.

7. Set options in the Comment Moderation area as desired:

   ▲ **Hold a comment in the queue if it contains more than *n* links** automatically holds a comment for moderation if it contains more than the number of links you specify.

   ▲ To hold a comment for moderation based on content, enter match words or phrases in the box at the bottom of the area. Be sure to enter each word or phrase on its own line.

Continued on next page...

SETTING DISCUSSION OPTIONS

Continued from previous page.

8. To automatically delete a comment based on its content, enter match words in the Comment Blacklist box at the bottom of the page. Be sure to enter each word on its own line.

9. To prevent comments from being entered from IP addresses known for comment spam, turn on the **Blacklist comments from open and insecure proxies** check box.

10. Click Update Options to save your settings.

✔ Tips

- The second two options in the Usual settings for an article area can be overridden when you author a post. Simply toggle check boxes in the Discussion area in the right column of the Write Post window (**Figure 3**). We tell you more about these options in **Chapter 3**.

- If you turn on both e-mail optins in step 5 and enable comment moderation in steps 6 and 7, you'll get two e-mail messages for each approved comment.

- In step 7, you can click the Common spam words link to display information about spam words and a list of words that commonly appear in spam comments. This information can be found at codex.wordpress.org/Spam_Words.

- We tell you more about controlling comment spam later in this chapter.

- For additional control over who can comment, you can set options in the Membership area of the General Options administration panel. We tell you about those options in **Chapter 2**.

Figure 3 You can set comment and pingback features for a specific post or Page when writing it, as discussed in **Chapter 3**.

✖ Warning!

- Use the Comment Blacklist box with care! WordPress will automatically delete any comment that contains a listed word, even if that word is only part of another word in the comment. You will not receive any notification of comments deleted with this feature. When in doubt about including a word, put the word in the Comment Moderation box discussed in step 7 instead.

Permanent link   *Comment link*

Posting by E-Mail
April 11th, 2006

I set up posting by e-mail and test it.

This is a test to see if posting by e-mail works.

Posting by e-mail is a WordPress feature that enables you to post blog entries by sending an e-mail message to a secret e-mail address. The address is secret because if it weren't, then anyone could post to the blog.

If you're seeing this, it means I set it up correctly. If the first line is bold, that means formatting works, too. If you're not seeing this, then I'm writing to myself (it won't be the first time) and I'll have to check the setup.

Let's see how we do…clicking Send now!

Posted in WordPress Tips | Edit | 2 Comments »

Figure 4 You can click a post's permalink or comments link to view the post and its comments.

Viewing & Entering Comments

In most WordPress themes, comments appear only in a single post view—that is, a page that displays only one post at a time. You can view a post and its comments by opening the permalink for the post.

In most cases, comments will be entered on your blog by its visitors. But in many instances, you'll want to reply to a comment entered on your blog or write a comment on someone else's blog.

In this part of the chapter, we explain how to enter comments for a blog post.

✔ Tip

- A *permalink* is a permanent link for a post. We tell you more about setting options for permalinks in **Chapter 2**.

To view a post & its comments

Click the permalink for the post. This is normally the title of the post (**Figure 4**).

Or

Click the comment link in the post. This normally indicates how many comments the post has (**Figure 4**).

The post and its comments, along with a comment form, appear on a page (**Figure 1**).

✔ Tip

- When you click the comment link for a post, you are immediately taken to the comments area at the end of the post.

To enter a comment

1. If necessary, display the post and its comments as instructed on the previous page.

2. Scroll down to the comment form at the bottom of the post (**Figure 5a** or **5b**).

3. If necessary, enter the required information at the top of the form (**Figure 5a**).

4. Enter the text of your comment in the large text box at the bottom of the form.

5. Click Submit Comment.

✔ Tips

- How the comment form appears depends on whether you are already logged into the blog. **Figure 5a** shows the form for someone who is not logged in or has never left a comment on the blog. **Figure 5b** shows the form for someone who is logged in.

- If you are not logged in but have left a comment on the blog before, the comment form will look like the one in **Figure 5a** with the top fields filled in from information you provided the last time you entered a comment. This information is stored in a cookie in your Web browser.

- In step 4, your comment can include basic HTML commands for formatting.

- In step 5, the button for submitting the comment may be labeled differently, depending on settings for the blog's theme. **Figures 5a** and **5b** show the Default theme.

- Your comment may or may not appear immediately, depending on how moderation options have been set by the blog's administrator.

Figures 5a & 5b The comment form for a user who is not logged in (top) and for a user who is logged in (bottom).

1 Comment

1. e On April 18th, 2006 at 8:56 am, Skyler Alden said:
What a waste of perfectly good stuff Marty thought free casino best
[url=http://www.chosen-online-gambling.info]free casino best[/url] the outside I
was kind of quite around most people that is I was a online casinos
[url=http://www.chosen-online-gambling.info]online casinos[/url] I wasnt wearing
my seatbelt and had I been sitting upright I would free casino games
[url=http://www.chosen-online-gambling.info]free casino games[/url] Well
Eileenjeez thats hard for me to say Have you ever been in a play casino games for
free [url=http://www.chosen-online-gambling.info]play casino games for free[/url]
Take a quick look at the chips to make sure that you know the values, casino games
[url=http://www.chosen-online-gambling.info]casino games[/url] gutter into little
test tubes Marty glanced at them for a moment casino online games to play
[url=http://www.chosen-online-gambling.info]casino online games to play[/url]
trucks in the air above his home He shook his head and turned his casino bonus
[url=http://www.chosen-online-gambling.info]casino bonus[/url] tsuduki o matta
zuni watashi wa free casino bonuses
[url=http://www.chosen-online-gambling.info]free casino bonuses[/url] Marty was
about to climb in the back of the truck the countdown still casino on net
[url=http://www.chosen-online-gambling.info]casino on net[/url] reason it wouldnt
turn casino on the net [url=http://www.chosen-online-gambling.info]casino on the
net[/url] Good evening one said Agents Reese (points to his buddy) and Foley free
online casino [url=http://www.chosen-online-gambling.info]free online casino[/url]
and how you choose depends on a number of factors Are you playing for fun, free
online casino games [url=http://www.chosen-online-gambling.info]free online casino
games[/url] were on stage playing The Blue Tango in the middle of the dance floor
internet casino [url=http://www.chosen-online-gambling.info]internet casino[/url]
honest opinion internet casino gambling

Figure 6 An example of comment spam in a blog entry's comment area. Spambots try to fool spam catching software by composing lengthy entries with full sentences to hide URLs and advertising text.

Moderating Comments

When you allow blog readers and other visitors to enter comments about your posts, you also leave your blog open to inappropriate comments and comment spam.

An inappropriate comment is one that you don't think is appropriate for your blog. It could include foul language or it might attack you or another commenter. It could even provide information you don't want included on your blog, such as blatant advertisements, libelous accusations, or URLs for porn sites. You are the judge of what is and is not appropriate as a comment for your blog.

Comment spam (**Figure 6**) is far more annoying. Normally an advertisement for a product or service, comment spam often includes URLs to access a Web site where more information can be found. Comment spam is usually automatically generated and sent by programs called *spambots* which can hit a blog with dozens or even hundreds of comments in a matter of minutes. When mingled with real comments on your blog, they discourage readers from reading an entry's comments or adding their own.

All this means that as a blogger, you have a responsibility to keep undesirable comments and comment spam off your site. Your first tool for controlling comments is comment moderation. That's what this part of the chapter is all about.

✔ Tips

- This chapter assumes you have enabled comment moderation features as illustrated in **Figure 2**.

- We tell you more about preventing comment spam in the section titled "Dealing with Spam" later in this chapter.

To moderate comments in the Moderation panel

1. If necessary, log into your blog and display the Dashboard (**Figure 7**).

2. Click the Comments in moderation link.

   or

   Click the Manage button in the top row of buttons and then click the Awaiting Moderation button in the second row of buttons.

   The Moderation Queue administration panel appears (**Figure 8**).

3. Select a bulk action radio button for each comment you want to moderate:

   ▲ **Approve** approves the comment and displays it in the comments area for the entry.

   ▲ **Spam** marks the comment as spam and deletes the comment.

   ▲ **Delete** deletes the comment without marking it as spam.

   ▲ **Defer until later**, which is the default selection, does nothing with that comment.

4. Click the Moderate Comments button.

   Your settings are saved. Any comments you set as Approve, Spam, or Delete are removed from the Moderation Queue.

Figure 7 The number of comments in moderation appears in the Dashboard when you log in to your blog.

Figure 8 Use the Moderation Queue to approve or delete comments.

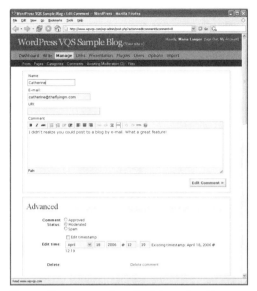

Figure 9 You can use a form like this one to edit a comment before approving it.

✔ Tips

■ Comments that appear in the Moderation Queue do not appear in your blog until you accept them.

■ To edit a comment, after step 2, click the Edit link for the comment you want to edit. Then use the comment editing form that appears (**Figure 9**) to modify comment contents. Click the Edit Comment button to save changes.

■ To view the post a comment is attached to, after step 2, click the View Post link for the comment. The post appears on its own WordPress page. You can click your browser's Back button to return to the Moderation Queue.

■ To delete a comment without moderating all comments, after step 2, click the Delete just this comment link for the comment you want to delete. Then click OK in the confirmation dialog that appears to permanently remove the comment.

■ In step 3, you can use links at the bottom of the Moderation Queue administration panel to moderate all comments at once. This is a quick way to set all comments the same without setting them individually. You must still click the Moderate Comments button to save your settings and complete the moderation.

To moderate comments from an e-mail notification

1. Open the e-mail message for the moderation request (**Figure 10**).

2. Click the appropriate link to approve or delete the comment.

   Your Web browser opens and displays the Moderation Queue administration panel. A message near the top of the window confirms that the comment has been approved (**Figure 11**) or deleted.

✔ Tips

- You can set options for e-mail notification of posted comments and comments held for moderation in the Discussion Options administration panel (**Figure 2**), which is discussed in detail earlier in this chapter.

- Other links in the e-mail request for moderation (**Figure 10**) enable you to view the post the comment is attached to, consult the Whois database for information about the commenter's IP address, and visit the Moderation Queue.

- If an e-mail notification informs you that a comment has been posted (**Figure 12**), you can still delete the comment. Just click the link in the message for deleting the comment.

Click one of these links to approve or delete the comment.

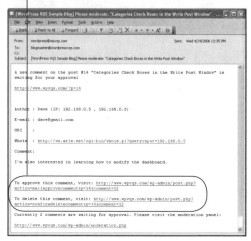

Figure 10 A request for moderation includes links to accept or delete a comment.

Figure 11 A message telling you that the comment has been approved or deleted appears at the top of the Moderation Queue.

Figure 12 Depending on Discussion Options settings, you may get a message like this one when a comment has been posted.

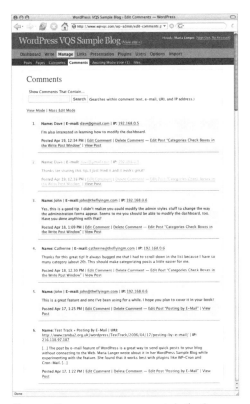

Figure 13 You can manage comments in the Comments administration panel.

Figure 14 The Comments administration panel in Mass edit mode.

Managing Comments

Once a comment has been added to your blog, it appears in the Comments administration panel. As shown in **Figure 13**, this window lists the 20 most recently posted comments and offers options for working with them, including searching for, editing, and deleting them.

To view the Comments administration panel

1. If necessary, log into your blog and display the Dashboard.

2. Click the Manage button in the first row of buttons.

3. Click the Comments button in the second row of buttons (**Figure 13**).

✔ Tip

- As shown in **Figure 13**, comments that are awaiting approval (comment 2 in the figure) are displayed in gray.

To switch between View mode & Mass edit mode

In the Comments administation panel (**Figure 13**), click the link for the mode you want:

◆ **View mode** (**Figure 13**) the entire text of each comment with links for working with it.

◆ **Mass edit mode** (**Figure 14**) displays abbreviated comment information for each comment with links for working with it. There's also a check box before each comment to make it easy to delete a bunch of comments at once.

To search for comments

1. In the Comments administration panel (**Figure** 13 or 14), enter a search word or phrase in the Show Comments That Contain box.

2. Click Search.

   A list of matching comments appears in the Comments administration panel (**Figure** 15).

To work with listed comments

In the Comment administration panel (**Figure** 13 or 14), click the link to perform the task you want:

◆ *E-mail address* opens your e-mail application and addresses a message to the e-mail address you clicked.

◆ *IP address* submits a Whois query for the IP address you click. The results appear on a Web page (**Figure** 16).

◆ **Edit Comment** or **Edit** displays a form you can use to edit the comment's content (**Figure** 9).

◆ **Delete Comment** or **Delete** permanently deletes the comment. You'll have to click OK in the confirmation dialog that appears to delete the comment.

◆ **Edit Post** "*post title*" displays the Write Post window containing the post content so you can edit it. This option is not available in Mass edit mode. We tell you about writing and editing posts in **Chapter** 3.

◆ **View Post** displays the post the comment is attached to in its own window with all comments. **View**, in Mass edit mode, also displays the post and its comment, but it zooms right to the comment you clicked the link for.

Figure 15 You can search for comments that contain a specific word or phrase.

Figure 16 You might find Whois information useful for tracking down an abusive commenter.

Latest Activity

Incoming Links More »
- No results found

Comments »

Comments in moderation (1) »
- Dave on Categories Check Boxes in the Write Post Window (Edit)
- John on Categories Check Boxes in the Write Post Window (Edit)
- Catherine on Categories Check Boxes in the Write Post Window (Edit)
- John on Posting by E-Mail (Edit)
- Test Track » Posting By E-Mail on Posting by E-Mail (Edit)

Posts »
- Posting by E-Mail
- Case sensitive WordPress install
- The Weather in Wickenburg
- Categories Check Boxes in the Write Post Window
- Handy: OmniDiskSweeper

Blog Stats

There are currently 7 posts and 5 comments, contained within 6 categories.

Figure 17
The Latest Activity area of the Dashboard lists the five most recently added comments and provides links for working with them.

To delete multiple comments

1. In the Comments administration panel, switch to Mass edit mode (**Figure 14**).

2. Turn on the check box beside each comment you want to delete.

3. Click the Delete Checked Comments button.

4. In the confirmation dialog that appears, click OK.

   The comments are removed from your blog.

To manage comments listed in the Dashboard

1. Log into your blog and, if necessary, display the Dashboard.

2. Click links under Comments in the Latest Activity area (**Figure 17**) to work with recent comments:

   ▲ » (after the Comments heading) opens the Comments administration panel (**Figure 13**).

   ▲ **Comments in Moderation** displays the Moderation Queue (**Figure 8**).

   ▲ *Post title* displays the comment on a post page.

   ▲ **Edit** displays a comment editing form (**Figure 9**).

Dealing with Spam

While it's possible to manually moderate and approve every single comment that is posted to your blog, this can be a cumbersome task when your blog is attacked by a spambot. You could be facing dozens or even hundreds of spam comments which could be very time-consuming to manually delete.

Fortunately, WordPress makes it possible to use plugins to help control spam. One plugin, Akismet Spam, is automatically installed and enabled in WordPress.com accounts and installed (but not enabled) in WordPress server installations. This service runs each comment through a number of tests at the Akismet server in an attempt to weed out and catch spam comments. Comments that may be spam are then listed without being posted to your blog, giving you an opportunity to make the final determination.

In this part of the chapter, we explain how to activate and use Akismet.

✔ Tips

- Take our advice: do not leave your blog open to comments without some kind of comment moderation or spam protection. Although spam protection takes a little work to set up and use, it's well worth the time and effort.

- If your blog is on a server installation of WordPress and you need more spam protection than what is available in Akismet, we highly recommend Dr. Dave's Spam Karma. This WordPress plugin uses a complex series of tests to determine whether a comment is legitimate or spam. You can find Spam Karma at unknowngenius.com/blog/wordpress/spam-karma. Spam Karma will not work with a WordPress.com blog.

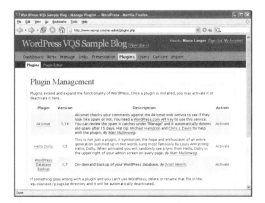

Figure 18 The Plugins Management administration panel on a WordPress server installation.

Figure 19 Conflicting messages may appear when you first activate Akismet.

Figure 20 Use this form to enter your API key.

To activate Akismet on a server-installed blog

1. If you have not already obtained an API key, follow the instructions in **Chapter 1** to create a WordPress.com account. An API key will be e-mailed to you.

2. Log into your blog and, if necessary, display the Dashboard.

3. Click the Plugins button. The Plugin Management administration panel appears (**Figure 18**).

4. Click the Activate link in the Action column for Akismet in the plugin list.

   Two conflicting messages appear at the top of the page; one says "Akismet is not active" and the other says "Plugin activated" (**Figure 19**).

5. Click the enter your WordPress.com API key link in the top message. The Akismet Configuration panel appears (**Figure 20**).

6. Enter your API key in the box and click Update API key. The Akismet Configuration panel reappears with your API key entered.

✔ Tips

- You do not need to follow these steps if your blog is hosted on WordPress.com. Akismet is already installed and configured for you.

- Although you must have a WordPress.com account to get an API key, you do not need to use that account for your blog.

- Your API key is displayed on the Your Profile administration panel in your WordPress.com account. We tell you about the Your Profile panel in **Chapter 5**.

- We tell you more about plugins in **Chapter 7**.

To moderate comments with Akismet

1. If necessary, log in to your blog and display the Dashboard.

2. Click the Manage button.

3. Click Akismet Spam in the second row of buttons. The Caught Spam administration panel appears (**Figure 21**).

4. To delete all comments listed in the panel, click the Delete all button.

   or

   To indicate that a listed comment is not spam, turn on the Not Spam check box beneath it and click Not Spam.

✔ Tips

- It's a good idea to check Akismet for caught spam at least once every two weeks to "rescue" any comments incorrectly identified as spam.

- Akismet will automatically delete spam after 15 days.

Figure 21 Comments that are identified as spam by Akismet are listed in the Caught Spam panel.

MODERATING COMMENTS WITH AKISMET

Working with Accounts

User Accounts

Every WordPress blog has at least one user who can add to and modify the blog's content.

On a WordPress.com account, there can be multiple users, but each user has to have his or her own WordPress.com account.

WordPress server installations also support multiple users, but they don't need to set up a WordPress.com account. Instead, each user has his own account and online identity within the blog.

In this chapter, we explain how to modify your WordPress account profile to set various options and change your password. We also explain how to add, modify, delete, and assign roles to users.

✔ Tip

■ In a WordPress server installation, if the Anyone can register option is enabled, site visitors can register and create their own accounts. We tell you about setting options in **Chapter 2**.

User Roles & Capabilities

The administrator of a blog can assign a different *role* to each user; the assigned role determines what *capabilities* or tasks that user can perform.

WordPress 2 supports five roles:

◆ **Subscriber** is the lowest level role. A subscriber can only read the blog.

◆ **Contributor** can do what a Subscriber can do, as well as create—but not publish—posts. Assign this role to someone you want to contribute content to the blog after approval.

◆ **Author** can do everything a Contributor can do, as well as upload files and publish posts.

Table 1

Roles and Capabilities for WordPress Users

Capability	Administrator	Editor	Author	Contributor	Subscriber
switch_themes	√				
edit_themes	√				
activate_plugins	√				
edit_plugins	√				
edit_users	√				
edit_files	√				
manage_options	√				
import	√				
moderate_comments	√	√			
manage_categories	√	√			
manage_links	√	√			
unfiltered_html	√	√			
edit_published posts	√	√			
edit_others_posts	√	√			
edit_pages	√	√			
upload files	√	√	√		
publish_posts	√	√	√		
edit_posts	√	√	√	√	
read	√	√	√	√	√

◆ **Editor** can do everything an Author can do, plus edit posts and Pages, moderate comments, and modify categories and links (or bookmarks). Think of the Editor as the Administrator's helper.

◆ **Administrator** has complete control over the entire blog.

Table 1 shows how the WordPress capabilities are distributed among the roles.

✖ Warning!

■ Do not assign the Administrator role to anyone who you either don't trust or who has a limited knowledge of WordPress. An Administrator can make drastic changes to a blog and its appearance!

✔ Tips

■ You can learn more about roles and capabilities in the WordPress Codex at `codex.wordpress.org/Roles_and_Capabilities`.

■ The WordPress Codex lists an additional 11 capabilities, named *level_0* through *level_10*. These capabilities apply to previous versions of WordPress and are supported for backwards compatibility.

USER ROLES & CAPABILITIES

Setting Your Profile & Personal Options

Each user account includes a profile, which is a collection of information about the user. Any user can access and modify his or her profile at any time, thus keeping the information accurate and up to date.

To view your profile

1. If necessary, log into your blog and display the Dashboard.

2. Click the Users link. The Your Profile and Personal Options administration panel should appear (**Figure 1**).

To modify your profile

1. Display the Your Profile and Personal Options administration panel (**Figure 1**).

2. Modify the fields in the Name area:

   ▲ **First name** is your first name.

   ▲ **Last name** is your last name.

   ▲ **Nickname** is a nickname or alias you may want to use online to identify yourself.

   ▲ **Display name publicly as** determines how your name appears on the blog—primarily when identified as a post author. The drop-down list includes various versions of the information in the Names area (**Figure 2**).

3. Modify or add information in the Contact Info area:

   ▲ **E-mail** is your e-mail address. This is a required field.

   ▲ **Website** is the URL for your Web site (if you have one).

   ▲ **AIM** is your AOL Instant Messenger account name.

Figure 1 The Your Profile and Personal Options administration panel.

Figure 2 Choose a version of your name from the drop-down list.

▲ **Yahoo IM** is your Yahoo Instant Messenger account name.

▲ **Jabber / Google Talk** is your Jabber or Google Talk account name.

4. If desired, enter a brief bio in the About yourself box.

5. To change your password, enter the same new password twice in the Update Your Password boxes.

6. To specify which editor appears in the Write Post or Write Page administration panel, toggle the check box under Personal Options. By default, WordPress uses the visual rich editor; turning off this check box displays the HTML editor.

7. Click Update Profile to save your changes.

✔ Tips

■ The Username field in the Name area cannot be modified.

■ If you change one of the Names area fields and want to use that revised name as your public name, you must first click Update Profile.

■ The About yourself information for a user can be displayed with by including `the_author_description` template tag in a theme's template file. We tell you more about themes and templates in **Chapter 6**.

■ We tell you more about writing posts and Pages with the visual rich editor and HTML editor in **Chapter 3**.

SETTING YOUR PROFILE & PERSONAL OPTIONS

Adding Users

If you have as WordPress.com blog, you can only add users who have WordPress.com accounts. If you have a WordPress server installation blog, you can add anyone you like as a user.

Either way, you add users with the Authors & Users administration panel. In this part of the chapter, we show you how.

✔ Tip

- We explain how to set up a WordPress.com account in **Chapter 1**.

To add a user to a WordPress.com blog

1. If necessary, log into your blog and display the Dashboard.

2. Click the Users button.

3. Click the Authors & Users button in the second row of buttons to display the Authors & Users administration panel (**Figure 3**).

4. Scroll down to the Add User From Community area.

5. Set options for the new user:

   ▲ **User E-Mail** is the user's e-mail address. If the user has more than one e-mail address, it must be the one associated with his WordPress.com account.

   ▲ **Role** is the role you want to assign to the user. Choose an option from the drop-down list (**Figure 4**).

6. Click Add User.

   The new user is added to the User List by Role area near the top of the window (**Figure 5**). An invitation e-mail is sent to the user you added (**Figure 6**).

Figure 3 The Authors & Users administration panel for a WordPress.com blog.

Figure 4 Choose a role from the drop-down list.

Figure 5 The new user is added to the User List by Role.

Figure 6 When a user is invited to join a blog, she gets a message like this one.

Figure 7 The Authors and Users administration panel for a WordPress server installation blog, with several users already added.

To add a user to a WordPress server installation blog

1. If necessary, log into your blog and display the Dashboard.

2. Click the Users button.

3. Click the Authors & Users button in the second row of buttons to display the Authors & Users administration panel (**Figure 7**).

4. Scroll down to the Add New User area.

5. Set options for the new user:

   ▲ **Nickname** is the user name and nickname for the new user.

   ▲ **First name** is the user's first name.

   ▲ **Last name** is the user's last name.

   ▲ **E-mail** is the user's e-mail address.

   ▲ **Website** is the URL for the user's Web site (if he has one).

   ▲ **Password (twice)** is a password for the user, entered twice.

6. Click Add User. The new user is added to the User List by Role area in the Authors & Users administration panel.

✔ Tips

■ The user can later change his nickname in the Your Profile and Personal Options administration panel as discussed earlier in this chapter.

■ By default, all new users are created with a role of Subscriber. You must edit the user to change his role; we explain how later in this chapter.

Working with User Accounts

Once you have set up a user account, you can make changes to it:

◆ Edit the user profile information (Word-Press server installation blogs only).

◆ Change a user's role.

◆ Delete the user account.

You do both of these things with the Authors & Users administration panel (**Figure** 3 or 7).

To edit a user's profile

1. In the Authors & Users administration panel (**Figure** 7), click the Edit link for a user.

2. Make changes in the Edit User adminis-tration panel (**Figure** 8). The options are the same as those in the Your Profile and Personal Options adminstration panel discussed earlier in this chapter, but you can also change the user's role.

3. Click Update User to save your changes.

To change a user's role

1. In the Authors & Users administration panel (**Figure** 3 or 7), turn on the check box beside each user whose role you want to change.

2. In the Update users area, select the Set the Role of checked users to option and choose a role from the drop-down list.

3. Click Update. The roles are changed for the user(s) you checked.

Figure 8 Use the Edit User administration panel to change profile options for a user.

Figures 9a & 9b The confirmation screen that appears when you remove a users varies depending on whether it's a WordPress.com blog (top) or a WordPress server installation blog (bottom).

To remove a user

1. In the Authors & Users administration panel (**Figure 3** or **7**), turn on the check box beside each user you want to remove.

2. In the Update users area:
   ▲ For a WordPress.com blog, select the Remove checked users from blog option.
   ▲ For a WordPress server installation blog, select the Delete checked users option.

3. Click Update.

4. For a WordPress.com blog, the Remove Users from Blog administration panel appears (**Figure 9a**). Continue to step 5.

   or

   For a WordPress server installation blog, the Delete Users administration panel appears (**Figure 9b**). Select one of the options:
   ▲ Delete all posts and links deletes all posts and links added by the user you are deleting.
   ▲ Attribute all posts and links to enables you to choose another user to become owner of the deleted users posts and links.

5. Click Confirm Removal or Confirm Deletion.

✔ Tip

■ When you remove a user from a Word-Press.com blog, the user's account remains active, but the user no longer has access to your blog.

✖ Warning!

■ When you remove a WordPress.com user, all posts attributed to that user will also be permanently removed. This cannot be undone.

REMOVING USERS

Customizing Themes

WordPress Themes

Figure 1 The Default theme, before customization.

Figure 2 The Default theme, after applying some of the theme modifications suggested in this chapter.

The appearance and content of your Word-Press blog depends on the code in the *theme* applied to it. WordPress uses the instructions in the theme's files to display and format your blog's contents.

WordPress makes extensive use of *PHP* to add intelligence to your blog's pages. It also uses XHTML and CSS, which are commonly used to create Web pages, to determine the formatting of the blog's pages.

Although you can set some basic options for your blog in the administration panels (as we explain in **Chapters 1** and **2**), to change your blog's appearance and content you need to edit the theme.

This chapter explains how themes work, what they include, and how you can modify them to customize the appearance and content of your WordPress blog (**Figures 1** and **2**).

✔ Tips

■ The information in this chapter applies only to server installations of Word-Press—not WordPress.com blogs.

■ To make the most of this chapter, you should have at least a basic knowledge of HTML and CSS. Although you don't need to know PHP, understanding a few basic concepts will allow you to edit theme files without "breaking" them.

Installing Other Themes

Many people have created themes they are willing to share with other WordPress users. These developers usually also allow you to modify their themes. This makes it easy to start with a theme you like and customize it so it meets your needs.

Installing a theme takes only minutes. Just download the theme file and upload its folder to your blog's themes folder. Once installed, you can activate it with the Themes administration panel.

✔ Tips

- There are many theme repositories, some of which are listed in **Appendix A**.

- Be sure to read any terms and conditions for a theme so you know what kind of use and modification the theme's developer allows.

- We explain how to choose or activate a theme in **Chapter 1**.

Figure 3 Here's an example of the Connections theme being downloaded from the Theme Browser available on AlexKing.org. Maria uses a heavily customized version of this theme on her wickenburg-az.com site.

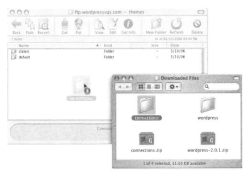

Figure 4 In this example, we're using Fetch to upload the connections theme folder to the themes directory for a WordPress blog.

Figure 5 The new theme folder appears in the themes directory.

Figure 6 Here's what the theme installed in **Figures 4** and **5** looks like after activation. This particular theme does not include a preview image.

To install a theme

1. Locate a theme you like and download it to your computer (**Figure 3**).

   or

   Create your own theme and store its files in a folder.

2. If the theme folder is compressed, expand it.

3. Use your FTP client to copy the theme folder to /wp-content/themes/ on the server (**Figures 4** and **5**).

4. Follow the instructions in **Chapter 1** to choose or activate the theme you installed (**Figure 6**).

✔ Tips

- Theme folders *must* go inside the themes directory inside the wp-content directory.

- Some themes require additional plugins or other files. Refer to the theme's documentation for details. We tell you more about plugins in **Chapter 7**.

- It's a good idea to view your site right after activating a new theme to make sure it looks okay. If it doesn't look right, you can always re-activate the previously activated theme.

- **Appendix B** provides detailed instructions on how to use popular FTP clients.

INSTALLING THEMES

Theme File Languages

WordPress is a system that allows you to focus on writing content, instead of managing your web pages. It uses *themes*—sets of template files written in XHTML and PHP—to work with the posts you write to make them available to visitors as Web pages and RSS feeds. Cascading style sheets (CSS) provide display information for formatting and layout. If you intend to modify or create themes, you need to understand at least a little about what these things are and how they interact.

The Default theme for WordPress contains approximately 20 items: PHP files, a preview screenshot, a Cascading Style Sheet, and a folder containing images and another PHP file. Other themes may have fewer or more files.

Some themes may offer more features than the Default theme, such as components for Google's Adsense or photo sharing, while others may offer fewer features, perhaps omitting the sidebar, footer, or other files.

MySQL

Your posts and related information are stored in a MySQL database. The database also stores links, if you enter them, user information, page content, and WordPress settings.

When visitors access a page of your blog or your blog's RSS feed, the database provides the correct content. Although the database is effectively invisible it is fundamental to your WordPress blog.

XHTML

WordPress uses *XHTML* (eXtensible Hyper-Text Markup Language), the currently recommended version of *HTML* (HyperText Markup Language). If you intend to edit any of the HTML in your WordPress theme you should be familiar with the rules of XHTML.

HTML is a static language that provides structure to a web page. HTML cannot interact with the MySQL database. This means that you can set up a page in HTML and give it headings and lists and so forth, but you can't use HTML to call up specific information on demand from the database.

You can identify the HTML portions of a page by the angle brackets around the code, for example:

```
<h2 class="center">Not Found</h2>
```

✔ Tips

- ■ Tags and attributes *must* be lower case:
  `<div class="entry">`

- ■ All tags must be closed:
  `<p>My paragraph.</p>`

- ■ Close image tags, breaks and other empty tags with a space and slash within the opening tag: `<br />`

- ■ Tags must be correctly nested:
  `<p>My <em>emphasis</em>.</p>`

- ■ Attributes must have a value
  `<input type="submit" />`

- ■ Values must be quoted:
  `<img src="test.jpg" alt="Test. " />`

- ■ Validate your code as it must be correct.

- ■ If you're looking for a good guide to XHTML, check out Liz Castro's *HTML for the World Wide Web with XHTML and CSS: Visual QuickStart Guide.*

PHP

WordPress uses PHP to create *template tags*—special commands that WordPress uses to find and retrieve data from the MySQL database. These PHP template tags work with a template's HTML to assemble and display blog pages.

You can identify the PHP portions of a page by the angle brackets and question marks that enclose them. For example: <?php get_header(); ?>. Note the space after <?php and before ?>.

Some sections of PHP may contain several lines that are spread throughout a template and intermingled with HTML. **Code 1** shows

Code 1

PHP and HTML in the index.php file

```php
<?php if (have_posts()) : ?>
  <?php while (have_posts()) : the_post(); ?>
    <div class="post" id="post-<?php the_ID(); ?>">
      <h2><a href="<?php the_permalink() ?>" rel="bookmark" title="Permanent Link to
      <?php the_title(); ?>"><?php the_title(); ?></a></h2>
      <small><?php the_time('F jS, Y') ?> <!-- by <?php the_author() ?> --></small>
      <div class="entry">
        <?php the_content('Read the rest of this entry &raquo;'); ?>
      </div>
      <p class="postmetadata">Posted in <?php the_category(', ') ?> |
      <?php edit_post_link('Edit', '', ' | '); ?>  <?php comments_popup_link('No Comments
      &#187;', '1 Comment &#187;', '% Comments &#187;'); ?></p>
    </div>
  <?php endwhile; ?>
  <div class="navigation">
    <div class="alignleft"><?php next_posts_link('&laquo; Previous Entries') ?></div>
    <div class="alignright"><?php previous_posts_link('Next Entries &raquo;') ?></div>
  </div>
<?php else : ?>
  <h2 class="center">Not Found</h2>
  <p class="center">Sorry, but you are looking for something that isn't here.</p>
  <?php include (TEMPLATEPATH . "/searchform.php"); ?>
<?php endif; ?>
```

Figure 7 If you "break" the PHP code in a template file, an error message will appear in your blog.

an example from the `index.php` file; the PHP code is black while the HTML is gray.

You don't need to know how to write or edit PHP to modify a theme, but you do need to be able to recognize which parts of a template file you should leave intact. If you "break" the PHP—in other words, introduce errors into the code—you'll see an error message like the one in **Figure 7** when you view your blog.

Although some theme modifications in this chapter rely on editing the PHP, if you follow the instructions carefully and make sure you have working backups, you shouldn't get into trouble, even if you don't know any PHP.

✔ Tips

- If you want to learn more about PHP, check out Larry Ullman's *PHP for the World Wide Web: Visual QuickStart Guide*.

- You can find a complete list of WordPress 2 template tags in the WordPress Codex, `codex.wordpress.org/Template_Tags`.

CSS

The structure of a page comes from the HTML, the content is drawn together by PHP from the MySQL database. CSS gives the whole thing shape, form, and color.

WordPress themes make extensive use of CSS to create complex layouts, many of which include multicolumn text, graphical elements, and other design features. In most well-designed themes, CSS determines the size, font, and color of text; the layout of the page's header, body, sidebar, and footer; and the positioning of graphic elements with or beneath text.

To modify or create your own look and feel for your blog, you'll need some understanding of CSS.

✔ Tip

- If you're looking for a good guide to CSS, check out Liz Castro's *HTML for the World Wide Web with XHTML and CSS: Visual QuickStart Guide*.

The Loop

The Loop consists of PHP and HTML code that gets and displays posts for a page. The Loop is a key component of a WordPress theme.

Loop basics

When broken down to its simplest form (**Code 2**), The Loop is actually quite simple:

```php
<?php if (have_posts()) : ?>
```

This starts by querying the database to determine whether there are posts to display. If there are, the next commands are executed; if not, WordPress skips ahead to the end of The Loop.

```php
<?php while (have_posts()) :
the_post(); ?>
```

This line of code tells WordPress to get post information. It starts The Loop's actual loop—a collection of code that is repeated for each item. In this case, the code inside the loop is repeated for each post. The actual number of posts it is repeated for is determined by WordPress settings, as discussed in **Chapter 2**.

```php
<?php the_content(); ?>
```

This line tells WordPress to display the contents of the post.

```php
<?php endwhile; ?>
```

This closes the loop when the specified number of posts have been retrieved and displayed.

```php
<?php endif; ?>
```

This is the end of The Loop.

Code 2

The Loop's Basic Code

```php
<?php if (have_posts()) : ?>
  <?php while (have_posts()) : the_post(); ?>
    <?php the_content(); ?>
  <?php endwhile; ?>
<?php endif; ?>
```

THE LOOP

Figure 8 The Default theme displays a Search form if there are no posts to display.

Beyond the Basics

Of course, **Code 2** is an extremely basic example. Although it will work in an `index.php` file as is—try it and see for yourself!—it omits much of the information readers expect to see, such as the post title, the post author, the post date, and so on. To add this information, insert the appropriate tags between the second and fourth line of this example.

✔ Tips

■ Anything inside The Loop will appear with every post. For example, you may wish to add a small image to each post to mark a special event such as Christmas. If you add it inside the loop the image will appear once with each post. If you add it outside the loop it will appear once for the whole page.

■ Some template tags can only be used in The Loop. That's because those tags retrieve and display information that is specific to a post, such as the author's name or the post date and time.

The Loop in the Default theme

In the Default theme, The Loop is much more complex. **Code 3** on the next page shows the code required by The Loop in black and additional content and formatting code in gray.

As you can see, this version of The Loop includes far more template tags. It also calls on other worker files, with their own template tags, that are part of the theme. All these tags send requests to the database and display the results that include the post title, the author name, the post date, and comment links (**Figure 1**). If there is nothing to display, WordPress tells you and displays a Search form (**Figure 8**).

The post in The Loop

The contents of the blog post itself is represented by one single line of code within The Loop.

In **Code 2**, it's `<?php the_content(); ?>`, which simply displays the post content.

In **Code 3**, from the Default theme, it's `<?php the_content('Read the rest of this entry &raquo;'); ?>`. This includes instructions to create a link to any part of the post that follows a special `<!--more-->` tag inserted by the post author within the post. The wording of the link is: *Read the rest of this entry »*.

Code 3

The Loop in the Default theme's index.php file

```php
<?php if (have_posts()) : ?>
  <?php while (have_posts()) : the_post(); ?>
    <div class="post" id="post-<?php the_ID(); ?>">
      <h2><a href="<?php the_permalink() ?>" rel="bookmark" title="Permanent Link to
      <?php the_title(); ?>"><?php the_title(); ?></a></h2>
      <small><?php the_time('F jS, Y') ?> <!-- by <?php the_author() ?> --></small>
      <div class="entry">
        <?php the_content('Read the rest of this entry &raquo;'); ?>
      </div>
      <p class="postmetadata">Posted in <?php the_category(', ') ?> |
      <?php edit_post_link('Edit', '', ' | '); ?>  <?php comments_popup_link('No Comments
      &#187;', '1 Comment &#187;', '% Comments &#187;'); ?></p>
    </div>
  <?php endwhile; ?>
  <div class="navigation">
    <div class="alignleft"><?php next_posts_link('&laquo; Previous Entries') ?></div>
    <div class="alignright"><?php previous_posts_link('Next Entries &raquo;') ?></div>
  </div>
<?php else : ?>
  <h2 class="center">Not Found</h2>
  <p class="center">Sorry, but you are looking for something that isn't here.</p>
  <?php include (TEMPLATEPATH . "/searchform.php"); ?>
<?php endif; ?>
```

header.php   The Loop   footer.php   sidebar.php

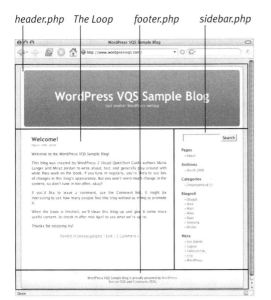

Figure 9 The file, index.php, which includes The Loop, calls header.php, sidebar.php, and footer.php to build the home page.

Components of the Default Theme

Studying the Default theme is a great way to learn about WordPress themes as designed by the WordPress development team and experienced users. As you work with WordPress, you'll find that most well-designed themes follow the basic structure of the Default theme.

The Default theme contains approximately 20 files, each of which has a specific function. Here's a quick overview of each file and its purpose.

✔ Tips

- ■ The default theme was developed by Michael Heilemann. You can visit his blog and learn more about his work at binarybonsai.com.

- ■ If you're developing a theme that can't be viewed by the public—for example, one on a testing server—you can include the name of each file in the body of the file. Then, when you view a page, you can see which template controls each part of it. Remove the file names before using the theme on a publicly accessible blog.

Home page components

These core files together create the blog's home page (**Figure 9**):

- ◆ **index.php** is the most important file. This file loads when a visitor views the home page of your blog. It calls header.php, sidebar.php, and footer.php to build the page. The most important code it contains is The Loop, which we explain on the previous few pages.

Continued on next page...

Continued on next page...

Continued from previous page.

◆ **header.php** contains standard information for the head section of any web page: document type declaration, character set, title, styles, and a call to `style.css`. It also opens the body section and includes the content of the header that appears at the top of your blog pages.

◆ **sidebar.php** handles everything you see in the narrow right column. It includes a search form, optional author information, introductory text for category and date archives, links to pages, categories and archives, your blogroll or links list, and a section called meta with a login link and other items. PHP code controls which items are displayed under various circumstances.

◆ **footer.php** adds the powered by WordPress and RSS links, an optional page load timer, a comment by the designer of the theme, and the closing tags for the page.

◆ **style.css** contains cascading style sheet code used to display your blog pages. It begins with the name and description details for the theme, then provides typography, color, margin, border, and other display settings. It ends with a comment from the designer.

Figure 10 The single.php template produces a page like this one. Note that some of its content comes from other template files, like header.php, comments.php, and footer.php.

Figure 11 The search.php template displays search results.

Other blog entry template files

These files also display blog entries or related comments:

◆ **single.php** provides the content and layout of the page displaying full text for a single post (**Figure 10**).

◆ **archive.php** provides the content and layout of pages displaying entry archives by date or category.

◆ **comments-popup.php** displays the form that allows visitors to leave comments.

◆ **comments.php** displays various messages related to comments. For example, it might advise that comments are closed or that the visitor must log in to enter a comment.

◆ **search.php** provides the content and layout of the page displaying search results (**Figure 11**).

◆ **searchform.php** creates the search form that appears in the sidebar and elsewhere.

◆ **attachment.php** displays a special attachment page when you click the link for an attachment in a post. If it's an audio attachment, clicking the audio icon plays the audio. If it's another type of attachment, clicking the attachment link downloads the linked file.

Page templates

WordPress's Page feature, which we discuss in detail in **Chapter 3**, displays Web pages of information from your WordPress MySQL database other than blog entries.

The Default theme has three of these templates:

◆ **page.php** provides the default content and layout of stand-alone Pages. Use this template to create Pages with whatever static information you want to display.

◆ **archives.php** is a template you can use to create a special archive Page. It builds a Web page that lists blog archives by date and category.

◆ **links.php** is a template for creating a special links Page. It builds a Web page that lists all links by link category (**Figure 12**).

To use these templates, you must choose the template from the Page Template menu when using the Write Page administration panel (**Figure 13**).

✔ Tips

■ The Archives and Links Page templates (archives.php and links.php) do not include The Loop. As a result, Pages based on these templates do not display any title or content text you may have entered when creating the Page.

■ We tell you more about creating Pages and managing links in **Chapter 3**.

Figure 12 WordPress can create a links page automatically if you create a blank page using the links.php page template.

Figure 13 Choose the template you want to use from the pop-up menu.

Figure 14 The screenshot.png file appears in the Themes administration panel.

Administrative files

These files are used internally by WordPress for administrative tasks.

◆ **functions.php** is used for modifying the theme's header colors, as discussed in **Chapter 1**. You should not edit this file unless you have a very good knowledge of PHP.

◆ **screenshot.png** is a thumbnail image for the theme. It appears in the Themes administration panel (**Figure 14**).

◆ **404.php** displays a formatted error message if a visitor attempts to view a page that does not exist and the server returns a *404 Not Found* message.

◆ **images** contains images for the default theme's appearance. The header-img.php file contains the programming to allow you to change the default theme's colors through the Header Image and Color section in the Presentation administration panel.

✔ Tip

■ You can learn more about creating a custom Error 404 page at codex.wordpress.org/Creating_an_Error_404_Page.

File Permissions

To modify theme files, they must be *writable*—that is, their file permissions must be set to allow modification. Here's a quick overview of file permissions and how they apply to WordPress theme files, as well as instructions on how to change them.

Unix file permissions basics

All of the files and directories on a Unix operating system server have *permissions* settings. Permissions control who may work with a file and what kind of access they have.

There are three kinds of access:

◆ **Read** (r) allows the user to view a file.

◆ **Write** (w) allows the user to change a file.

◆ **Execute** (x) allows the user to run a program or open a directory.

In addition, there are three types of users who work with files:

◆ Owner

◆ Group

◆ Others

As shown in **Table 1**, a numeric permissions equivalent is associated with each type of access and each type of user. Adding the applicable values together determines the permissions setting for a file.

For example, the circled values in **Table 2** correspond to read and write permissions for owner, group, and others. Adding the values together (400+200+40+20+4+2) results in a permissions setting of 666. This is the appropriate setting for a WordPress theme file if you want to edit that file with WordPress's built-in Theme Editor.

Table 1

File Permissions			
User Type	Read	Write	Execute
Owner	400	200	100
Group	040	020	010
Others	004	002	001

Table 2

File Permissions for WordPress Theme Files			
User Type	Read	Write	Execute
Owner	400	200	100
Group	040	020	010
Others	004	002	001

✔ Tip

■ You can change permissions for a file or directory with FTP client software or with the file manager tools made available by your ISP.

Figure 15a In this example, we're using CuteFTP on Windows to change the permissions of a theme file.

Figure 15b Here's Fetch on a Macintosh changing the permissions of a theme file.

To change a file's permissions with an FTP client

1. Use your FTP client software to connect to the server and view the file for which you want to change permissions.

2. Select the file's icon.

3. Use the appropriate command to view permissions for the file. For example, in Cute FTP, the command is File > Properties, and in Fetch, the command is Remote > Get Info.

4. A window that displays file information, including permissions, should appear (**Figures 15a** and **15b**). Toggle check boxes or enter a Unix equivalent value to set the permissions as desired for the file.

5. Click OK (**Figure 15a**) or Apply (**Figure 15b**) to save your settings.

✔ Tip

■ How you connect to your server varies depending on your FTP client software. FTP software is covered in more detail in **Appendix B**.

To change file permissions with a file manager

1. Use your Web browser to visit the online Control Panel for your Web site.

2. Click the link for the File Manager (**Figure 16**).

3. Navigate to the file whose permissions you need to change. You can click on a folder icon to open it.

4. Click the name of the file you want to change to view its properties (**Figure 17**).

5. Click Change Permissions (**Figure 18**).

6. Set permissions as desired.

7. Click Change to activate the new permissions (**Figure 19**).

✔ Tips

- Your file manager may show permissions as a set of numbers, for example, 666, or it may show check boxes for what the Owner, Group, and Others may do. **Figure 19** shows both sets of information, although it uses different terminology for the permission categories.

- Each ISP's file manager is different. If you have trouble using your ISP's file manager, contact your ISP for help.

Figure 16 Your ISP should offer a control panel for accessing Web site features. Here's the control panel for HostMe.co.nz, which is Miraz's ISP. (Maria's ISP, GoDaddy.com, does not offer a Web interface for changing file permissions.)

Figure 17 In this example, the permissions for each file appears in the list beside its name. Click the name of the file you want to change to view its properties.

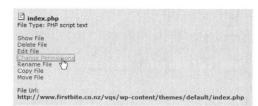

Figure 18 Click Change Permissions.

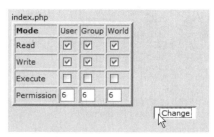

Figure 19 After setting permissions as desired, click Change.

Figure 20 The Theme Editor offers a Web-based interface for modifying your theme's template files.

Tools for Modifying Theme Files

WordPress makes it easy for you to customize your blog's theme and to make it truly your own. You do this by making changes to the theme's template files.

There are two ways to modify theme files: with the Theme Editor or with a text editor.

The Theme Editor

The *Theme Editor*, which is built into WordPress, allows you to make changes to writable files with your Web browser. You simply log into your WordPress blog and access the Theme Editor administration panel (**Figure 20**). Select the theme you want to modify, make changes, and save them.

There are several benefits to using the Theme Editor:

◆ You can use the Theme Editor to edit theme files from any computer with an Internet connection.

◆ No special software is required—other than a Web browser.

There are drawbacks to using the Theme Editor, too:

◆ The Theme Editor can only edit existing and installed theme files. You cannot create a new theme file or folder and then edit it.

◆ If you make an error while editing with the Theme Editor, you have to remember what you did and manually fix it.

THE THEME EDITOR

Text editors

You can also use a text editor to edit theme template files (**Figure 21**). This offers the flexibility of editing the file on your own computer, with a software tool well-suited for the task.

Of course, to edit a theme file on your computer, you have to get it there. There are two ways to do that:

◆ Use an FTP client to download the file you want to edit. When you're finished editing it, use the FTP client to upload it back to the server.

◆ Use the FTP capabilities built into the text editor to open the file on the server. Then, after making changes to the file, simply save it; it's automatically saved back to the server. Keep in mind that not all text editors include this feature.

✔ Tips

■ Be sure to use a plain text editor and not a word processor. Word processors, like Microsoft Word and even TextEdit, can introduce additional characters into a text document—characters that can wreak havoc with your code.

■ **Appendix C** provides some information about using text editors, including instructions for opening text files on a server with two different text editor programs.

Figure 21 In this example, we're using TextWrangler on a Macintosh to edit the index.php file. Text editors like this one have features such as code coloring and indentation that make them good tools for editing code.

Modifying Theme Files

Once you've chosen your tool to modify a theme file, you can make changes as desired to customize the appearance and functionality of your site. In general, this is a four-step process:

1. Open the file you want to change.

2. Make changes as desired.

3. Save your changes.

4. Test to be sure your changes resulted in the desired effect.

This section explains how to use the Theme Editor or a text file to modify theme template files. We provide suggestions for specific modifications later in this chapter.

✔ Tips

- Before making any changes to a file that already works, copy all the text and paste it into a plain text file stored on your computer. If the changes you make break your blog you can retrieve the original text and paste it back in.

- You can test your changes by merely viewing the pages of your blog that will be affected by the change.

- Be sure to refresh or reload your browser window when viewing your blog after making any changes.

- If you cannot see the effect of your change, try restarting your browser, switching to another browser, or adding a ? (question mark character) at the end of the page address when loading the page. Any of these techniques should force a refresh.

To use the Theme Editor

1. If necessary, log into your WordPress blog and navigate to the Dashboard administration panel.

2. Click the Presentation button.

3. Click the Theme Editor button to display the Theme Editor (**Figure 20**).

4. Use the Select theme to edit drop-down list to choose the theme whose files you wish to edit and click Select.

5. In the list of theme files on the right side of the window, click the link for the file you want to edit. The file's name appears near the top of the window and its contents appear in the scrollling list.

6. Edit the file as you wish.

7. Click the Update File button near the bottom of the window to save your changes. A message near the top of the window confirms that the file has been edited successfully (**Figure 22**).

8. View your blog to confirm that your changes appear as intended.

✔ Tip

- If a theme file is not writable, a message appears near the bottom of the Theme Editor window (**Figure 23**). Follow the instructions earlier in this chapter to change the permissions for the file to 666 so it is writable, then reload the Theme Editor page and try again.

Figure 22 A message appears at the top of the Web browser window to indicate that your change has been saved.

Figure 23 If you can't edit a file, the Theme Editor tells you.

USING THE THEME EDITOR

To use a text editor

1. Use FTP client software to download the file to your computer and open it with your text editor.

   or

   Use your text editor to open the file directly from the server.

2. Edit the file as you wish.

3. Use your text editor to save the file to your computer and then use your FTP client software to upload the file to the server.

   or

   Use your text editor to save the file directly back to the server.

4. View your blog to confirm that your changes appear as intended.

✔ Tip

■ Make backups of files *before* editing them—it's easy to make disastrous changes. If you mess up you can simply replace the broken file with a known working copy.

USING TEXT EDITORS

Creating a New Theme

Sometimes you might make enough changes to a theme that it becomes an entirely new theme based on the original. In that case, you could create a new theme with its own folder.

To create a new theme

1. In Windows Explorer or Mac OS Finder, select the theme folder on which you want to base your new theme (**Figure 24**).

2. Use the Copy and Paste commands (Windows or Mac OS) or Duplicate command (Mac OS) to duplicate the folder (**Figure 25**).

3. Rename the duplicate folder (**Figure 26**).

4. Open the `style.css` file in the new folder and edit the information at the beginning of the file to reflect your theme's name, URI, author, and other information (**Figure 27**).

5. Modify the new theme's files to reflect your design ideas.

✔ Tips

- When naming files and folders for the Web, use only letters, numbers, hyphens, and underscore characters. Keep file names short.

- The Theme Name and Description you enter in `style.css` displays in the Themes administration panel (**Figure 6**).

- After installing and applying your new theme, you can create a screenshot of the home page of your blog, save it as `screenshot.png`, and place it in the theme's folder. This enables you to see a preview of the theme in the Themes administration panel (**Figure 6**). We explain how to install a theme earlier in this chapter.

Figure 24 Select the folder for the theme on which you want to base your new theme.

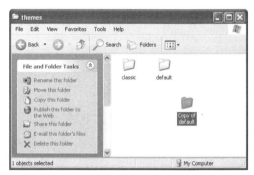

Figure 25 Duplicate the folder.

Figure 26
Rename the duplicate folder.

Figure 27 Edit the information at the top of the style.css file to identify your theme.

Modifying the Appearance with CSS

In a well-designed WordPress theme, fonts, colors, layout, and typography are all controlled by cascading style sheets (**CSS**). The primary place to modify these is in the file style.css. In the Default theme, a few styles related to images are also set in header.php.

In the Default theme, style.css groups the style rules into categories:

- ◆ **Typography & Colors** controls the font, font size, font color, and background color of text on each page.

- ◆ **Structure** specifies the page layout. In the Default theme, that's a group of four "boxes"—header, content, sidebar, and footer—encompassed in a page box. This is all done with CSS, not HTML tables.

- ◆ **Headers** provides additional formatting for header content.

- ◆ **Images** provides alignment information for images.

- ◆ **Lists** provides formatting information for ordered and unordered lists.

- ◆ **Form Elements** includes formatting information for search, entry, and comment forms.

- ◆ **Comments** formats comment elements.

- ◆ **Sidebar** provides formatting information for the sidebar.

- ◆ **Calendar** provides formatting instructions for the calendar, which may be displayed in the sidebar.

- ◆ **Various Tags & Classes** includes formatting instructions for elements such as blockquotes, acronyms, and horizontal rules.

✔ Tip

- ■ To modify the settings in style.css, you should have a good understanding of CSS. Experimentation is okay, but be sure to check your blog's appearance after every change.

To modify a blog's styles

1. Make a copy of your `style.css` file for safekeeping.

2. Open Stylesheet with the Theme Editor or `style.css` with a text editor (**Figure 28**).

3. Modify the style rules to fit your design.

4. Save or upload the modified file to replace the original.

5. Visit your blog to check that it works as expected.

6. If the blog does not appear as expected, repeat steps 2 through 5 to fix the problem or restore the `style.css` file with the backup copy you made in step 1—you did follow step 1, didn't you?

✔ Tips

- We explain how to edit theme files with the Theme Editor or a text editor earlier in this chapter.

- If you're not sure what a CSS style is used for, consult the theme template files to learn which PHP or HTML codes call it.

- Use Comments to keep notes about the stylesheet. For example, you might add a comment to explain how an instruction works (**Figure 28**).

- CSS comments take this form:
  `/* comment goes here */`.

- If you can't see the effects of your CSS modifications load `style.css` directly into your browser to check that the browser is accessing the latest version.

- It's a good idea to validate the CSS to make sure it conforms to W3C recommendations. We explain how near the end of this chapter.

Figure 28 The style.css file for the Default theme, opened in the TextWrangler text editor. Note the two comments near the top of the window.

Figure 29 Create a header image that's 760 pixels wide and 200 pixels high.

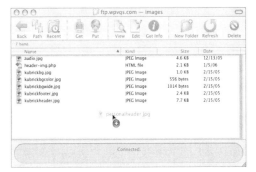

Figure 30 Copy the personalheader.jpg file into the images folder for the Default theme. In this example, we're using Fetch on a Mac.

```
/*  To ease the insertion of a personal header
    that you simply drop in an image called 'pe
    directory. Dimensions should be at least 76
    get cropped off of the image. */
    /*
    #headerimg { background: url('<?php blogin1
    */
</style>
```

Figure 31 The header image style information is commented out to deactivate it.

```
/*  To ease the insertion of a personal header
    that you simply drop in an image called 'pe
    directory. Dimensions should be at least 76
    get cropped off of the image. */

    #headerimg { background: url('<?php blogin1

</style>
```

Figure 32 Remove the comment codes to activate the header image style information.

Figure 33 Your image appears as the header image.

To change the Default theme's header image

1. Prepare an image at least 760 pixels wide and 200 pixels high (**Figure 29**).

2. Save the image with the name personalheader.jpg.

3. Use your FTP client software to put the image in /wp-content/themes/default/images (**Figure 30**).

4. Open Header with the Theme Editor or header.php with a text editor.

5. Locate the line that begins with #headerimg { background: (**Figure 31**) and remove the commenting code from the lines before and after it (**Figure 32**).

6. Save or upload the modified file to replace the original.

7. View your blog. Your image should appear in place of the default header image (**Figure 33**).

✔ Tips

■ As you can see, the designer of the Default theme made it very easy to replace his image with yours. Although the code for his header image appears earlier in the header.php file, when you follow step 5, header image code is activated that supercedes the earlier code and replaces the image.

■ This is a good example of how CSS information can appear in a file other than style.css.

To change the Default theme's header text appearance

1. Open Stylesheet with the Theme Editor or style.css with a text editor.

2. Scroll down to the h1 and #headerimg .description selectors in the Typography and Colors section (**Figure 34**).

3. To modify the appearance of your blog's name in the header:

   ▲ Change the size of text by editing the font-size attribute for h1.

   ▲ Change the alignment of text by editing the text-align attribute for h1.

4. To modify the appearance of your blog's description in the header:

   ▲ Change the size of text by editing the font-size attribute for #headerimg .description.

   ▲ Change the alignment of text by editing the text-align attribute for #headerimg .description.

5. If necessary, scroll down a little farther to the selector for h1, h1 a, h1 a:hover, h1 a:visited, #headerimg .description (**Figure 34**).

6. To change the color of all header text, edit the color attribute for h1, h1 a, h1 a:hover, h1 a:visited, #headerimg .description.

7. Save or upload the modified file (**Figure 35**) to replace the original.

8. View your blog. The text in the header should reflect your changes (**Figure 36**).

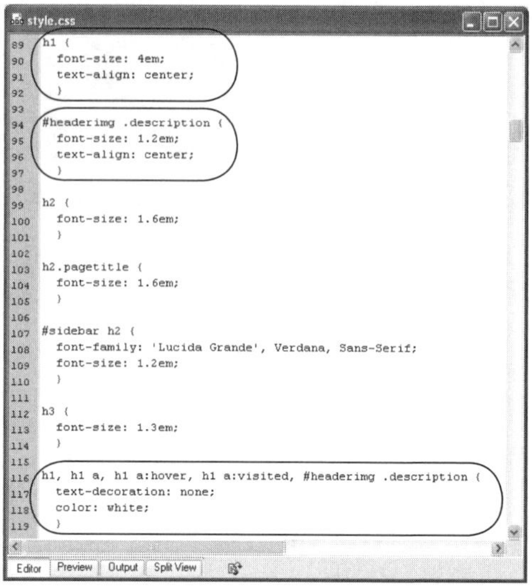

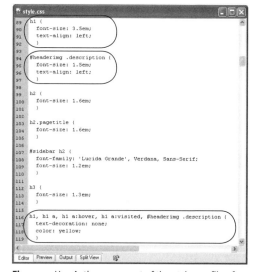

Figure 34 Scroll down to the part of the style.css file that contains the selectors you want to modify. In this example, we're using HTML-Kit on Windows.

Figure 35 Here's the same part of the style.css file after a few changes.

Figure 36 Your changes appear the next time you view your blog.

Figure 37 All of this style information in the header.php file must be removed to set custom colors in style.css.

```
/* Begin Typography & Colors */
body {
    font-size: 62.5%; /* Resets 1em to 10px */
    font-family: 'Lucida Grande', Verdana, Arial, Sans-Serif;
    background-color: #d5d6d7;
    color: #333;
    text-align: center;
    }

#page {
    background-color: white;
    border: 1px solid #959596;
    text-align: left;
    }

#header {
    background-color: #73a0c5;
    }
```

Figure 38 The beginning of the style.css file has three examples of a background-color attribute. Just keep in mind that two of these attributes are redefined later in this file.

Figure 39 In this example, we've changed the back-ground colors for all parts of the page.

To change the background colors

1. Open Header with the Theme Editor or header.php with a text editor.

2. Delete the lines for the style definitions. These lines begin with <style type="text/css" media="screen">and end with </style> (**Figure 37**).

3. Save or upload the modified file to replace the original.

4. Open Stylesheet with the Theme Editor or style.css with a text editor.

5. To set the background colors, modify or add a background-color attribute for the following rules:

   ▲ body controls the entire Web page (**Figure 38**).

   ▲ #page controls the page content other than the header, footer, and sidebar. Be sure to modify the background-color attribute in the *second* occurrence of the #page rule.

   ▲ #header controls the page header. Be sure to modify the background-color attribute in the *second* occurrence of the #header rule.

   ▲ #footer controls the page footer.

   ▲ #sidebar controls the sidebar. This rule must be added.

6. Save or upload the modified file to replace the original.

7. View your blog to check your changes (**Figure 39**).

Continued on next page...

CHANGING BACKGROUND COLORS

133

Continued from previous page.

✔ Tips

■ Wondering why you deleted the style definitions in step 2? Here's the explanation. The styles in header.php override any styles in style.css because they are referenced *after* style.css. The lines you deleted tell WordPress to use images in wp-content/themes/default/images for background and shading on blog pages. By deleting them, you make it possible to set colors in style.css.

■ In the Default theme's style.css file, #page and #header are defined twice, each time with a background-color attribute. The second attribute is the one that will be used for your Web pages. If desired, you can "clean up" the style.css file by deleting the second background-color attribute for each of these styles.

■ To add a rule for the background color of the sidebar, copy all three lines for the #footer rule and paste them right beneath the #footer rule. Change #footer to #sidebar in the pasted-in rule to create the new rule. Then change the background-color attribute to the desired color. **Figure 40** shows what it might look like when you're done.

■ You can define the background colors at any point in the stylesheet.

■ If your style changes don't appear to be having an effect, check for typos, missing semicolons, and other errors which may make your stylesheet invalid. You might also want to set your browser's cache setting to 0 (zero) to force all page components to refresh each time you load a page.

```
#footer {
    background-color: #0000cc;
    }

#sidebar {
    background-color: #6699ff;
    }
```

Figure 40 You can create a #sidebar rule by copying, pasting, and modifying the #footer rule.

Figure 41 Example of a post as it appears on the Default theme's home page.

Figure 42 In this example, the entry is split using a <!--more--> tag after the first paragraph. WordPress automatically creates a link for viewing the entire entry.

Modifying Post-Related Content

In the Default template, the index.php file includes The Loop. As discussed earlier in this chapter, The Loop contains PHP code to insert blog database content, such as a post's title, date, author name, content, and comments. You can modify The Loop to rearrange, remove, or add components, even if you don't know PHP. All you need to know is which PHP commands display each component—and how you can safely move, remove, or add them.

Figure 41 shows a typical post as it appears on the home page in the Default theme. In **Code 4** on the next page, the PHP code that actually displays this information is in black while the additional PHP and HTML that make up links and formatting are in gray. Here's a quick look at the PHP that's doing all of the display work:

```
<?php the_title(); ?>
```
displays the post title. Because it's surrounded by <a> and </a> HTML tags, the text appears as a link. The URL for the link is determined by more PHP code that retrieves the permanent link for the post; clicking the link displays the post on its own page using single.php.

```
<?php the_time('F jS, Y') ?>
```
displays the post date. Although it uses the the_time template to get the information from the database, the formatting instructions within the parentheses tell WordPress to display the date as shown in **Figure 41**.

```
<?php the_content('Read the rest of
this entry &raquo;'); ?>
```
displays the post itself. If the post is split using a <!--more--> tag, a link will appear (**Figure 42**) so the reader can click it and read the rest of the post.

Continued on next page...

Continued from previous page.

`<?php the_category(', '); ?>`
displays the category assigned to the post.
If there is more than one category, each
category name is separated by a comma
and a space.

`<?php edit_post_link ('Edit', '', ' | '); ?>`
displays a link you can click to edit the post.
This link only appears to site visitors who are
logged in and have either authored the post
or have administrative access.

Code 4

Post-related PHP code in the Default theme's index.php file

```php
<?php if (have_posts()) : ?>
  <?php while (have_posts()) : the_post(); ?>
    <div class="post" id="post-<?php the_ID(); ?>">
      <h2><a href="<?php the_permalink() ?>" rel="bookmark" title="Permanent Link to
      <?php the_title(); ?>"><?php the_title(); ?></a></h2>
      <small><?php the_time('F jS, Y'); ?> <!-- by <?php the_author() ?> --></small>
      <div class="entry">
        <?php the_content('Read the rest of this entry &raquo;'); ?>
      </div>
      <p class="postmetadata">Posted in <?php the_category(', '); ?> |
      <?php edit_post_link('Edit', '', ' | '); ?>  <?php comments_popup_link('No Comments
      &#187;', '1 Comment &#187;', '% Comments &#187;'); ?></p>
    </div>
  <?php endwhile; ?>
  <div class="navigation">
    <div class="alignleft"><?php next_posts_link('&laquo; Previous Entries') ?></div>
    <div class="alignright"><?php previous_posts_link('Next Entries &raquo;') ?></div>
  </div>
<?php else : ?>
  <h2 class="center">Not Found</h2>
  <p class="center">Sorry, but you are looking for something that isn't here.</p>
  <?php include (TEMPLATEPATH . "/searchform.php"); ?>
<?php endif; ?>
```

```
<?php comments_popup_link('No Comments
&#187;', '1 Comment &#187;', '% Com-
ments &#187;'); ?>
```
displays a link that indicates the number of comments. A reader can click the link to display the post on its own page, along with its comments and a comment entry form.

As you can see, it isn't difficult to dissect and analyze the contents of a PHP file. Just look up the template tags you find in the file to see what they do. Your best reference is the WordPress Codex's Template Tags Web page, codex.wordpress.org/Template_Tags.

On the following pages, we show you how to change post-related blog content: the date, author, category, comment line, and text linking to the remainder of a longer post. There are plenty more ways to customize your blog, but these examples should give you a practical starting point and help you understand how to modify the theme files without breaking anything.

✔ Tips

- We tell you more about PHP and HTML in template files earlier in this chapter. If you skipped that part of the chapter, you might want to go back and review it now.

- The Loop is not always included in index.php. In many themes, it is part of a post.php file that is not included in the Default template.

- To see how PHP coding translates into what you see on your blog, view the source of the page in your browser. You can usually do this by choosing a Source or View Source command from browser's View menu.

- Related PHP commands can be separated by stretches of HTML (**Code 4**). When cutting and pasting, be careful to retain all related PHP code.

- Use comments to keep notes and reminders in the file. These can help you remember how or why you included specific code. HTML comments take this form: <!-- *comment goes here* -->.

- It's a good idea to validate the XHTML of an edited template to make sure it conforms to W3C recommendations. We explain how near the end of this chapter.

To change the date format

1. Open Main Index Template with Theme Editor or `index.php` with a text editor.

2. Locate the following code:
   `<?php the_time('F jS, Y'); ?>`

3. Edit the date format between the parentheses and single quote marks. **Table 3** provides a list of commonly used characters for the date format parameter. Note that these characters are case-sensitive and can be combined with punctuation and other characters to format the date.

4. Save or upload the modified file to replace the original.

5. View your blog to make sure the new format is what you expected (**Figures 43a and 43b**).

✔ Tips

- WordPress uses standard PHP date formatting. You can find a complete list of PHP date formatting options at `us2.php.net/date`.

- The part you edit is inside the parentheses and surrounded by single quotes. Both are important. Make sure you retain both the brackets and the quotes.

- Make your blog more user-friendly by spelling out the month as a word and the year with 4 digits. Blogs are viewed by people from all over the world. Some will understand 7/5/06 to be the fifth of July while others will read it as the seventh of May.

Table 3

Partial List of PHP Date & Time Format Characters		
Character	**Description**	**Example**
j	1- or 2-digit day of month	3
d	2-digit day of month	03
D	3-character day name	Wed
l	Full-text day name	Wednesday
S	Ordinal suffix for day of month	rd
n	1- or 2-digit month number	6
m	2-digit month number	06
M	3-character month name	Jun
F	Full-text month name	June
y	2-digit year number	07
Y	4-digit year number	2007
g	1- or 2-digit hour number (12-hour clock)	5
h	2-digit hour number (12-hour clock)	05
G	1- or 2-digit hour number (24 hour clock)	8
H	2-digit hour number (24-hour clock)	08
i	2-digit minute number	09
s	2-digit second number	32
a	Lowercase am/pm	am
A	Uppercase AM/PM	AM

Case sensitive WordPress install
Wednesday, March 22, 2006

Case sensitive WordPress install
22-Mar-06

Figures 43a & 43b These two examples use the following format codes: l, F j, Y (top) and j-M-y (bottom).

Case sensitive WordPress install

March 22nd, 2006 by Miraz Jordan

Figure 44 Displaying the author name for a post in the Default theme is as easy as removing a pair of comment tags.

Case sensitive WordPress install

Written by **Miraz Jordan** on March 22nd, 2006 at 7:12 pm

Figure 45 This example switches the date and time and adds additional information and text.

To add the author's name

1. Open Main Index Template with Theme Editor or index.php with a text editor.

2. Locate the following code:
   `<!-- by <?php the_author(); ?> -->`

3. Delete the comment tags (`<!--` and `-->`). The new code should look like this:
   `by <?php the_author(); ?>`

4. Save or upload the modified file to replace the original.

5. View your blog to make sure the author name appears the way you expected (**Figure 44**).

✔ Tips

■ As you can see in this example, the author name code is already in the index.php file in the Default template. The comment tags around it simply deactivate it. You can use comment tags to deactivate any code you like without actually deleting it from the file.

■ The way the author name appears depends on settings for the author's user profile. We tell you about user profile options in **Chapter 5**.

■ You can take this example a step further by switching the author name and date so it looks like the example in **Figure 45**, change the code from:

   ```
   <?php the_time('F jS, Y'); ?> by
   <?php the_author(); ?>
   ```

   to:

   ```
   Written by <strong><?php the_
   author(); ?></strong> on <?php
   the_time('F jS, Y'); ?> at <?php
   the_time('g:i a'); ?>
   ```

   Get the idea?

To change the "more" link text

1. If a recent blog post does not include a `<!--more-->` tag, edit a post to insert one.

2. Open Main Index Template with Theme Editor or `index.php` with a text editor.

3. Locate the following code:
   `<?php the_content('Read the rest of this entry &raquo;'); ?>`

4. Modify the text between the single quotes so it says what you want it to say. For example: `<?php the_content('Read more...'); ?>`

5. Save or upload the modified file to replace the original.

6. View your blog to make sure the more link text for a post with a `<!--more-->` tag appears the way you expected (**Figure 46**).

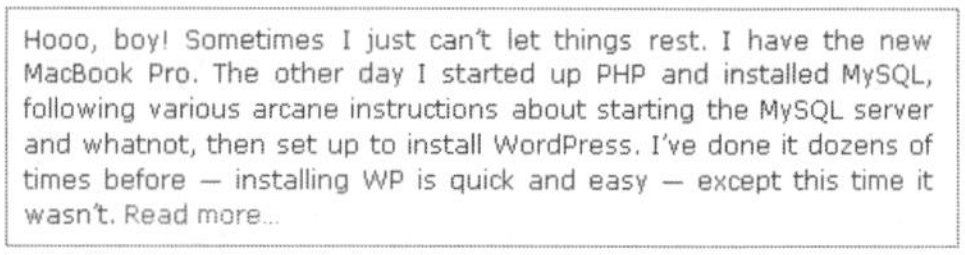

✔ Tip

■ The more link text is only visible for posts which have been divided with the `<!--more-->` tag. (Although this tag looks like a comment, it isn't; spaces between the word *more* and the hyphens are missing.) We tell you more about using this tag in posts in **Chapter 3**.

Hooo, boy! Sometimes I just can't let things rest. I have the new MacBook Pro. The other day I started up PHP and installed MySQL, following various arcane instructions about starting the MySQL server and whatnot, then set up to install WordPress. I've done it dozens of times before — installing WP is quick and easy — except this time it wasn't. Read more...

Figure 46 A more link can say anything you want.

Figure 47 In this example, the link separators have been changed to bullet characters.

To change the post footer's link separator character

1. Open Main Index Template with Theme Editor or `index.php` with a text editor.

2. Locate the following code:
```
<?php the_category(', '); ?> | <?php
edit_post_link('Edit', '', ' | '); ?>
```

3. Replace the two pipe (|) characters with the character you prefer. The first is between the `the_category` and the `edit_post_link` tags, each of which create links. The second is a parameter for the `edit_post_link` tag.

4. Save or upload the modified file to replace the original.

5. View your blog to make sure the new link separators appear the way you expected (**Figure 47**).

✔ Tips

- The `edit_post_link` tag includes its own separator parameter because the Edit link only appears under certain circumstances, as discussed earlier in this chapter. If the link does not appear, the separator shouldn't appear either, right?

- To use a special character as a separator, you must enter its HTML code. For example, `&bull;` is the code entered to display a bullet character like the ones shown in **Figure 47**. You can find a list of character codes on the Web at `www.web-source.net/symbols.htm`.

CHANGING SEPARATOR CHARACTERS

To change the category separator

1. Open Main Index Template with Theme Editor or index.php with a text editor.

2. Locate the following code:
   `<?php the_category(', '); ?>`

3. Replace the text within the single quotes (a comma and a space) with whatever separator characters you prefer.

4. Save or upload the modified file to replace the original.

5. View your blog to make sure the new category separators appear the way you expected (**Figure 48**).

✔ Tips

- Category separators are only visible for posts which have more than one category assigned to them.

- To use a special character as a separator, you must enter its HTML code. For example, & is the code entered to display an ampersand character like the ones shown in **Figure 48**. You can find a list of character codes on the Web at www.web-source.net/symbols.htm.

- Make sure you separate links on your Web pages with more than just space characters. Otherwise, multiple links will appear to run together as one long linked phrase.

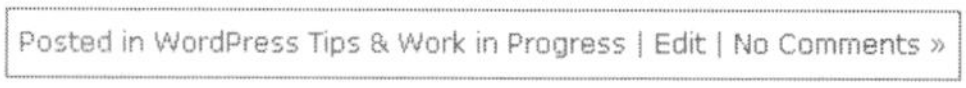

Posted in WordPress Tips & Work in Progress | Edit | No Comments »

Figure 48 Here, the category separator has been changed from a comma to an ampersand.

Posted in WordPress Tips, Work in Progress | Edit Post | No Comments »

Figure 49 In this example, we changed Edit to Edit Post. The result: undesirable word wrap when there are two categories.

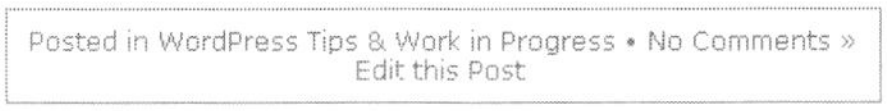

Posted in WordPress Tips & Work in Progress • No Comments » Edit this Post

Figure 50 Here's a better solution: putting the edit post link text on its own line.

To change the edit post link text

1. Open Main Index Template with Theme Editor or index.php with a text editor.

2. Locate the following code:
   ```
   <?php edit_post_link('Edit', '', ' |
   '); ?>
   ```

3. Replace the word Edit with whatever text you prefer.

4. Save or upload the modified file to replace the original.

5. View your blog to make sure the edit post link text appears the way you expected (**Figure 49**).

✔ Tips

- The edit post link text is only visible if you have editing rights and are logged in.

- The edit_post_link tag has three parameters separated by commas: the text that appears as a link, the text that appears before the link, and the text that appears after the link.

- You could also place the edit post link on a separate line. **Figure 50** shows how it would look if you changed:
   ```
   Posted in <?php the_category(', ');
   ?> | <?php edit_post_link('Edit',
   '', ' | '); ?>  <?php comments_
   popup_link('No Comments &#187;',
   '1 Comment &#187;', '% Comments
   &#187;'); ?>
   ```

   to:
   ```
   Posted in <?php the_category('
   &amp; '); ?> &bull; <?php comments_
   popup_link('No Comments &#187;',
   '1 Comment &#187;', '% Comments
   &#187;'); ?><?php edit_post_
   link('Edit this Post', '<br />',
   ''); ?>
   ```

To change the comment link text

1. Open Main Index Template with Theme Editor or index.php with a text editor.

2. Locate the following code:

```
<?php comments_popup_link('No Comments &#187;', '1 Comment &#187;', '% Comments &#187;'); ?>
```

3. Change the text within the single quotes as follows:

   ▲ To change the text that appears if there aren't any comments (**Figure 51**), replace the text within the first set of single quotes.

   ▲ To change the text that appears if there is only one comment (**Figure 52**), replace the text within the second set of single quotes.

   ▲ To change the text that appears if there is more than one comment (**Figure 53**), replace the text within the third set of single quotes. Be sure to include the % character if you want the number of comments to appear; it will be replaced by the number of comments.

   Figures 51 through **53** illustrate what the following code might look like with zero, one, and two comments:

```
<?php comments_popup_link('Would you care to make a comment? ', 'There is 1 Comment', 'There are % Comments'); ?>
```

4. Save or upload the modified file to replace the original.

5. View your blog to make sure the comment link text appears the way you expected (**Figures 51, 52,** and **53**).

Posted in WordPress Tips | Edit | Would you care to make a comment?

Posted in Life Beyond WordPress | Edit | There is 1 Comment

Posted in Work in Progress | Edit | There are 2 Comments

Figures 51, 52, & 53 You can change the text that appears when there are no comments, one comment, or more than one comment.

Validating Theme Files

WordPress uses CSS and XHTML to display Web pages. To help ensure consistent behavior from one Web browser to another on all computer platforms, it's a good idea to validate the CSS and XHTML in your theme files. The validation process will either confirm that the files are compliant with W3C recommendations or point out problems that may require attention to achieve full compliance.

Fortunately, there are online tools that will check your CSS and XHTML for you. All you do is visit a Web page, enter the URL you want checked, and click a button. Within seconds, the file is checked and a report appears onscreen.

In this part of the chapter, we explain how to validate the CSS and XHTML in your theme files.

✔ Tip

■ In addition to using the validation services discusssed here, you should view your blog with as many different browsers and computer platforms as possible.

To validate CSS

1. Use a Web browser to visit `jigsaw.w3.org/css-validator` (**Figure 54**).

2. To validate a CSS file that is already online, enter the URI for the CSS file in the Address box of the Validate by URI area. It should be something like `http://www.example.com/wp-content/themes/default/style.css` or `http://www.example.com/wordpress/wp-content/themes/default/style.css`, depending on whether you installed WordPress in your root Web directory or in a `wordpress` folder.

   or

   To validate a CSS file that has not yet been uploaded to your site, click the Browse button in the Validate by File Upload area. Then use the File Upload dialog that appears to locate, select, and open the CSS file you want to upload. It's path appears in the Local CSS file box (**Figure 55**).

3. Click Check in the appropriate area.

4. A report of problems and potential problems appears (**Figure 56**). Review the report.

5. If the report includes any errors, fix them in your CSS. Then repeat steps 1 through 5 again until all errors have been resolved.

✔ Tip

■ Not all items on the CSS Validator's report require action (**Figure 56**). Some are just recommendations to make your CSS better.

Figure 54 The CSS Validator at w3.org.

Figure 55 You can browse to or enter the path for a file on your hard disk.

Figure 56 The CSS validator displays warnings as well as errors.

Figure 57 You can access an XHTML validator on the w3.org Web site.

Figure 58 Even if the page looks fine, it might contain errors.

To validate XHTML pages

1. Use a Web browser to visit `validator.w3.org` (**Figure** 57).

2. To validate a theme file that is already online, enter the URL for the blog page you want to validate in the Address box of the Validate by URL area. It could be any page of your blog.

3. Click Check.

4. A report of problems appears (**Figure** 58). Review the report.

5. If the report includes errors, fix them in the theme file in which they appear. Then repeat steps 1 through 5 again until all errors have been resolved.

✔ Tips

- Tracking down errors listed in the report by line number isn't as easy as it might seem. Remember, each Web page for your blog can be made up of several php files. Sometimes it's easier to track down the error by the content that appears with it.

- In many cases, fixing a single error near the top of the list will have a ripple effect that fixes a bunch of other errors further down in the list. For that reason, it's always a good idea to work out the problems from the top of the list down.

To use a validation feed

1. Create a validation feed address by appending your site's URL to the end of:

   ```
   http://www.benhammersley.com/tools/
   validate.cgi?url=
   ```

   Here's an example from Miraz's test site:

   ```
   http://www.benhammersley.com/tools/
   validate.cgi?url=http://miraz.info/
   vqs/index.php.
   ```

2. Add the URL to your RSS aggregator.

3. Periodically check the feed.

   ▲ If no problems are found, there will be no items in the feed.

   ▲ If your home page contains invalid code, you will see one or more items in the feed that identify the error(s) found (**Figure 59**).

✔ Tips

- The Safari and Opera Web browsers include an aggregator.

- The Wizz RSS News Reader extension for Firefox is available from `addons.mozilla.org/firefox/424`.

Figure 59
The Wizz RSS feed reader I added to Firefox shows that a post has problems.

Using Plugins

Figure 1 The Plugins page in the WordPress Codex provides additional information about plugins, as well as links to plugin repositories.

Plugins

Plugins are special files that make it easy to add extra functions and features to your server-installed WordPress blog. They include PHP code that adds functions or perform other tasks. Some work their magic simply by being activated, while others also require you to edit files, modify posts, or carry out other actions.

For example, a plugin may trap comment spam, show post headlines from other blogs, or display all the photos you've uploaded. There are hundreds of plugins available to you in dozens of categories.

In this chapter we explain how to activate and deactivate plugins and, if necessary, set plugin options. We also show you some plugins we find particularly useful.

✔ Tips

- You can find links to lists of plugins at codex.wordpress.org/Plugins (**Figure 1**). **Appendix A** includes additional resources for finding plugins.

- Plugins can be added to WordPress server installations only, so if you have a WordPress.com blog, this chapter won't provide much useful information for you—except some good reasons to run your own WordPress installation!

Obtaining Plugins

If you want to use a plugin that isn't part of a standard WordPress installation, you'll have to obtain a copy of it. How you do this depends on how the plugin is made available:

◆ Most plugins are available as downloads. You click a link and download the plugin or an archive file containing the plugin and support files.

◆ Some very simple plugins are available only as plain text viewable in your Web browser. The code for these files must be copied and pasted into a plain text file and saved on your computer.

In this section, we explain how to use either method to obtain a plugin.

✔ Tip

■ Some plugins are available only from the plugin author's Web site.

To download a plugin

1. Locate the plugin you want through an Internet search or a plugin directory.

2. Click the appropriate link to download the plugin to your computer (**Figure 2**).

3. If a dialog like the one in **Figure 3a** or **3b** appears, choose an application from the menu and click OK.

   The plugin file(s) should appear in your default downloads location (**Figure 4**).

✔ Tip

■ Most downloadable plugins are archived with the ZIP compression scheme. Step 3 normally opens the archive file so you can see and use its contents. If the file is downloaded as a ZIP file and is not opened automatically, you can double-click its icon to open it.

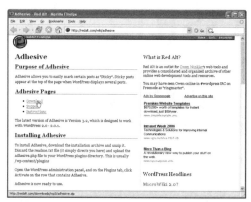

Figure 2 Click a download link to download the plugin.

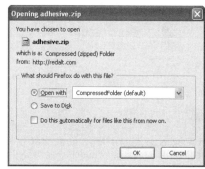

Figures 3a & 3b A dialog like this may ask how you want to open the downloaded file. These illustrations are from Firefox for Windows (top) and Firefox for Mac OS (bottom).

Figure 4 An example of the contents of a plugin archive file.

Figure 5 When you click a link to a PHP file, Safari displays the file's code in a Web browser window.

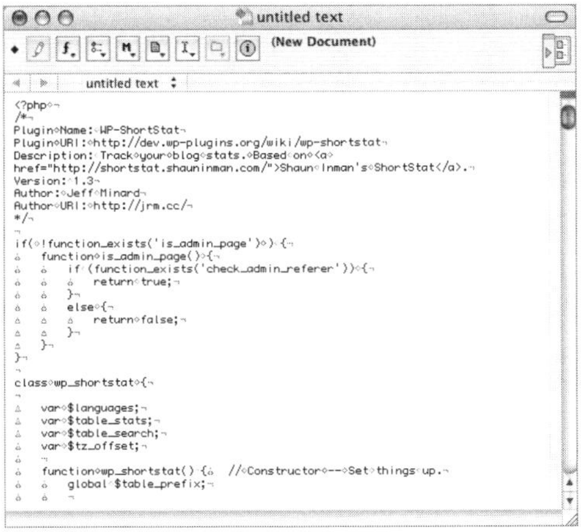

Figure 6 Paste the PHP code into an empty text file. In this illustration, invisible characters are displayed so we can track down and kill extra characters at the beginning or end of the file.

Warning: Cannot modify header information - headers already sent by (output started at /home/firstb/public_html/vqs/wp-content/plugins/wp-shortstat.php:1) in **/home/firstb/public_html/vqs/wp-admin/plugins.php** on line **16**

Figure 7 Here's an example of an error message that might appear if a plugin file includes extra characters. A similar message might appear if a plugin file becomes corrupted.

To create a plugin file from a code listing

1. Locate the plugin you want through an Internet search or a plugin directory.

2. Click the appropriate link to display the the plugin file's code in your Web browser window (**Figure 5**).

3. Select the text of the plugin from the opening <?php to the closing ?>.

4. Choose Edit > Copy or press ⌃C (Windows) or ⌘C (Mac OS).

5. Open your favorite text editor application and use it to create a new, empty text file.

6. Position the insertion point in the new document and choose Edit > Paste or press ⌃V (Windows) or ⌘V (Mac OS). The PHP code is pasted in (**Figure 6**).

7. If necessary, delete any extra text or other characters from the start and end of the document. The file must start with <?php and end with ?>.

8. Save the file with the name suggested by the creator of the plugin. Be sure to include the .php file name extension.

✔ Tips

- How a PHP file appears depends on your browser. For example, although clicking a link in Safari displayed the code you see in **Figure 5**, clicking the same link in Firefox offered to download the file as instructed on the previous page.

- Don't skip step 7! You may see an error message in your blog (**Figure 7**) if a plugin includes any extra characters.

- To help identify extra characters, it's a good idea to show invisible characters when working with PHP files in your text editor (**Figure 6**).

Installing Plugins

Once you have a plugin you want to use, you need to install and activate it.

Most plugins are completely installed in the plugins folder inside your wp-content folder. That means you'll copy the plugin's files or the folder in which the plugin files reside directly into the plugins folder.

Some plugins require special installation. For example, the WP-UserOnline plugin Maria uses on her blogs requires php files to be installed in several places in her blog folder.

There is no universal set of instructions for all plugin installations. You should follow the instructions provided by the plugin developer. You can usually find instructions and other documentation in a ReadMe file that came with the plugin (**Figure 4**) or on the developer's Web site where you downloaded the plugin (**Figure 2**). Pay special attention to the following instructions:

◆ Where should the plugin files be installed?

◆ Does the plugin require any other plugin to work?

◆ Do you need to change permissions for any file or folder for the plugin to work?

◆ Do you need to manually set configuration options in the plugin file itself?

◆ What modifications need to be made to your theme's template files after activation for the plugin to work?

✔ Tip

■ If plugin installation instructions aren't followed correctly, the plugin either won't work or will generate error messages.

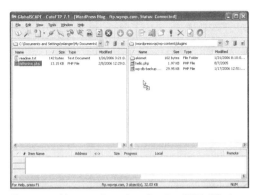

Figure 8 In this example, we're using Cute FTP in Windows to copy a plugin file to the plugins folder for a blog.

To install a plugin

1. Obtain the plugin as explained in the previous section.

2. Copy the plugin file(s) to the appropriate location(s) as instructed by the plugin developer using an FTP client (**Figure 8**).

3. Activate the plugin from the Plugin Management administration panel as discussed a little later in this chapter.

4. Follow other developer instructions to change permissions, modify theme files, and perform other configuration tasks as required.

5. Check your blog to make sure it is functioning as expected.

✔ Tips

- We explain how to use some popular FTP client software packages in **Appendix B**.

- Some plugins depend on other plugins for functionality. For an example, Duh Gallery, which we cover later in this chapter, requires the Exec-PHP plugin.

- Some plugins require you to change permissions on one or more files or folders. We explain how to do this in **Chapter 6**.

- If you need to edit other WordPress files be sure to make backups before you start. If something goes wrong you can easily revert to a known working copy.

- After making changes to your theme files, be sure to validate them using the XHTML validator at `validator.w3.org`. This can prevent errors caused by invalid codes or typing mistakes. We explain to validate HTML at the end of **Chapter 6**.

INSTALLING PLUGINS

To update a plugin

1. Obtain the updated plugin.

2. In the Plugin Management administration panel, deactivate the installed version of the plugin.

3. Upload the new plugin file(s) as instructed in the plugin documentation to replace the existing plugin file(s).

4. Use the Plugin Management administration panel to activate the plugin.

5. Check the plugin documentation for any other files you may need to edit. Make any necessary modifications.

6. Check your blog to make sure it is functioning as expected.

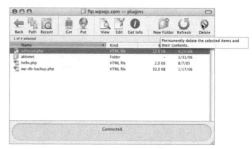

Figure 9 You can use an FTP client like Fetch, shown here, to delete plugins you no longer plan to use.

✔ Tip

■ When you update WordPress, be sure to check for updates to your plugins. In the past, some WordPress updates changed how the software worked, causing some plugins to fail.

To remove a plugin

1. In the Plugin Management administration panel, deactivate the installed version of the plugin.

2. Use your FTP client to delete all files for the plugin that you installed (**Figure 9**).

3. Check your blog to make sure it is functioning as expected.

✔ Tip

■ If the plugin required you to modify theme files, be sure to remove the modifications. Otherwise, you may see error messages in your blog.

UPDATING A PLUGIN

Figure 10 The Plugin Management administration panel shows all installed plugins. This illustration shows the three plugins that are part of a WordPress installation (Akismet, Hello Dolly, and WordPress Database Backup) as well as the one we installed in **Figure 8** (Adhesive). One plugin (Akismet) is enabled.

Managing Plugins

The Plugin Management administration panel (**Figure 10**) is your primary interface for working with plugins. You can use this panel to activate or deactivate plugins and get more information about a plugin. For some plugins, the Plugin Management panel also offers links to configure a plugin.

In this part of the chapter, we introduce the Plugin Management administration panel and explain how you can use it to manage your installed plugins.

✔ Tips

- A plugin will not appear in the Plugin Management administration panel unless it is properly installed.

- If a plugin malfunction prevents you from accessing your blog or the Plugin Management administration panel, use FTP to remove or rename the problem plugin. Doing so will deactivate it so you can access your blog or the Plugin Management panel again.

To display the Plugin Management administration panel

1. If necessary, log in to your WordPress blog and display the Dashboard.

2. Click the Plugins button. The Plugin Management administration panel appears, displaying a list of all installed plugins (**Figure 10**).

To get information about a plugin

In the Plugin Management administration panel (**Figure 10**):

◆ Click the name of the plugin in the Plugin column to visit its home page (**Figure 11**).

◆ Read information in the Description column to learn more about what the plugin does and follow links to the developer's Web site and other information.

To activate a plugin

1. Open the Plugin Management administration panel (**Figure 10**).

2. Click the Activate link beside the plugin you want to activate (**Figure 12**).

3. The page refreshes and a note near the top of the page indicates that the plugin has been activated (**Figure 13**).

4. Perform any other installation tasks required by the plugin. Consult the plugin's documentation for detailed instructions.

5. Visit your blog to make sure everything is working as you intended.

✔ Tips

■ An active plugin is displayed in the Plugin Management administration panel with a green background.

■ If an installed and activated plugin does not work as you expected, deactivate it. You can use the plugin's documentation or contact the plugin developer to troubleshoot and fix the problem.

Figure 11 Clicking the Akismet link takes you to the plugin's Web site.

Figure 12 Click the Activate link.

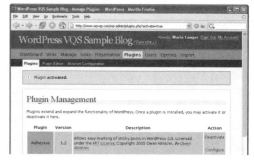

Figure 13 WordPress confirms that the plugin has been activated.

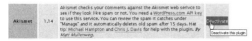

Figure 14 To deactivate a plugin, click the Deactivate link.

To deactivate a plugin

1. Open the Plugin Management administration panel (**Figure 10**).

2. Click the Deactivate link beside the plugin you want to deactivate (**Figure 14**).

3. The page refreshes and a note near the top of the page indicates that the plugin has been deactivated.

4. Perform any other deinstallation tasks related to the plugin. This includes, but is not limited to, deactivating related plugins and reverting modifications to theme files. Consult the plugins documentation for details.

5. Visit your blog to make sure everything is working as intended.

✔ Tip

■ If you don't plan to use a plugin again, you can remove it. We explain how earlier in this chapter.

DEACTIVATING PLUGINS

Setting Plugin Options

Plugin developers aren't aways consistent about how they allow access to plugin configuration options. Generally speaking, you can find links to view and set plugin options in any of the following places:

Figure 15 Configuration options for a plugin.

◆ The Action column of the Plugin Management administration panel sometimes includes a configure link for a plugin (**Figure 13**). Clicking that link opens the administration panel for the plugin (**Figure 15**).

◆ The Dashboard may display additional buttons to access plugin options (**Figure 16**).

Figures 16, 17, & 18 Buttons to access plugin configuration options can appear almost anywhere in the administration panel hierarchy.

◆ Clicking the Manage button from the Dashboard may display additional buttons to access plugin options (**Figure 17**).

◆ Clicking the Options button from the dashboard may display additional buttons to access plugin options (**Figure 18**).

How do you learn where to find access to configuration options? Read the documentation that came with the plugin!

✔ Tip

■ Not all plugins have configuration options. Some just come preset and work as designed without setting anything.

To set plugin options

1. If necessary, log in to your WordPress blog and display the Dashboard.

2. Access the administration panel for the plugin (**Figure 15**).

3. Set options as desired.

4. Click the Save, Update, or similar button to save your changes.

Hello, Dolly *lyric appears here*

Figure 19 A random line from the lyrics appears near the top of the administration panel.

```
k?php
/*
Plugin Name: Hello Dolly
Plugin URI: http://wordpress.org/#
Description: This is not just a plugin, it symbolizes the hope and
enthusiasm of an entire generation summed up in two words sung most
famously by Louis Armstrong: Hello, Dolly. When activated you will
randomly see a lyric from <cite>Hello, Dolly</cite> in the upper
right of your admin screen on every page.
Author: Matt Mullenweg
Version: 1.5
Author URI: http://photomatt.net/
*/

// These are the lyrics to Hello Dolly
$lyrics = "Hello, Dolly
Well, hello, Dolly
It's so nice to have you back where you belong
You're lookin' swell, Dolly
I can tell, Dolly
You're still glowin', you're still crowin'
You're still goin' strong
We feel the room swayin'
While the band's playin'
One of your old favourite songs from way back when
So, take her wrap, fellas
Find her an empty lap, fellas
Dolly'll never go away again
Hello, Dolly
Well, hello, Dolly
It's so nice to have you back where you belong
You're lookin' swell, Dolly
I can tell, Dolly
You're still glowin', you're still crowin'
You're still goin' strong
We feel the room swayin'
While the band's playin'
One of your old favourite songs from way back when
Golly, gee, fellas
Find her a vacant knee, fellas
Dolly'll never go away
Dolly'll never go away
Dolly'll never go away again";

// Here we split it into lines
$lyrics = explode("\n", $lyrics);
// And then randomly choose a line
$chosen = wptexturize( $lyrics[ mt_rand(0, count($lyrics) ) ] );
```

Figure 20 You can replace the *Hello, Dolly* lyrics with lyrics from one of your favorite songs.

Plugins Installed with WordPress

A standard WordPress server installation includes three plugins:

◆ **Akismet** by Matt Mullenweg attempts to identify and weed out comment spam using the Akismet Web service. We explain how to use Akismet—as well as why comment spam prevention is important—in **Chapter 4**.

◆ **Hello Dolly** by Matt Mullenweg displays a random lyric from the musical *Hello, Dolly* in the upper-right corner of every administration panel. It's not terribly useful, but it's fun.

◆ **WordPress Database Backup** by Scott Merrill makes it easy to backup your posts, Pages, links, and comments.

In this part of the chapter, we explain how to set up and use Hello Dolly and WordPress Database Backup. Akismet is covered in detail in **Chapter 4**.

To use Hello Dolly

1. In the Plugin Management administration panel, activate Hello Dolly. A note appears at the top of the page that the plugin has been activated.

2. View the top-right corner of any Dashboard window to see a lyric from Hello, Dolly (**Figure 19**).

✔ Tip

■ If you'd rather see lyrics from a different song, open the Hello Dolly plugin with a text editor (**Figure 20**) and paste in new lyrics. Be sure to keep each line of the song on a separate line in the text editor.

USING HELLO DOLLY

To back up your database with WordPress Database Backup

1. Set the permissions on the wp-content directory to 777 (**Figure 21**).

2. In the Plugin Management administration panel, activate WordPress Database Backup.

3. Click the Manage button near the top of the window.

4. Click the Backup button in the second row of buttons. The Backup administration panel appears (**Figure 22**).

5. Select the backup option you prefer:

   ▲ **Save to server** creates a backup file and saves it in the indicated location on the server.

   ▲ **Download to your computer** creates a backup file, temporarily saves it on the server, sends it to your browser for download, and then deletes it from the server.

   ▲ **Email backup to** creates a backup file, temporarily saves it on the server, e-mails it to the address you provide, and then deletes it from the server.

6. Click the Backup! button at the bottom of the page. WordPress shows a page with a progress indicator (**Figure 23**) while it creates a compressed file in the backup directory.

7. When the backup is complete, one of three things happens, depending on what you selected in step 5.

   ▲ If you selected Save to server, Word-Press displays a download link beneath the progress bar (**Figure 24**). You can click the link to download the backup file to your computer. The backup file is removed from the server.

Figure 21
You can use an FTP client, like Fetch, to set permissions for the wp-content folder.

Figure 22 The Backup administration panel.

Figure 23 A progress bar appears while the backup file is being created.

Figure 24 A download link appears beneath the progress bar.

Figure 25 A dialog like this one may appear when the backup file is downloaded.

Figure 26 If the backup is e-mailed to you, a dialog like this appears when it is complete.

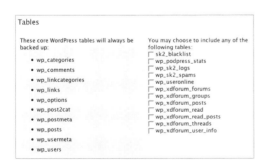

Figure 27 If your database includes additional tables maintained by plugins, you'll see them listed in the Backup administration panel, too.

▲ If you selected Download to your computer, the backup file automatically begins downloading to your computer. If a dialog like the one in **Figure 25** appears, select Save to Disk and click OK. The file is downloaded to your default downloads folder and removed from the server.

▲ If you selected Email backup to, WordPress displays a dialog (**Figure 26**); you can click OK to dismiss it. The file is e-mailed to the address you provided and removed from the server.

✔ Tips

■ We explain how to change permissions for a directory in **Chapter 6**.

■ It's best to keep your backup files on a computer other than the server. This way, if the server goes down, you won't lose both your blog and its backup.

■ If other plugins add data to the database, the WordPress Database backup administration panel will list those tables with check boxes (**Figure 27**). Turn on all the check boxes before clicking Backup! to include all database content in the backup file.

■ WP-Cron is another plugin by Scott Merrill that works with WordPress Database Backup to automatically back up the database daily.

✖ Warning!

■ WordPress Database Backup does *not* back up your theme files, plugins, uploaded images, or any other blog content or configuration files that are not part of the database. You can use FTP software to back up your entire site by downloading it from the server to your computer or by backing up the blog folder to some other media.

Other Useful Plugins

As we mentioned earlier in this chapter, there are hundreds of WordPress plugins. These plugins offer many possibilities for enhancing your blog.

In the remainder of this chapter, we introduce you to some of the plugins we use by telling you what they do and where to obtain them and providing basic setup information. Keep in mind that most of these plugins offer far more features and customization options than what we have room to discuss in this book. Check the developer's documentation for detailed instructions on how to install, configure, and use the plugin.

✔ Tips

■ You can find links to lists of plugins at codex.wordpress.org/Plugins (**Figure 1**). **Appendix A** includes additional resources for finding plugins.

■ Although most plugins are available for free, plugin developers work hard to build, test, document, support, and enhance their plugins. If you like a developer's plugin, let him know by sending a donation. Even a few dollars can go a long way to showing developers how much you appreciate their work.

Adhesive

Adhesive lets you designate a post as *sticky*, meaning it will stay at the top of the Home Page and relevant Archive or Category pages, rather than scrolling down the pages when newer content is added. This is especially useful for presenting important information or announcements about your blog or one of its categories.

Adhesive was developed by Owen Winkler and can be downloaded from redalt.com/wiki/adhesive.

To install and configure Adhesive

1. Follow the instructions earlier in this chapter and in the Adhesive documentation to install and activate Adhesive.

2. In the Plugin Management administration panel, click the Configure button in the Action column beside Adhesive. The Configure Adhesive administration panel opens (**Figure 15**).

3. Set options as desired:

   ▲ **Categories only** makes posts sticky on category pages only—not on the home page.

   ▲ **Display date** displays the date instead of a date banner on posts. (This feature is not supported by all themes.)

   ▲ **Date Banner** is formatted text that can appear instead of the date for a sticky post. (This feature is not supported by all themes.)

4. Click the Update button to save your settings.

To make a post sticky

1. In the Write Post administration panel for a new or existing post, expand the Post Status area (**Figure 28**).

2. Turn on the Sticky check box.

3. Complete and publish the post.

✔ Tips

- We explain how to create and edit posts in **Chapter 3**.

- In the Manage Posts administration panel, the word *Sticky* appears before the title of a sticky post (**Figure 29**).

- To remove the sticky feature from a post, follow the above steps but turn off the Sticky check box in step 2. When you publish the post, it will fall into the normal chronology of the blog's other posts.

Figure 28 When you activate Adhesive, a Sticky check box appears in the Post Status area.

Figure 29 Sticky posts are identified in the Manage Posts administration panel.

ADHESIVE

Figure 30 Use CG-Feedread to display information from other feeds in your blog.

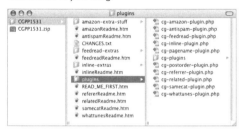

Figure 31 The contents of the CGPP1531 folder and its plugins folder.

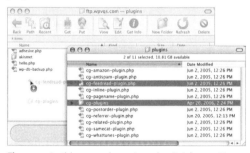

Figure 32 In this example, we're using Fetch on a Mac to install the CG-Feedread files.

Figure 33
You can use your FTP software to set a folder's permissions.

CG-Feedread

CG-Feedread is an RSS/Atom aggregation script to pull in feeds and display titles or posts from other sites on your blog (**Figure 30**).

CG-Feedread is by David Chait of ChaitGear. It's part of the CG-PowerPack, which can be downloaded from www.chait.net/index.php?p=238. Be sure to download the most recent version; although it may say it's for WordPress 1.5.1, it'll also work with Word-Press 2.

✔ Tips

- Although the CG-PowerPack package includes several plugins, we're only covering CG-Feedread in this book. Explore the other plugins on your own.

- In the future, the Chaitgear plugins may move to chaitgear.com.

To install & activate CG-Feedread

1. Open the CGPP1531 folder you downloaded. It contains all of the files that make up the CG-PowerPack package (**Figure 31**).

2. Open the plugins folder (**Figure 31**).

3. Use your FTP client to upload the cg-feedread-plugin.php file and cg-plugins folder to the plugins folder in your wp-content folder (**Figure 32**).

4. On the server, set the permissions for the wp-content/plugins/cg-plugins/cache_feedread folder to 777 (**Figure 33**).

5. In the Plugin Management administration panel, activate the CG-Feedread plugin.

✔ Tip

- We tell you more about using FTP software in **Appendix B**.

To use CG-Feedread

1. Use your favorite text editor to open the theme template file in which you want to display the feeds. In most cases, this will be sidebar.php, but it could be another file.

2. Insert the following code where you want the feed to appear, substituting the feed's URL for the italicized URL shown here:

   ```
   <?php $feedUrl = "http://example.com/index.rss"; // an example

   $feedOut = getSomeFeed($feedUrl, 5, false, "feed-example", '', 20, false);

   if ($feedOut) echo $feedOut; ?>
   ```

   Figure 34 shows an example using the Default theme's sidebar.php file.

3. Save the edited file.

4. Check your blog to see if the modifications are functioning as expected. You should see a list of five headlines from the feed you specified in step 2. In our example, we used the feed from TiKouka; we can now see five headlines from that blog in the sidebar of our test blog (**Figure 30**).

✔ Tips

- The second line of code in step 2 includes seven parameters you might want to modify to better meet your needs:
  - ▲ `$feedUrl` is the feed URL.
  - ▲ `5` is the maximum number of items.
  - ▲ `false` (the first instance) tells CG-Feedread not to show article details or body.
  - ▲ `"feed-example"` is the name of the feed's cache on your server. It must be unique.

Figure 34 In this example, we're inserting the code for CG-Feedread into the sidebar.php file.

- ▲ `''` (an empty string) is for filtering a feed by category or key word. Normally, you'd leave this as shown here.
- ▲ `20` is the maximum number of characters to display for each item.
- ▲ `false` (the second instance) strips out any HTML from the displayed text.

- You can find additional information about CG-Feedread parameters in the feedreadReadme.htm file in the CGPP1531 folder (**Figure 31**).

Exec-PHP

Exec-PHP makes it possible to include PHP code within the posts and pages of your blog. It is required for certain plugins to work, including Duh Gallery, which is discussed on the next page.

Exec-PHP was written by Sören Weber and can be found at www.soeren-weber.net/post/2005/08/18/50/.

✔ Tip

- Be sure to read the documentation for Exec-PHP on it's Web page to fully understand how it works and how it may impact your site's security.

To install & activate Exec-PHP

Follow the instructions earlier in this chapter and on the Exec-PHP Web page to install and activate Exec-PHP.

Duh Gallery

Duh Gallery enables you to display all the photos you've uploaded to your blog as a gallery organized by date (**Figure 35**).

Duh Gallery was written by Nate Ritter and can be found at blog.perfectspace.com/2006/03/28/duh-gallery-the-simple-wordpress-photo-gallery-plugin/.

✔ Tip

- Duh Gallery only displays images that were uploaded using the Upload feature of the Write Post or Write Page administration panel. It does not display images uploaded via FTP. We explain how to upload images in **Chapter 3**.

To install, activate, & configure Duh Gallery

1. Follow the instructions earlier in this chapter and on the Duh Gallery Web page to install and activate Duh Gallery.

2. Display the Miscellaneous Options administration panel (**Figure 36**).

3. Confirm that the path for uploading files is valid, and, if necessary turn on the check box marked Organize my uploads into month- and year-based folders.

4. Click the Update Options button.

✔ Tip

- We tell you about setting Miscellaneous Options in **Chapter 2**.

Figure 35 Duh Gallery makes it easy to display a gallery of images uploaded to your blog.

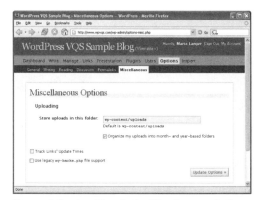

Figure 36 Check settings in the Miscellaneous Options administration panel.

Figure 37 Use the Write Page panel to create a Photo Gallery Page.

Figure 38 The page first appears with links to years.

Figure 39 Clicking an image displays a larger version of it.

To use Duh Gallery

1. Upload images to your blog using the upload feature in the Write Post or Write Page administration panel.

2. Use the Write Page administration panel to create a new Page with at least the following line of code:

   ```
   <?php do_action('duh_gallery'); ?>
   ```

   Be sure to give the Page a title and enter any other text you want to appear. **Figure 37** shows an example.

3. Click Create New Page to publish the page.

4. Visit the Page you just created (**Figure 38**). Use the year and month links to reveal the images in various folders (**Figure 35**). You can also click an image to view a larger version (**Figure 39**).

✔ Tips

- We explain how to upload files in **Chapter 3**.

- Although you can use Duh Gallery code in a post, it may be more practical to use it on a Page so your photo gallery is more easily accessible.

- If you normally use the Rich Text Editor for editing posts and Pages you may need to switch to HTML view to successfully enter the PHP code.

- Read the instructions on Duh Gallery's Web page for details on customizing it.

Event Calendar

Usually, posts dated in the future don't appear in your blog until the date and time set within them. The Event Calendar plugin makes them available right away. This enables you to create a calendar of upcoming events (**Figure 40**), each of which are tied to a blog entry that can provide additional event details. Best of all, events scroll off the calendar and events list automatically when they have passed.

Event Calendar was written by Alex Tingle. It can be found at blog.firetree.net/2005/ 07/18/eventcalendar-30.

✔ Tip

■ Maria makes extensive use of Event Calendar to list upcoming holidays, Town Council Meetings, and other events on her local area Web site, wickenburg-az.com.

To install, activate, & configure Event Calendar

1. Upload the eventcalendar3 folder and eventcalendar3.php file to the plugins folder in your wp-content folder (**Figure 41**).

2. In the Plugin Management administration panel, activate the Event Calendar plugin.

3. If necesssary, display the Manage Categories administration panel and add a new category named *Events* (**Figure 42**).

4. Click Options and then click Event Calendar to display the Event Calendar Options administration panel (**Figure 43**).

5. Choose Events from the Event category drop-down list (**Figure 44**).

Figure 40 Event Calendar makes it easy to maintain a calendar of upcoming events—right in your blog.

Figure 41 Copy the eventcalendar3 folder and eventcalendar3.php file to your plugins folder.

Figure 42 If you don't already have a category created for events, add one.

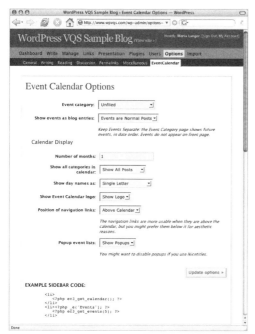

Figure 43 You can set options for Event Calendar in its administration panel.

Figure 44 Be sure to choose the Events category from the Event category drop-down list.

6. To display events only in the Events category and not on the front page of your blog, choose Keep Events Separate from the Show events as blog entries drop-down list.

7. Set Calendar Display options as desired.

8. Click the Update options button to save your settings.

✔ Tips

- In step 3, you can name the event calendar category anything you like. Just be sure to choose that category in step 5.

- Consult the Read Me file that comes with Event Calendar for more information about setting options and customizing the appearance of your calendar. It also explains a problem that may crop up with early versions of WordPress 2, and how to deal with that problem by editing some files. We were not affected by the problem and did not have to edit any files.

INSTALLING & CONFIGURING EVENT CALENDAR

To use Event Calendar

1. Use your browsers Copy command to copy the Example Sidebar Code at the bottom of the Event Calendar Options administration panel (**Figure 43**).

2. Use your favorite text editor to open the sidebar.php file for your theme.

3. Use the Paste command to paste the code where you want the calendar of events to appear (**Figure 45**).

4. Save the sidebar.php file.

5. Use the Write Post administration panel to create one or more posts for future events. For each event, be sure to set the Post Timestamp to the correct future date and time and set the Categories to Events (**Figure 46**).

6. View your blog. You should see a calendar and a list of Events in the Sidebar (**Figure 40**). Click the link for an event to see its details on a blog entry page.

✔ Tip

- We tell you all about creating posts in **Chapter 3**.

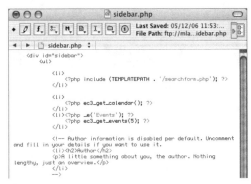

Figure 45 In this example, we've pasted the Event Calendar code into the sidebar.php file for the default theme.

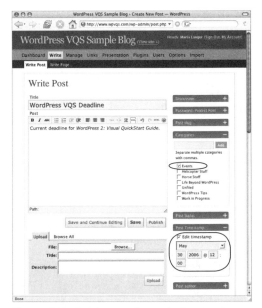

Figure 46 It's vital that you choose the Events category and set a future date and time when creating a post for an event.

Figure 47 Keywords can be displayed at the bottom of a post.

Jerome's Keywords Plugin

Jerome's Keywords Plugin enables you to tag your posts with one or more keywords (**Figure 47**). Blog visitors can then click a keyword for a post to see other posts with the same keyword assigned. This makes posts in your blog easier to find by topic, without relying on category.

Jerome's Keywords Plugin was written by Jerome Lavigne and can be downloaded from vapourtrails.ca/wp-keywords.

✔ Tip

- The keywords you assign with Jerome's Keywords Plugin are also recognized and indexed as tags by Technorati. You can learn more about Technorati and how it can help drive visitors to your blog for free at www.technorati.com.

To install Jerome's Keywords Plugin

Follow the instructions earlier in this chapter and on the Jerome's Keywords Plugin Web page to install and activate the plugin.

To use Jerome's Keywords Plugin

1. Open the template file containing The Loop for your theme. Normally, this will be the index.php or post.php file

2. Insert the following code inside The Loop, but after the post (**Code 1**):

   Tags: <?php the_post_keytags(); ?>.

3. Save the file.

4. In the Write Post window for your blog, enter keywords in the Keywords box below the post editing area (**Figure 48**).

5. Publish the post.

6. View your blog and look at a post with keywords. The keywords should appear below the post (**Figure 47**).

✔ Tips

- We tell you more about The Loop in **Chapter 6**.

- You can also add keywords for posts you have already composed and published. The Keywords box appears in the Write Post window when creating a new post or editing an existing one. We tell you more about writing and editing posts in **Chapter 3**.

Code 1

Inserting Jerome's Keywords Plugin template tag in The Loop

```php
<?php while (have_posts()) : the_post(); ?>

  <div class="post" id="post-<?php the_ID(); ?>">

    <h2><a href="<?php the_permalink() ?>" rel="bookmark" title="Permanent Link to <?php the_title(); ?>"><?php the_title(); ?></a></h2>

    <small><?php the_time('F jS, Y') ?> <!-- by <?php the_author() ?> --></small>

    <div class="entry">

      <?php the_content('Read the rest of this entry &raquo;'); ?>

    </div>

    <p class="postmetadata">Posted in <?php the_category(', ') ?> | <?php edit_post_link('Edit', '', ' | '); ?> <?php comments_popup_link('No Comments &#187;', '1 Comment &#187;', '% Comments &#187;'); ?></p>

    Tags: <?php the_post_keytags(); ?>

  </div>

<?php endwhile; ?>
```

Figure 48 A Keywords box appears in the Write Post window, right beneath the Post box.

Figure 49 The default theme with Random Header installed.

Figure 50 The components of the Random Header plugin.

Figure 51 Upload the images you prepared to the theme's image folder.

Random Header

The Random Header plugin loads a different header image every time the page is loaded or refreshed (**Figure 49**). This adds variety to your site's pages.

Random Header was written by Kamiel Martinet and can be downloaded from www.martinet.nl/wp-site/random-header-plugin. That's also where you can see Random Header in action; the site's page header will automatically change each time you reload the page.

To install & use Random Header

1. Open the randomheader Folder you downloaded. It should contain plugin file, a folder, and a readme file (**Figure 50**).

2. Upload the randomheader.php file and the randomheader folder to the plugins folder in your blog's wp-content folder.

3. Use an image editor to prepare some header images. Each image should be at least 760 pixels wide by 200 pixels high.

4. Upload the header images to your theme's images folder; for example, wp-content/themes/default/images (**Figure 51**).

5. In the Plugin Management administration panel, activate the Random Header plugin.

6. Click the Options button and then click the Random Header button to display the Random header options administration panel (**Figure 52**).

7. If the ID of the header element for your theme is not *header*, enter the correct ID in the Header ID box and click the Save options button.

Continued on next page...

Continued from previous page.

8. In the Add new header image area, choose an image from the drop-down list (**Figure 53**). The picture is displayed beneath the drop-down list (**Figure 54**).

9. Click the Add image button. The image is displayed in the Header images section, with a Delete link beside it (**Figure 55**).

10. Repeat steps 8 and 9 for each image you uploaded in step 4.

11. View your blog and refresh or reload the page a few times. The header image should change randomly with each refresh.

✔ Tips

- You can learn the ID of the header element in your theme by consulting the `style.css` file for your theme. The header element is the style that contains the header image in its defintion. In many cases, this will be *header*.

- To add additional images in the future, repeat steps 3, 4, 8, and 9. The new images will be pooled in with the ones originally added for display.

- To remove an image from the header image rotation, click the Delete link beside it in the Header images area (**Figure 55**). This prevents the image from being displayed but does not delete it from your server.

Figure 52 The Random header options administration panel.

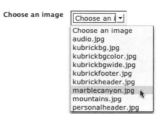

Figure 53 Choose an image from the drop-down list.

Figure 54 The image appears beneath the list.

Figure 55 Added images appear in the Header images area.

INSTALLING & USING RANDOM HEADER

Figure 56 In this example, we used Customizable Post Listings to show the three most recent posts in the sidebar.

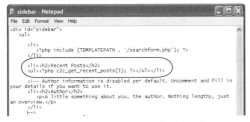

Figure 57 Insert code into your sidebar.php file.

Customizable Post Listings

The Customizable Post Listings plugin allows you to add quick lists of recent posts, recently commented posts, recently modified posts, and random posts, as well as other post listings your sidebar. In this example, we show you how to add a list of recent posts (**Figure 56**).

Customizable Post Listings was written by Scott Reilly of Coffee2Code. It can be found at www.coffee2code.com/archives/2004/08/27/plugin-customizable-post-listings.

✔ Tip

■ To learn how to add other listings with Customizable Post Listings, consult the documentation on its Web page. That's where you'll find code examples and plugin support.

To install Customizable Post Listings

Follow the instructions earlier in this chapter and on the Customizable Post Listings Web page to install and activate the plugin.

To use Customizable Post Listings

1. Use your favorite text editor to open the sidebar.php file for your theme.

2. Insert the following code where you want the recent post listing to appear (**Figure 57**):

   ```
   <li><h2>Recent Posts</h2>
   ```

   ```
   <ul><?php c2c_get_recent_posts(3);
   ?></ul></li>
   ```

3. View your blog. The sidebar should display dates and titles for the three most recent posts (**Figure 56**).

Search Pages Plugin

The Search Pages Plugin allows visitors to search both posts and Pages. The default WordPress search does not include Pages.

Search Pages was written by David B. Nagle based on a hack by Rob Schlüter. You can find it at randomfrequency.net/wordpress/search-pages.

To install & use Search Pages Plugin

1. Follow the instructions earlier in this chapter and on the Search Pages Plugin Web page to install and activate the plugin.

2. View your blog's search form.

3. Search for a word you know is contained within a Page but not a post. The results appear on a search results page (**Figure 58**).

Figure 58 With the Search Pages Plugin installed and activated, search results can include pages.

Figure 59 You can designate any WordPress page to be your site's home page with the static front page plugin.

Figure 60 Be sure to set the Post Slug option to *home*.

Static Front Page

The static front page plugin allows you to set a WordPress Page as the home page of your blog.

The static front page plugin was written by Denis de Bernardy and can be found at semiologic.com/software/static-front.

To install & use the static front page plugin

1. Follow the instructions earlier in this chapter and on the static front page plugin Web page to install and activate the plugin.

2. Open the Write Page administration panel for a new or existing WordPress page (**Figure 60**).

3. Create or edit the page as desired.

4. In the Post slug text box enter the word *home* (**Figure 60**).

5. Click Create New Page or Save to publish the page.

6. View your blog's Home Page. The page you just created or modify should appear as the Home page. (**Figure 59**).

INSTALLING & USING STATIC FRONT PAGE

Subscribe to Comments

The Subscribe to Comments plugin allows visitors to subscribe to a post's comments by toggling a check box when they enter a comment for that post (**Figure 61**). Each time a new comment is entered for that post, the subscribers get the comment delivered to them by e-mail (**Figure 63**). This makes it possible for blog readers to keep track of a post's discussion without manually checking in for comments.

Subscribe to Comments was written by Mark Jaquith based on code originally by Jennifer ("ScriptyGoddess"). It can be found at `txfx.net/code/wordpress/subscribe-to-comments`.

To install Subscribe to Comments

1. Open the `subscribe-to-comments` folder. It contains several files (**Figure 62**), including `subscribe-to-comments.php` and `wp-subscription-manager.php`

2. Upload `subscribe-to-comments.php` to the `plugins` folder in your `wp-content` folder.

3. Upload `wp-subscription-manager.php` to the root directory of your blog—that is, the directory that also contains `wp-config.php`.

4. In the Plugin Management administration panel, activate the Subscribe to Comments plugin.

Leave a Reply

Name (required)
Mail (will not be published) (required)
Website

Submit Comment

☐ Notify me of followup comments via e-mail

Figure 61 When you install Subscribe to Comments, a Notify me check box appears beneath the comment form.

Figure 62 Subscribe to Comments comes with several files.

Figure 63 When you subscribe to a post's comments, you get an e-mail message each time a comment is entered and approved for that post.

To test Subscribe to Comments

1. If necessary, log out of your blog and view it without being logged in.

2. View the comments form for any post. A Notify me of followup comments via e-mail check box should appear beneath the Submit Comment button (**Figure 61**).

3. Fill in the comment form, using an e-mail address other than the one associated with an administrator account or the account for the post author. Submit the comment.

4. Enter a second comment, using any e-mail address. You should receive an e-mail message at the first e-mail address with the contents of the second comment and instructions on managing your subscriptions (**Figure 63**).

✔ Tips

- The Notify me check box does not appear when you are logged in as administrator or author of the post.

- If the Notify me check box does not appear in step 2 and you are definitely logged out of your blog, your theme may have a conflict with the plugin. To learn how to fix the problem, consult the Subscribe to Comments Wiki page at dev.wp-plugins.org/wiki/Subscribe ToComments.

- If comment moderation is enabled, you may have to approve the comments in step 4 before you receive notification by e-mail. We explain how to moderate and approve comments in **Chapter 4**.

WP-ContactForm

The WP-ContactForm plugin allows you to offer a contact form (**Figure 64**) in addition to, or instead of, an e-mail link. The main benefit of this is that the form shields your e-mail address from e-mail harvesting robots that collect e-mail addresses for spamming purposes.

WP-ContactForm was written by Ryan Duff and can be downloaded from ryanduff.net/projects/wp-contactform.

✔ Tip

- The WP-ContactForm plugin offers a quick and easy way to create a Contact Page (**Figure 64**)

To install WP-ContactForm

1. Upload the wp-contact-form folder to the plugins folder in your wp-content folder.

2. In the Plugin Management administration panel, activate the WP-ContactForm plugin.

3. Click the Options button at the top of the administration panel and then click the Contact Form button. The Contact Form Options administration panel appears (**Figure 65**).

4. Set the options as desired:

   ▲ **E-mail address** is the address you want the contact message sent to.

   ▲ **Subject** is the subject of the contact message, as it will appear in your e-mail application.

   ▲ **Success Message** is the message that appears to the user when the contact form is successfully submitted.

Figure 64 You can use WP-ContactForm to create a contact page for your site.

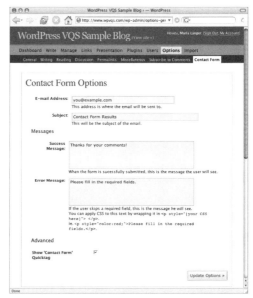

Figure 65 Set options in the Contact Form Options administration panel.

Insert Contact Form button

Write Page

Page Title

Contact Us!

Page Content

B *I* ABC | ☰ ☰ | ☵ ☵ | ☰ ☰ ☰ | ∞ ☒ ☒ ☒ ☐ | ⅋ ⅋ HTML ⃝ ⬚

Got something to say about this site or its content? Use the Contact Form below.

<!--contact form-->

Path: p

Figure 66 Creating a contact form is as easy as inserting a line of code in a post or Page.

▲ **Error Message** is the message that appears to the user when the contact form cannot be successfully submitted—normally due to an incomplete form.

▲ **Show 'Contact Form' Quicktag** adds a button to the post or page editing window (**Figure 66**) to make it easy to insert the code for the contact form.

5. Click the Update Options button.

To insert a contact form

1. In the post or Page editing area of a Write Post or Write Page window, insert the following line of code where you want the form to appear (**Figure 66**):

   `<!--contact form-->`

   or

   While composing a post or Page position the insertion point where you want the contact form to appear and click the Insert Contact Form button (**Figure 66**).

2. Publish or save the post or Page.

3. View the post or Page you created in your blog to confirm that the Contact Form appears as expected (**Figure 64**).

✔ Tip

■ Although the Contact Form code resembles an HTML comment, it is lacking the spaces required for a normal comment. The correct form is:

   `<!--contact form-->`

   where the only space is between the words `contact` and `form`.

WP-ShortStat

The WP-ShortStat plugin provides visitor statistics for your blog on a ShortStat admin-sitration panel within WordPress (**Figure 67**).

WP-ShortStat was written by Jeff Minard and can be downloaded from jrm.cc/archives/blog/wp-shortstat/.

To use WP-ShortStat

1. Follow the instructions earlier in this chapter and on the WP-ShortStat Web page to install and activate the plugin.

2. Click the Dashboard button in the administration panel and then click the ShortStat button. The ShortStat adminis-tration panel with statistics for your site appears.

✔ Tips

- Statistics start accumulating when you install WP-ShortStat. When you first view the ShortStat administration panel, there may not be any statistics to see.

- If you have trouble getting ShortStat to work with WordPress 2.0.2, there is a fix available by Pascal VanHecke. Visit pascal.vanhecke.info and use the search feature to search for *ShortStat*. The page that appears includes a link to the fix.

Figure 67 ShortStat provides all kinds of statistics for your site's visitors.

Adding Other Content

Adding Other Content

Chapter 7 discusses some useful plugins for adding features to your server-installed WordPress blog. If there's no suitable plugin available for the content you want to add, you may be able to get the desired result by adding coding directly to your theme's files.

In this chapter we suggest some possibilities for extending your blog beyond what's possible with plugins. We show you how to display information about the blog's author, easily add distinctive images to posts from different authors, see statistics about the blog, use a favicon, and perhaps make a little money with Google AdSense. Since these tasks all require you to edit theme files, this chapter applies only to server-installed WordPress blogs and not to WordPress.com blogs.

In this chapter, we mainly show you how to add content to the sidebar, but of course, you're free to include it wherever you wish. Just remember, as explained in **Chapter 6**, any code you include inside The Loop will be attached to each post and may appear multiple times on one page. Code outside The Loop, or in the header, sidebar, or footer will appear only once per page.

Continued on next page...

Continued from previous page.

✔ Tips

- Although most of the instructions in this chapter apply specifically to the Default WordPress theme, you can use similar or identical code in your own theme files to add the same features.

- Whenever you edit your blog's theme files you run the risk of creating coding errors. To keep your blog running smoothly, validate your pages frequently. We explain how in **Chapter 6**.

- Remember to always view your blog after saving changes to the files; even valid code may be incorrect.

- In the examples in this chapter we show you how to add code directly to your theme files. Another way to do this is to put the code in a separate file and then include that file in the theme. We explain how to do this at the end of this chapter.

- Most items in the Default theme's sidebar are part of a list; you should usually wrap sidebar items in list tags if you're using the Default theme.

- Although this chapter suggests that you edit theme files in a text editor, you can also use WordPress's built-in theme editor. We explain how to modify theme files in **Chapter 6**.

Figure 1 The Author Profile code is commented out until you're ready to use it.

Figure 2 Here's an example of Miraz's profile.

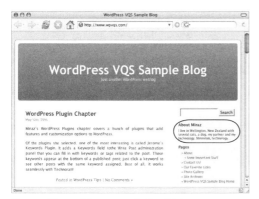

Figure 3 The profile appears in the sidebar.

✔ Tips

- Remember to include your name. You may also want to include a photo (using an IMG tag) and perhaps an e-mail address.

- If you have a lot to say about yourself consider creating a Page. **Chapter 3** explains how to create Pages.

Author Profile

Many bloggers forget that the rest of the world doesn't know who they are. They write about their work, leisure, opinions, friends, and family, but don't provide their name, leaving visitors to hunt through the blog for clues.

By default, a WordPress installation does not display any information about the blog's owner or author. But space is reserved in the Default theme's sidebar, ready for you to activate it. Here's how.

To add an author profile to the sidebar

1. Open the Default theme's `sidebar.php` file in a text editor.

2. Locate the following section of code (**Figure 1**):

   ```
   <!-- Author information is disabled
   per default. Uncomment and fill in
   your details if you want to use it.

   <li><h2>Author</h2>

   <p>A little something about you, the
   author. Nothing lengthy, just an
   overview.</p>

   </li>

   -->
   ```

3. Delete the first and last lines to remove the commenting codes.

4. If desired, change the heading *Author* to something you prefer.

5. Replace the default text between the `<p>` and `</p>` tags with information about yourself (**Figure 2**).

6. Save the edited file.

7. View your blog to see your new author profile in the sidebar (**Figure 3**).

Author Photos

If your blog has more than one author, you might like to include author photos with their posts. It's easy to do this automatically by associating each author with an image file using a clever piece of coding. The trick is that each author has a unique ID on the blog; just use photos whose file names use that same ID.

✔ Tip

- Maria's `wickenburg-az.com` (**Figure 4**) is a good example of a blog using author photos.

To discover author IDs

1. Follow the instructions in **Chapter 5** to view the Authors & Users administration panel for your blog (**Figure 5**).

2. In the leftmost column, note the ID of each author.

✔ Tip

- If your blog has many authors, you can print the Authors & Users administration panel page (**Figure 5**) for reference.

Figure 4 Maria's wickenburg-az.com site makes extensive use of author photos.

Figure 5 Each user's ID appears in the Authors & Users administration panel.

Figure 6
Create an image
you want to associ-
ate with an author.
Here's Miraz.

To prepare author photos

1. Use your image editing software to create an image for an author (**Figure 6**).

2. Save the image as a JPEG, GIF, or PNG format file using the author's ID as the file name with the appropriate filename extension. For example, using the user list shown in **Figure 5**, Miraz's image, if saved in JPEG format, would be named 2.jpg.

3. Repeat steps 1 and 2 for each author you want to provide an image for.

4. Upload the author images to your server within the main WordPress main directory. For our example, we uploaded them to wp-content/images/authors.

✔ Tips

- In step 1, for best results the image file's dimensions and file size should be small—less than 150 pixels square and less than 10Kb.

- If your blog entries are usually very short, use smaller images.

- If you like your entries to have a uniform look, be sure to use the same size for all author images.

- In step 2, all images must be saved in the same format with the same file extension.

- To prevent missing image errors in some browsers, you should create images for all blog authors. If you don't want to display an image for a specific author, create a 1x1 pixel image with the same background color as your blog's entry area and save it with that author's ID.

To add author photos to posts

1. Open the Default theme's `index.php` file in a text editor.

2. Add the code shown in **Code 1** within The Loop where you want the author's photo to appear. Here's a breakdown of the code so you can understand how it works:

```
<img src="<?php get_bloginfo
('url'); ?>wp-content/images/
authors/<?php the_author_ID();
?>.jpg"
```

This code uses the `get_bloginfo` tag to get the URL of the blog's home page, then appends the rest of the path to the author images folder. The `the_author_ID` tag supplies the user ID for the author, which is appended to the file name extension. (This example assumes you are using JPEG format files.) The result is the start of an `img src` tag with the complete URL for the post's author image file.

```
class="auth"
```

This applies a style to the image which will be defined later in these instructions.

```
alt="<?php the_author(); ?>. "
```

This uses the `the_author` template tag to get the name of the author as alternate text.

```
title="<?php the_author(); ?>. "
```

This uses the `the_author` template tag to get the name of the author as title text.

```
/>.
```

This completes the `img src` tag.

3. Save the edited file.

4. Open the Default theme's `style.css` file in a text editor.

Code 1

Author Photo Code Inserted in The Loop

```php
<?php if (have_posts()) : ?>

 <?php while (have_posts()) : the_post();
?>

    <div class="post" id="post-<?php
the_ID(); ?>">

      <h2><a href="<?php the_permalink()
?>" rel="bookmark" title="Permanent Link to
<?php the_title(); ?>"><?php the_title();
?></a></h2>

      <small><?php the_time('F jS, Y') ?>
by <?php the_author() ?></small>

      <div class="entry">

        <img src="<?php get_
bloginfo('url'); ?>wp-content/images/
authors/<?php the_author_ID(); ?>.jpg"
class="auth" alt="<?php the_author(); ?>.
" title="<?php the_author(); ?>. " /><?php
the_content('Read the rest of this entry
&raquo;'); ?>

      </div>

      <p class="postmetadata">Posted in
<?php the_category(', ') ?> | <?php edit_
post_link('Edit', '', ' | '); ?>  <?php
comments_popup_link('No Comments &#187;',
'1 Comment &#187;', '% Comments &#187;');
?></p>

    </div>

 <?php endwhile; ?>

 <div class="navigation">

    <div class="alignleft"><?php next_
posts_link('&laquo; Previous Entries')
?></div>

    <div class="alignright"><?php previous_
posts_link('Next Entries &raquo;') ?></div>

 </div>

 <?php else : ?>

 <h2 class="center">Not Found</h2>

 <p class="center">Sorry, but you are
looking for something that isn't here.</p>

 <?php include (TEMPLATEPATH . "/
searchform.php"); ?>

<?php endif; ?>
```

Figure 7 Each entry should display the photo of its author.

5. Insert the following line of code at the end of the file:

```
img.auth { float: left;
margin-right: 1em; }
```

This code aligns the image on the left with 1 em of spacing between the image and the text that will flow around it.

6. Save the edited file.

7. View posts written by different authors to make sure that each one has the related image (**Figure 7**).

✔ Tips

- The image code must be anywhere within The Loop for each author's image to appear near their post. **Chapter 6** provides more information about The Loop.

- The Loop does not always appear in the index.php file for a theme. If you're not using the Default theme, you may find it in a different file—for example, post.php.

- Be sure to use the correct file name extension for your image file. These instructions assume you have saved the images in JPEG format.

- If you don't want text to wrap around the image, you can omit the class="auth" code and skip steps 4 through 6.

Blog Statistics

The Dashboard displays information about the number of posts, comments, and categories in your blog (**Figure 8**). You may want to share this information with your visitors. Fortunately, it's easy. You just copy some code from one file and paste it into another. Here's how you can put blog statistics in the footer.

To include blog statistics in the footer

1. Open the index.php file in the wp-admin folder (*not* your theme folder) with a text editor.

2. If necessary, display line numbers.

3. Locate the text starting at line 100 and ending at line 110 (**Figure 9**) and copy it. This code counts the numbers of posts, comments, and categories and then displays the counts.

4. Open the footer.php file for your theme with a text editor.

5. Paste the copied text after this line:
   <div id="footer">

6. Save the footer.php file. The footer now includes code to count posts, comments, and categories and to display the count.

7. View your blog to see the new information (**Figure 10**).

Figure 8 The Dashboard displays basic blog stats.

Figure 9 Select the code that will display the stats.

Figure 10 The stats appear in the blog's footer.

a favicon

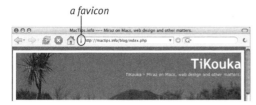

Figure 11 A favicon appears in the Location or Address bar in a Web browser window.

Figure 12
Here's a 32x32 image based on our book's cover, all ready to be converted into a favicon.ico file.

Favicons

A *favicon* is a specially formatted graphic that you can use to uniquely represent your blog. In most Web browsers the favicon appears at the left end of the Location or Address bar (**Figure 11**), and may appear beside Bookmarks or in browser tabs.

✔ Tip

- Favicons work with regular Web sites as well as blogs.

To create a favicon

1. Use graphics editing software create an image that is either 16 or 32 pixels on each side in either 8-bit or 24-bit color (**Figure 12**).

2. Save the image file in Windows icon (ico) format with the name favicon.ico.

✔ Tip

- If your image editing software does not support ico format and you have an image you want to convert into a favicon, you can use the Generate FavIcon service at www.chami.com/html-kit/services/favicon. Just follow the instructions that appear onscreen to create and download the completed favicon.ico file.

CREATING A FAVICON

To add a favicon to your blog

1. Upload the favicon.ico file to the theme folder for your site—for example: wp-content/themes/default.

2. Open the header.php file for your theme with a text editor.

3. Add these lines within the head portion of the file (**Figure 13**):

   ```
   <link rel="shortcut icon"
   href="<?php bloginfo('template_
   directory'); ?>/favicon.ico" />
   ```

4. Save your changes.

5. View your blog to see the new favicon (**Figure 14**).

✔ Tips

- You may have to Refresh or Reload a page in your Web browser before you can see the favicon.

- If you change the favicon you may have to clear the browser cache or try a different browser to see the new favicon.

- Some browsers do not support favicons. Firefox, Internet Explorer, Safari, and Opera are good browsers for checking favicon display.

Figure 13 Insert the code within the head tags in the header.php file.

Figure 14 The new favicon appears in the address bar.

Figures 15a As shown in this example from Miraz's blog, AdSense for Content displays ads related to the content of your blog.

Figure 15b In Maria's blog, the ads appear as text in the page footer. Although this isn't as profitable a placement as the sidebar or top of a page, it earns some revenue and doesn't distract blog visitors.

Google Ads

Many bloggers find Google AdSense a good source of additional income to help defer the cost of running a server or paying ISP costs.

AdSense provides contextual ads for your blog's visitors (**Figures 15a** and **15b**). For example, if you've written a post about taking your dog to the vet, the ads may be for veterinary products, dog breeders, dog beds, and other dog or vet-related products and services. The ads displayed change according to the content of the page on which they appear. You earn a small amount when a visitor clicks on a Google AdSense ad.

As we explain in this section, it takes only a moment to include AdSense code in your blog.

✔ Tips

- These instructions assume you have already visited www.google.com/adsense, set up an AdSense account, and followed the instructions to create the AdSense for Content code for your blog. If you haven't done these things, do it now. You can find instructions on the Google AdSense site.

- Be sure to consult the Google AdSense terms and conditions for information about what you may and may not do with AdSense code.

To add AdSense code to your blog's sidebar

1. Follow the instructions on the Google AdSense site to create and display the AdSense for Content code for your blog (**Figure 16**).

2. Click in the Your AdSense code box to select the code.

3. Choose Edit > Copy or press Ctrl C (Windows) or ⌘ C (Mac OS) to copy the code to the clipboard.

4. Open sidebar.php for your theme in a text editor.

5. Position the insertion point where you want the Google ad to appear.

6. Choose Edit > Paste or press Ctrl V (Windows) or ⌘ V (Mac OS) to paste in the contents of the clipboard (**Figure 17**).

7. Save the edited file.

8. View your blog to see the ads (**Figure 18**).

✔ Tips

■ In most themes, the sidebar items are in a list. To maintain this formatting, you should precede the AdSense code with `<li>` and follow it with `</li>` (**Figure 17**).

■ When setting code options, be sure to specify dimensions for the ad that correspond to the ad location. For example, a vertical layout works best in the sidebar (**Figure 18**) while a horizontal layout works best in a header (**Figure 15a**) or footer (**Figure 15b**).

■ In general, visitors tend to notice and click on ads high up on the page. You can find more detailed recommendations for positioning ads at www.google.com/ support/adsense/bin/answer.py?answer =17954&topic=371.

Figure 16 Your AdSense code appears in a box like this.

Figure 17 Paste it into the theme file.

Figure 18 The ad appears when you view the blog.

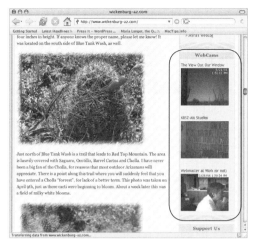

Figure 19 One of Maria's blogs, wickenburg-az.com, has three WebCams on the home page.

WebCam Images

A WebCam is a camera that regularly uploads new images to a Web server for display on one or more Web pages. The Web page displaying the WebCam image uses an `img src` tag that includes the URL to the image. As a result, the latest version of the image automatically appears when the page is loaded.

Once you have a WebCam set up, it's easy to include the image in your WordPress blog. In this section, we explain how to display a WebCam image in the sidebar of your blog (**Figure 19**).

✔ Tips

- ■ These instructions assume that you have already set up a WebCam and that the images are already being uploaded regularly to an Internet-accessible server. Instructions for setting up WebCam hardware and software are beyond the scope of this book.

- ■ WebCam images are not animated and do not automatically refresh. It may be necessary to clear your Web browser's cache or restart your Web browser to display a revised image, depending on the browser and its settings.

- ■ For best results, the WebCam image should be sized so it fits where you want to display it. For example, if you plan to display the image in the sidebar, as discussed here, the image should be narrow enough to fit in the sidebar.

To add a webcam image

1. Consult your WebCam software to get the complete URL for the WebCam image file (**Figure 20**).

2. Open the sidebar.php file for your site in a text editor.

3. Insert the following code where you want the image to appear:

   `<li><img src="http://www.example.com/pathtoimage.jpg" alt="Webcam. " /></li>`

   Be sure to use the URL you obtained in step 1 (**Figure 21**).

4. Save the edited file.

5. View your blog to see the WebCam image (**Figure 22**).

✔ Tips

- The Default WordPress sidebar is 190 pixels wide. For best results use a Web-Cam image with a width less than 190 pixels.

- You can also create a Page with a larger version of the image and more information about what visitors are viewing. Then you can link the sidebar image to the Page you created. We explain how to create Pages in **Chapter 3**.

Figure 20 In this example from EvoCam WebCam software, the Location box displays the FTP upload location. This is easily converted into an http:// URL. (Miraz can be such a ham.)

Figure 21 Insert the code where you want the image to appear.

Figure 22 The WebCam image appears in the sidebar.

Figure 23 You can save code in a separate file.

Figure 24 Then use an include statement to reference the other file. As you can see here, the search form in the sidebar is also referenced using an include statement.

Including Files

Some of the modifications in this chapter involve including large chunks of code in a theme file such as the sidebar or footer. Another approach is to create a separate file containing the additional code. You can then reference the additional file from the source file with a single line of PHP code. Here's how.

To include a file in the theme

1. Use your text editor to create a separate file containing the code you wish to include, for example, the AdSense code discussed earlier in this chapter.

2. Save the new file in your theme's folder with a unique name, followed by the .php extension. For example, you might call a file containing AdSense code adsense.php (**Figure 23**).

3. Insert the following line of code where you would have inserted the code that's in the new file:

   `<?php include (TEMPLATEPATH . '/filename.php'); ?>`

   Be sure to use the correct filename (**Figure 24**).

4. Save the changes.

5. View your blog to ensure that it's working as expected.

✔ Tip

- The TEMPLATEPATH variable indicates the directory in which the active theme's templates are stored.

INCLUDING FILES

Blogging Tools

Blogging Tools

In **Chapter 3** we describe how to add content to your WordPress blog by using the posting and editing tools in the Dashboard. Another possibility is to use stand-alone software. Such software is particularly useful if you post to more than one blog, enjoy clipping items from web pages and other sources such as RSS aggregators and posting those clips to your blog, and if you prefer to compose posts while offline.

You are able to use stand-alone software to interact in certain ways with your blog because of a file called `xmlrpc.php`. This file is located in the root directory for your blog and makes it possible for you to create new posts, edit existing posts, assign existing categories, and so on, but you don't have the full scope and power that the WordPress Dashboard gives you. For example, you can't add users or moderate comments.

In this chapter we explain how to use some of these applications to write and edit posts on your WordPress blog. First gather the information you'll need: blog address, username, password, address of the xmlrpc file. If you use WordPress on your own server, rather than at WordPress.com, you may also need the address, username, and password for your FTP server. Then install and set up the blog client and start posting.

Continued on next page...

Continued from previous page.

Each application mentioned here is capable of much more that, but is beyond the scope of this book. We simply aim to show you the basics for posting text and images, and editing existing posts. Check each application's documentation for complete instructions for using all its features.

✔ Tips

- The client ID for WordPress blogs is usually 1.

- A typical address for the xmlrpc file is http://www.example.com/xmlrpc.php or http://blogname.wordpress.com/xmlrpc.php. If your blog is in a sub-directory then the address will include that, for example: http://www.example.com/blog/xmlrpc.php.

- If you installed WordPress on your own server, make sure that an uploads folder exists and is writable, i.e., permissions are set to 777, before trying to upload a file or image with an external application.

- When you include images in a post, check the alt text. Alt text should function as a text replacement for the image.

- When you include files in a post, check the link text. Link text for a file should include an indication of file size and format, for example: Tuesday podcast (1.5Mb, MP3).

Figure 1 The BlogJet Account Wizard steps you through the setup process for BlogJet.

Figure 2 The Edit connection settings window with Host and xmlrpc information from Miraz's test blog which is in the vqs subdirectory on Miraz's site.

Figure 3 Enter your Username and Password. Choose to save the password if you prefer not to enter the password each time you use the software.

BlogJet

BlogJet is a weblog client for Windows available from blogjet.com. A 30-day trial version is free. We used version 1.6.2 in writing this chapter.

Extensive support and documentation are available at blogjet.com/support.

To set the BlogJet preferences

1. Open BlogJet. If you have no accounts already set up the Account Wizard is displayed.

2. Choose I have a blog! and click the Next button (**Figure 1**).

3. Fill in the form on the Edit connection settings window (**Figure 2**):

   ▲ **Provider** allows you to choose from various blogging systems. Select WordPress (direct upload) to interact with WordPress.

   ▲ **Host** is the address for your domain, without the http:// protocol. For example: www.firstbite.co.nz or wpvqs.wordpress.com. If your blog is in a sub-directory on your own server do not include that sub-directory name.

   ▲ **Page** is the address for the xmlrpc file. Start this address with a slash, for example: /xmlrpc.php. If you installed your blog in a sub-directory on your own server, include that sub-directory name here, for example: /vqs/xmlrpc.php.

4. Click the Next button. The Wizard moves on to the Enter username and password window (**Figure 3**).

Continued on next page...

SETTING BLOGJET PREFERENCES

Continued from previous page.

5. Enter your username and password. If you do not wish to enter your password each time you use BlogJet then turn on the check box to Save password.

6. Click the Next button.

7. Select the Use default upload location radio button in the File Upload Configuration window (**Figure 4**).

8. Click the Next button. The Enter Account Title and Address window is displayed.

9. If necessary, edit the information here or if it is correct, simply click the Finish button (**Figure 5**). The New Post window is displayed.

   ▲ **Enter the title for this account:** give this account a name that is meaningful to you. If you use BlogJet to post to several blogs, this name will let you know which one you're working with.

   ▲ **Address of your blog page:** the address for your blog should appear here. If this is incorrect it suggests you have entered incorrect information on an earlier screen.

Figure 4 The File Upload Configuration screen. The default upload location should be suitable for most blogs.

Figure 5 Edit the account name and blog address if necessary, or just click Finish.

Figure 6
Get Recent Posts
from the Blog
menu with BlogJet.

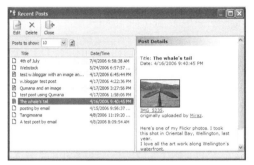

Figure 7 BlogJet's Recent Posts window here shows 10 recent posts. The post I have selected from the list is previewed on the right.

Figure 8
Choose Post and Publish
from the Blog menu to
send the post to your
blog with BlogJet.

To edit an existing post

1. Open BlogJet. The New Post window opens.

2. Choose Blog > Get Recent Posts (**Figure 6**). The Recent Posts window is displayed (**Figure 7**).

3. Double-click an existing post in the list of Recent Posts to open it for editing.

4. Make changes as you wish.

5. When you have finished editing choose Blog > Post and Publish (**Figure 8**). BlogJet sends the edited post to your blog to replace the previous content and closes the window. A New Post window opens.

To create a new post

1. Open BlogJet. The New Post window opens.

2. Create your post:

   ▲ **Title**: the title you enter here will appear as the heading for your post.

   ▲ **Category**: click the arrow beside the drop-down box to choose from any categories already set up on your blog.

   ▲ **The Normal tab**: type your text into the Normal tab (**Figure 9**). BlogJet creates the HTML for you. Include images or other files as required. The next sections show how.

   ▲ **The Code tab**: view and edit BlogJet's HTML code here (**Figure 10**), or add your own HTML. The Code tab helps with a code-completion pop-up. Files and images display a local path until the post has been sent to the server.

   ▲ **Properties**: in this tab you can set various options for a post, including the date and time stamp, comment options, and keywords (**Figure 11**).

3. When you have finished editing choose Blog > Post & Publish (**Figure 8**). BlogJet sends the post to your blog and opens a blank New Post window.

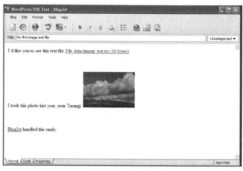

Figure 9 BlogJet's Normal tab allows you to just write your post, without worrying about HTML.

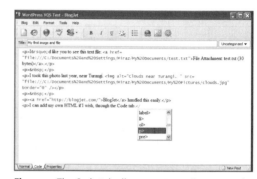

Figure 10 The Code tab allows you to easily enter and edit HTML. Before you upload a file or image the path refers to your computer. After upload the path changes to reflect the file's location on the server.

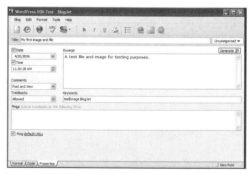

Figure 11 The Properties tab allows you to set many options for a post, including date and time, keywords and discussion options.

Figure 12
Attach a file with
BlogJet from the
Tools menu.

Figure 13 BlogJet's File Attachment dialog.
You need to click the button beside the file
name to browse your computer for the file.

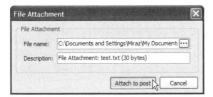

Figure 14 We've found the file we want and
click the Attach to post button.

To add a file to a post

1. Open BlogJet and create a new post or
   edit an existing post.

2. Place the cursor where you wish the file
   to be inserted.

3. Choose Tools > Attach File (**Figure 12**).
   The File Attachment dialog box opens.

4. To upload a file from your computer click
   the dots at the end of the File name text
   field (**Figure 13**). The Browse dialog box is
   displayed.

5. Choose the file to upload from your
   computer and click the Open button. The
   File Attachment dialog box is displayed
   again showing the path to the local file
   and a Description field.

6. Click the Attach to post button (**Figure
   14**). The file is attached and a link is
   added to the post as shown in **Figure 9**.

7. When you have finished adding files to
   your post choose Blog > Post & Publish
   (**Figure 8**). BlogJet sends the post and
   attachments to your blog and opens a
   blank New Post window.

ADDING FILES TO POSTS

To add an image to a post

1. Open BlogJet and create a new post or edit an existing post.

2. Place the cursor where you wish the image to be inserted.

3. Choose Format > Insert Image (**Figure 15**). The Insert Image dialog box is displayed.

4. Click the Browse button to find an image on your computer. The Open dialog box is displayed.

5. Choose the image to upload from your computer and click the Open button. The Insert Image dialog box is displayed again showing the path to the local file and the Alternate text.

6. Edit the alternate text and set the other settings as you wish.

7. Click the OK button (**Figure 16**).

8. The image is added to the post at the position of the cursor. **Figure 9** shows a post after an image has been added.

9. When you have finished choose Blog > Post & Publish (**Figure 8**). BlogJet sends the post and attachment to your blog and opens a blank New Post window.

Figure 15
Include an image in a BlogJet post with the Insert Image command in the Format menu.

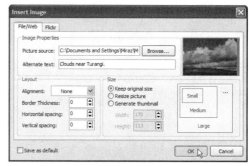

Figure 16 Edit the alternate text and set the other options as you desire then click OK to upload the image with BlogJet.

Figure 17 The Ecto Account Wizard steps you through the setup process for Ecto.

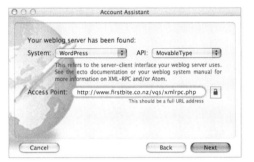

Figure 18 Ecto's Account Assistant has found the settings for our blog.

Figure 19 Enter the username and password for your blog.

Ecto

Ecto is a weblog client for Macintosh OS X and Windows available from ecto.kung-foo.tv. A 21-day trial version is free. We used version 2 for the Macintosh when writing this chapter.

Ecto has comprehensive Help files at ecto.kung-foo.tv/docs.

To set the Ecto preferences

1. Open Ecto. If you have no accounts already set up the Account Assistant is displayed.

2. Enter the address of your blog and click the Next button (**Figure 17**). Ecto attempts to download settings for your blog.

3. Confirm the settings are correct (**Figure 18**):

   ▲ **System**: this should be set to WordPress.

   ▲ **API**: MovableType is the correct choice. API stands for application programming interface. This refers to the set of instructions that allow other applications to interact with your blog in certain ways, such as creating and editing posts.

   ▲ **Access Point**: this is the address for your blog's xmlrpc file.

4. Click the Next button. The Username and Password window is displayed (**Figure 19**).

5. Enter your username and password, then click the Next button. The account name window is displayed (**Figure 20**).

Continued on next page...

SETTING ECTO PREFERENCES

Continued from previous page.

6. Give this account a name that is meaningful to you. If you use Ecto to post to several blogs, this name will let you know which one you're working with.

7. Click the Next button. Ecto attempts to connect to your blog and displays a Default settings window (**Figure 21**). See **Chapter** 2 for more information on the specific settings.

8. Click the Next button. Ecto displays a confirmation window (**Figure 22**).

9. Click the Finish button to exit the Account Assistant. Ecto displays the Entries & Drafts window (**Figure 23**) for interacting with your blog.

Figure 20 Name this account in Ecto.

Figure 21 Ecto allows you to set defaults for posting to your blog.

Figure 22 Ecto confirms your settings. Click the Finish button to exit the Account Assistant.

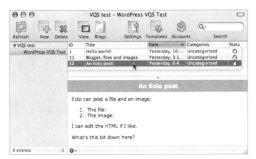

Figure 23 Ecto's main Entries & Drafts window resembles an e-mail application.

Figure 24 Edit a post in a separate window.

Figure 25 You've edited an existing post. Should Ecto publish it as a new post or as a change to the existing post?

To edit an existing post

1. Open Ecto.

2. Double-click an existing post in the Entries & Drafts window (**Figure 23**) to open it for editing. The post opens into an editing window (**Figure 24**).

3. Make changes as you wish.

4. When you have finished choose Draft > Publish. Ecto displays an alert (**Figure 25**).

5. Choose the action Ecto should take:

   ▲ **Send New**: the post will appear as a new post in your blog; the original post remains unchanged.

   ▲ **Cancel**: the alert is dismissed; no new post is created; the original post remains unchanged.

   ▲ **Send Edit**: this changed post replaces the original.

6. Click the button to choose the action to take. The post edit window is closed and the Entries & Drafts window is displayed (**Figure 23**).

To create a new post

1. Open Ecto and choose File > New Drafts. The New Draft window opens (**Figure 26**).

2. Create your post:

   ▲ **Title**: the title you enter here will appear as the heading for your post.

   ▲ **Main**: type your post in the rich text area immediately below the Title field. Click the A button at bottom left of the window to use the rich text editor, and the <> button beside it to use the HTML editor.

   ▲ **Extended entry**: use this field to enter content that should not appear on the front page of your blog. For more on this feature of WordPress see **Chapter 3**.

   ▲ **Options**: in this tab you can set various options for a post, including comment options, categories, and keywords.

   ▲ **Formatting**: in this tab you can set straight or smart quotes and choose a script to apply, if you have installed one.

3. Choose options as required from the Draft menu to modify the date, preview the post, manage trackbacks, and validate the HTML (**Figure 27**).

4. When you have finished choose Draft > Publish. Ecto closes the post window, sends the post to your blog and refreshes the list of posts in the Entries & Drafts window (**Figure 23**).

✔ Tips

■ If the Options tab is not visible choose Draft > Toggle Display > Options to make it visible.

■ Hover over the buttons in the window to see a Tooltip showing what each button does.

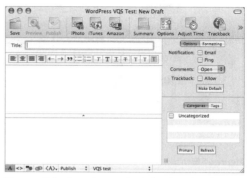

Figure 26 The Ecto New Draft window is rich with toolbars and buttons.

Figure 27 The Ecto Draft menu provides options to modify the post date, manage trackbacks, add photos and attachments and even to validate the code.

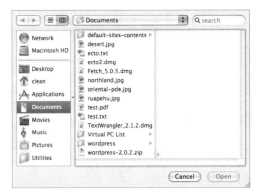

Figure 28 After you choose Add Attachment from the Draft menu, a standard Open dialog box allows you to choose a file to attach to your post.

Figure 29 By default Ecto displays a thumbnail image in the post for an attached file.

To add a file to a post

1. Open Ecto and create a new post or edit an existing post.

2. Place the cursor where you wish the file to be inserted.

3. Choose Draft > Add Attachment. The Open dialog box is displayed (**Figure 28**).

4. Navigate your hard drive and select the file to add to your blog, then click the Open button. Your file is added to the post, with a thumbnail image (**Figure 29**).

5. When you have finished editing choose Draft > Publish. Ecto closes the post window, sends the post to your blog and refreshes the list of posts in the Entries & Drafts window (**Figure 23**).

✔ Tip

■ If you prefer a text link for your attachment double-click the file thumbnail and explore the options in the Attachment settings dialog box.

To add an image to a post

1. Open Ecto and create a new post or edit an existing post.

2. Place the cursor where you wish the image to be inserted.

3. Choose Draft > Import from iPhoto. Select an image from the iPhoto browser dialog box that appears and click Import. (**Figure 30**). Skip to step 5.

   or

   Choose Draft > Add Attachment. The Open dialog box is displayed (**Figure 28**).

4. Navigate your hard drive and select the image to add to your blog then click the Open button. Your image is added to the post.

5. Double-click the image. The Attachment settings dialog box is displayed.

6. Click the Basic tab and edit the image alt text to meet best practice requirements (**Figure 31**). Confirm or edit other settings as you wish.

7. Click the Apply button when you have finished. The settings are saved and you are returned to editing the post.

8. When you have finished editing choose Draft > Publish. Ecto closes the post window, sends the post to your blog and refreshes the list of posts in the Entries & Drafts window (**Figure 23**).

✔ Tips

- There can be many reasons why visitors to your blog may not see images. Alt text replaces any images that are not visible.

- End alt text with a full stop followed by a space, otherwise it can just blend in to your text and look like a mistake.

Figure 30 Choose the image from your iPhoto library through the Ecto iPhoto browser.

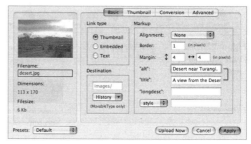

Figure 31 Edit the image alt text and confirm other settings in Ecto's comprehensive Attachment settings dialog box.

Figure 32 When you first start MarsEdit it displays a Getting Started screen. Enter your blog's name and address to begin.

Figure 33 MarsEdit could not successfully obtain the settings it needed, so edit them manually.

MarsEdit

MarsEdit is a weblog client for Macintosh OS X available from www.ranchero.com. A 30-day trial version is free. We used version 1.1.2 in writing this chapter.

Extensive help is available from the application's Help menu.

To set MarsEdit preferences

1. Open MarsEdit. If you have never used it before a Getting Started window is displayed (**Figure 32**).

2. Fill in the name and URL of your blog:
   - ▲ **Weblog name**: use a name that is meaningful to you. If you use MarsEdit to post to several blogs, this name will let you know which one you're working with.
   - ▲ **Weblog URL**: the address for your blog. For example: http://www.firstbite.co.nz/vqs or http://wpvqs.wordpress.com.

3. Click the OK button. MarsEdit attempts to automatically obtain the settings it requires. If it has a problem it will display an alert (**Figure 33**). Click the Edit Settings button to continue setting the preferences or the Cancel button to continue to the main MarsEdit window with incorrect settings.

4. If you choose to Edit Settings by hand the Blog settings dialog is displayed (**Figure 34**).

5. Click on the System tab button to configure the base settings:
   - ▲ **Name** is any name you wish to use for your blog inside MarsEdit. It does not need to be the same name that appears on your blog.

Continued on next page...

Continued from previous page.

▲ **Home URL** is the address for your blog. For example: `http://www.firstbite.co.nz/vqs` or `http://wpvqs.wordpress.com`.

▲ **Software** is the system your blog is using. Set this to WordPress.

▲ **RPC URL** is the address of the xmlrpc file. The address for this file is the address for your blog, followed by `/xmlrpc.php`. For example: `http://www.firstbite.co.nz/vqs/xmlrpc.php` or `http://wpvqs.wordpress.com/xmlrpc.php`.

▲ **Blog ID** is usually 1 for a WordPress blog.

▲ **Number of posts to download** is the number of recent posts MarsEdit will automatically download. We suggest you set this to a number between 10 and 30.

6. Click the OK button (**Figure 34**). The blog is added to the list of blogs in the Weblogs Drawer.

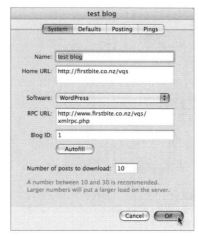

Figure 34 I have entered the settings for my blog in MarsEdit.

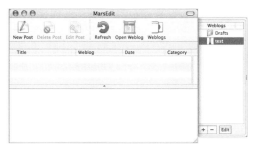

Figure 35 I have selected my 'test' blog in the MarsEdit Weblogs Drawer.

Figure 36 Supply your username and password so that MarsEdit can contact the server and interact with your blog.

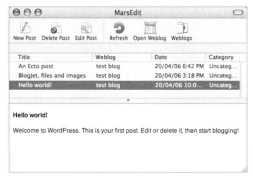

Figure 37 MarsEdit displays a list of recent posts, displaying the selected post in the Preview pane.

To edit an existing post

1. Open MarsEdit. If necessary, choose View > Show Weblogs to display the Weblogs Drawer.

2. Click once on the name of your blog in the Weblogs Drawer to select it (**Figure 35**).

3. Choose View > Refresh.

4. MarsEdit displays a dialog box requesting your username and password if you have never worked with this blog before, or have not saved the password. Enter the requested information (**Figure 36**). Click the OK button.

5. MarsEdit displays a list of recent posts in the MarsEdit window (**Figure 37**).

6. Double-click an existing post in the list of recent posts to open it for editing.

7. Make changes as you wish.

8. When you have finished editing choose File > Send to Weblog. MarsEdit sends the edited post to your blog to replace the previous content and closes the Post window. The list of recent posts in the MarsEdit main window is refreshed.

✔ Tips

■ Turn on the Store password in keychain check box to avoid having to enter the password each time you work with your blog.

■ MarsEdit allows you to also edit the time stamp, trackbacks, and enclosures. With a post open, check the Post menu for possibilities.

To create a new post

1. Open MarsEdit and choose File > New Post. The post window opens.

2. Create your post:

   ▲ **Title**: the title you enter here will appear as the heading for your post.

   ▲ **URL**: this field displays only for WordPress.com blogs, not for server-installed blogs (**Figure 38**). If you edit an existing WordPress.com post the URL field displays the URL for the post.

   ▲ **Text area**: write your post in the main text area.

   ▲ Assign categories to your post by choosing Post > Show Options. The Categories drawer is displayed (**Figure 39**). Check and uncheck categories as required.

   ▲ Use the HTML Tags pop-up in the Toolbar to help with entering HTML (**Figure 40**).

3. When you have finished editing choose File > Send to Weblog to send the post to your blog. The Post window closes and the post is added to the blog. The list of recent posts in the MarsEdit Main Window is refreshed.

Figure 38 The URL field is displayed in a Post window only if you are working with a WordPress.com blog.

Figure 39 Choose categories and set options for Formatting, Comments and TrackBacks in the Categories Drawer.

Figure 40 Use the HTML Tags pop-up to help enter HTML tags. The Custom pop-up allows you to create your own tags.

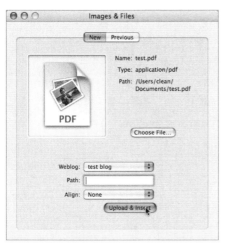

Figure 41 The MarsEdit Images & Files dialog box. Add new files with the Choose File button or browse files you've used previously by selecting the Previous tab.

Figure 42 MarsEdit has uploaded my file and image and entered the HTML code. I've edited the link text and alt text to meet standards of best practice. This post is ready to be sent to the server.

To add an image or file to a post

1. Open MarsEdit and create a new post or edit an existing post.

2. Place the cursor where you wish the file to be inserted.

3. Choose Window > Images & Files. The Images & Files window is displayed (**Figure 41**). Choose the settings to use:

   ▲ **Previous tab**: click on this tab to choose a previously uploaded image or other file.

   ▲ **Choose File**: click this button to upload an image or other file. In the dialog window that opens, navigate your hard drive and select the file to add to your blog then click the Open button.

   ▲ **Weblog**: use the pop-up to choose the blog to which you want to upload.

   ▲ **Path**: you can leave this blank unless you want to upload the file to a non-standard location.

   ▲ **Align**: choose an alignment for the image within the post. Although MarsEdit will write alignment code for images, it will not do so for files.

4. Click the Upload & Insert button. The file is uploaded to your blog, HTML coding is inserted in the Post window, and the Images & Files window remains open on screen.

5. Upload any further files, as required. Use the red Close button to close the window when you're finished.

6. Check the HTML coding added to the post, in particular editing image alt text and file link text to meet best practice requirements (**Figure 42**).

Continued on next page...

ADDING IMAGES OR FILES TO POSTS

Continued from previous page.

7. Choose File > Send to Weblog to send the post to your blog. The Post window closes and the post is added to the blog. The list of recent posts in the MarsEdit Main Window is refreshed.

✔ Tips

- Choose Post > Show Preview to preview your post before committing it to your blog.

- If you choose None for the image alignment MarsEdit creates an align tag with an empty value. This will cause validation problems. Either choose to align Right or Left or edit the HTML MarsEdit inserts to remove: `align=""`.

Figure 43 The w.bloggar Add Account Wizard steps you through the setup process for w.bloggar.

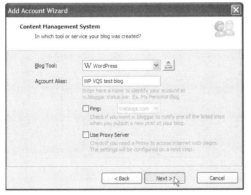

Figure 44 Choose WordPress as the Blog Tool and give your account a name.

Figure 45 Enter the address for the blog and the path to the xmlrpc file. My blog is in the vqs subdirectory so the Path begins with /vqs.

w.bloggar

w.bloggar is a free weblog client for Windows available from www.wbloggar.com. We used version 4 Full Setup for Mozilla in writing this chapter.

To set w.bloggar posting preferences

1. Open w.bloggar. If you have never set up an account before, the w.bloggar Add Account Wizard is displayed.

2. Select the Yes, I want to add it as a new account radio button to add an existing blog (**Figure 43**). Click the Next button.

3. Set the options in the Content Management System window (**Figure 44**):

   ▲ **Blog Tool**: choose WordPress.

   ▲ **Account Alias**: enter a memorable name, for example, it could be the name of your blog.

   ▲ **Ping**: turn on the check box if you wish to notify a service such as Technorati when you make a post. Use the pop-up to choose a service to notify.

   ▲ **Use Proxy Server**: turn this check box on if you know you use a proxy server. Most users are unlikely to need this. If you're unsure, consult your Internet service provider.

4. Click the Next button.

5. Complete the details in the Account Connection Settings window (**Figure 45**):

   ▲ **Host**: enter the address for your blog, without the http:// protocol. For example: www.firstbite.co.nz or wpvqs.wordpress.com.

Continued on next page...

Continued from previous page.

▲ **Path**: is the address for the xmlrpc file. Start this address with a slash, for example: /xmlrpc.php. If you installed your blog in a sub-directory on your own server, include that sub-directory name here, for example: /vqs/xmlrpc.php.

6. Click the Next button. The Account User and Password window is displayed.

7. Enter your User name and Password. If you do not wish to enter your password each time you use w.bloggar then turn on the Save Password check box. Click the Finish button (**Figure 46**).

8. The Wizard closes, the settings for posting text are saved, and the New Post window is displayed.

9. Choose Tools > Options to set the HTML preferences to use XHTML. The Options dialog box opens.

10. Click the Code Editor tab.

11. Turn on the Use XHTML Compatible Tags check box (**Figure 47**):

12. Click the OK button. The dialog box closes and the settings are saved.

✔ Tip

■ WordPress blogs use XHTML. Using code from HTML 4 and earlier will cause your blog to be invalid, which may cause problems for some visitors.

Figure 46 Enter the username and password.

Figure 47 Turn on XHTML compatible tags so your posts will use valid code.

Figure 48 Enter the FTP server address, username and password so you'll be able to upload files.

To set w.bloggar FTP preferences

1. Open w.bloggar.

2. Choose Tools > Blog Properties so you can enter settings for uploading images and other files. The Blog Properties dialog box opens.

3. Click the Upload tab.

4. Complete the details for the FTP Server settings panel (**Figure 48**):

   ▲ **Host**: enter the address of the FTP server.

   ▲ **Remote Path**: enter the path from the root directory of the server to the uploads folder.

   ▲ **Port**: this is usually 21.

   ▲ **User**: enter your user name for connecting via FTP to the server.

   ▲ **Password**: enter your password for connecting via FTP to the server.

   ▲ **URL to Link**: if you upload images and other files with w.bloggar, this is the address that will be used in the HTML of the post for linking to the files; for example, `http://example.com/blog/wp-content/uploads/`.

5. Click the OK button. The dialog box closes and the settings are saved.

To edit an existing post

1. Choose Tools > Posts > Last *n* Posts, where *n* represents one of the number options (**Figure 49**). The Recent Posts window is displayed (**Figure 50**).

2. Double-click a post. The Post opens in the Editor window.

3. Make changes as you wish.

4. When you have finished editing choose Tools > Post & Publish (**Figure 51**). An alert confirms the post was updated (**Figure 52**).

5. Click OK. The alert is dismissed and a New Post window opens.

Figure 49 Choose the number of recent posts to display with w.bloggar.

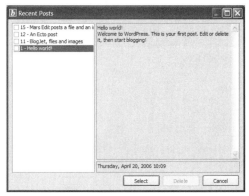

Figure 50 w.bloggar displays Recent Posts in a list on the left. The selected post is previewed in a pane on the right.

Figure 51 Choose Post & Publish from the Tools menu to send the edited post to the blog.

Figure 52 The edited post has been successfully updated.

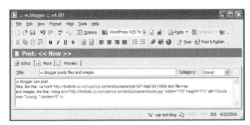

Figure 53 Use w.bloggar's Editor tab in the New Post window to type your post.

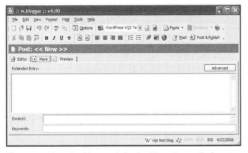

Figure 54 Use the More tab in the New Post window to add an extended entry, an excerpt, and keywords.

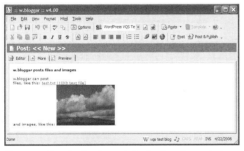

Figure 55 Use the Preview tab in the New Post window to preview your post.

Figure 56
The new post has been published.

To create a new post

1. Open w.bloggar. The post window opens.

2. Create your post:

   ▲ **Title:** the title you enter here will appear as the heading for your post.

   ▲ **Category:** click the arrow beside the drop-down box to choose from any categories already set up on your blog.

   ▲ **The Editor tab:** type your text into the Editor tab (**Figure 53**). The HTML code is created for you by w.bloggar. Include images or other files as required. The next sections show how.

   ▲ **The More tab:** in this tab you can add extended text, an excerpt and keywords (**Figure 54**). You can also click an Advanced button to access settings for comments, pings, trackbacks, to edit the date and time for the post, and to choose text filters, if you have them installed.

   ▲ **The Preview tab:** in this tab you can see a preview of your post (**Figure 55**).

3. When you have finished editing choose Tools > Post & Publish (**Figure 51**). The post is sent to your blog and an alert tells you that the post was successful (**Figure 56**).

4. Click OK. The alert is dismissed. A New Post window opens.

To add a file or image to a post

1. Open w.bloggar and create a new post or edit an existing post.

2. Place the cursor where you wish the file to be inserted.

3. Choose Tools > Upload File. The Upload File dialog box is displayed.

4. To upload a file from your computer click the dots at the end of the File text field (**Figure 57**). The Open dialog is displayed.

5. Choose the file to upload from your computer and click the Open button. The Upload File dialog box is displayed showing the path to the local file.

6. Choose what should be inserted:

   ▲ **Image on the post**: turn this on for images.

   ▲ **Link to the file**: turn this on for other files.

   ▲ **Edit the Tag before insert**: turn this on to edit the HTML before it is inserted into the post. We recommend you leave this off. If you turn it on w.bloggar allows you to add a title to an image but does not include any alt text. Since the rules of HTML require alt text you will then have to add alt text manually.

7. Click the Upload button (**Figure 58**). The file is uploaded to the server and the link or image coding is added to the post.

8. Edit image alt text and file link text to meet best practice requirements (**Figure 59**).

9. When you have finished editing choose Tools > Post & Publish (**Figure 51**). An alert confirms that the post was successful (**Figure 56**).

10. Click OK. The alert is dismissed and a New Post window opens.

Figure 57 Click the button beside the File field to call up the Open dialog box.

Figure 58 Clicking the upload button sends the file to the server and adds the image code or link text to the post.

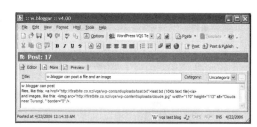

Figure 59 I've edited the inserted link and image code to make my blog more useful for visitors. This edited post is ready to be sent to the server.

ADDING FILES OR IMAGES TO POSTS

Advanced Tasks

Advanced Tasks

Earlier chapters explained the basics of setting up and using WordPress, but there are many more possibilities for working with your blog:

◆ Replace the list of posts on your Home Page with a static page.

◆ Get your hands dirty with the internals of the database.

◆ Bring in content from blogs on other systems.

◆ Have some fun podcasting.

◆ Check how many visitors your blog receives and which posts are most popular.

◆ Use custom fields.

◆ Set up multiple blogs.

In this chapter we show you some advanced tools for working with WordPress.

Creating a Static Home Page

A default WordPress install puts a list of recent posts derived from `wp-content/themes/default/index.php` on the home page of your blog. You may prefer the home page to have more static content, perhaps with links to your blog and to other sections of your site.

This is easy to achieve. One method is to use a plugin, such as the Static front page plugin discussed in **Chapter 7.** Another method is to make use of the way WordPress uses template files.

When a visitor calls up your Website Word-Press first looks in the theme folder for a template file called `home.php`. If it fails to find that file, it next looks in the theme folder for a template file called `index.php`. Since the default theme does include `index.php` but not `home.php` WordPress uses `index.php` to display your blog.

To create a static home page all you have to do is create a file called `home.php`, containing whatever WordPress template tags, text, images, and links you wish to use, and add it to the theme folder.

✔ Tips

- This technique applies only to WordPress installed on your own server and not to WordPress.com blogs.

- There is more information on the template hierarchy at: `codex.wordpress.org/Template_Hierarchy`.

Figure 1 I've created a very simply home.php file in my text editor.

Figures 2 & 3 Before and after: The standard home page based on index.php shows my one recent post (top). After adding home.php to the theme folder the front page shows my customized content: a few links to the various sections of my site, framed with the usual header, sidebar and footer (bottom).

To create a static home page

1. Use your text editor to create a new blank document that will become the home page for your site.

2. To give your page the same header, stylesheet, sidebar and footer as the rest of your WordPress site add these three lines of code:

   ```
   <?php get_header(); ?>
   ```

   ```
   <?php get_sidebar(); ?>
   ```

   ```
   <?php get_footer(); ?>
   ```

3. Save the file with the file name home.php. If you include only the code above, your Home Page will display the header, sidebar and footer, but no other content.

4. Add your own content after the line that reads: <?php get_header(); ?> (**Figure 1**).

5. Upload home.php to your blog's theme folder. It instantly supersedes index.php as the Home Page (**Figures 2** and **3**).

✔ Tips

- In the Default theme the content of a page is normally wrapped inside a div with the id of content and a class of narrowcolumn: <div id="content" class="narrowcolumn">*your content here*</div>. Ensure your new content has appropriate styling.

- If you wish to include posts on this static Home Page you need to include the coding for The Loop. **Chapter 6** has detailed information about how a theme is put together, including the function of The Loop.

Directly Accessing the Database

When you create a post, page, link, or user, WordPress stores the relevant information in its MySQL database. The normal way to interact with the database is through Word-Press' administration panels, or a blogging tool that works through the xmlrpc file, as we explain in **Chapter 9**.

It may also be possible to access the database directly if you've installed WordPress on your own server. WordPress.com blogs don't offer this possibility.

If your Web host provides a Control Panel as part of the hosting package you probably have access to both Manage Mysql for creating and removing databases, and to phpMyAdmin for working with databases. Another option is one of the many stand-alone programs or *clients* that provide a graphic user interface for working with MySQL, such as SQLyog for Windows (www.Webyog.com/sqlyog/index_sqlyogfree. php) or CocoaMySQL-SBG for Mac OS (www.theonline.org/cocoamysql).

Although working directly with the database requires a good knowledge of MySQL, just looking is a safe and easy way to learn more about WordPress and what it's doing behind the scenes. If you actually edit the database directly, rather than working through the administration panels, you may make changes that cause your blog to function incorrectly or even not work at all, so act cautiously and always make a backup before changing anything.

On the other hand, working directly with the database can save you hours of tedious labor if you need to make changes to large numbers of posts, and even allows you to do some things that are otherwise impossible with only administration panel access.

✔ Tips

■ This section on working with the database is not intended to be comprehensive; it is just a glimpse into the behind-the-scenes world of WordPress.

■ If you're looking for a good guide to MySQL, check out Larry Ullman's *MySQL Second Edition: Visual QuickStart Guide*, and *PHP and MySQL for Dynamic Web Sites: Visual QuickPro Guide*.

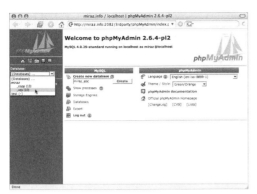

Figure 4 Choose the database to work with from the drop-down list.

Figure 5 Use the icons in the list of tables in the right-hand pane of the phpMyAdmin window to carry out many functions, including editing and deleting.

Figure 6 After selecting a table in the left-hand pane, view and edit its fields in the right-hand pane. Click the Browse button at the top of the window to display a list of posts in the selected table.

To edit a post with phpMyAdmin

1. Log in to the Control Panel your Web host provides.

2. Click on the link for phpMyAdmin. The phpMyAdmin Welcome window should appear.

3. Select the correct database from the Database drop-down in the left column (**Figure 4**). A list of tables in that database is displayed below the name of the database in the left column. Information relating to the table is displayed in the right-hand pane (**Figure 5**).

4. To see posts on your blog click on the table whose name contains 'posts'. For example, unless you changed the table prefix in the wp-config file when you installed WordPress, the posts table should be named wp_posts. The right-hand pane changes to display information about the fields within the wp_posts table.

5. Click on the Browse button from the buttons across the top of the right-hand pane. A list of posts is displayed (**Figure 6**).

6. Click the pencil icon beside any post to edit that post. The selected post opens, with editable fields (**Figure 7**).

7. Make changes as required.

8. When you have finished editing, scroll to the bottom of the window. If necessary select Save from the left-hand drop-down. Select an option from the right-hand drop-down, as explained on the next page and then click the Go button to save your changes (**Figure 8**) or the Reset button to restore the post to how it was before you changed it:

Continued on next page...

Continued from previous page.

▲ **Go back to previous page**: saves the changes you have made and then displays the list of posts.

▲ **Insert another new row**: saves the changes you have made and then opens a new blank row in the database. If you're working with the list of posts this is the same as starting a new post.

▲ **Go back to this page**: saves the changes you have made and continues to display the current row.

▲ **Edit next row**: saves the changes you have made and opens the next row for editing.

✔ Tips

■ Web hosts offer various versions and brands of Control Panels. The Control Panel your hosting service offers may not be exactly the same as we show here. It should however, be broadly similar.

■ Contact your Web host for more information and help with any Control Panel they offer.

Figure 7 A post open for editing in the phpMyAdmin interface. The body of the post is contained in the post_content field.

Figure 8 I save the edits by choosing Save from the dropdown and then clicking the Go button.

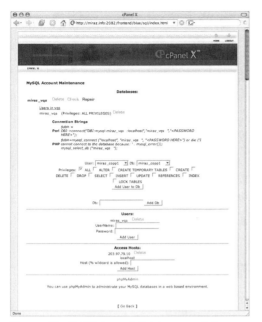

Figure 9 The MySQL Account Maintenance window.

Figure 10 After adding my IP address to the Access Hosts section of the MySQL Account Maintenance window I can now access my blog's database with a stand-alone client.

To allow access to stand-alone clients

1. Log in to the Control Panel your Web host provides.

2. Click on the link for Manage Mysql. The MySQL Account Maintenance window should appear (**Figure 9**).

3. Scroll to the section labelled Access Hosts (**Figure 10**).

4. Enter your computer's IP address in the Host text box.

5. Click the Add Host button. You should now be able to connect to the database from that IP address with a stand-alone client.

✔ Tips

- This kind of behind-the-scenes access to the database can raise security concerns; your Web host may not allow it. Contact the Web host for help and further information.

- If your computer does not have a static IP address or is behind a firewall you may need to contact your computer support or ISP for help and further information.

ALLOWING ACCESS TO STAND-ALONE CLIENTS

To edit a post with SQLyog

1. Enable access to the database, as explained in the previous instructions.

2. Open SQLyog. A nagware screen appears if you're using the free version. Click the bottom button to continue (**Figure 11**) or click one of the other buttons to learn about upgrades. The Connect to MySQL Host window is displayed (**Figure 12**).

3. Click the New button. Give the connection a name and click the OK button (**Figure 13**).

4. The Server panel becomes active. Enter the MySQL Host Address, User Name and Password details to connect to your blog (**Figure 14**). The information required here is the same as you entered in the wp-config file when you installed your blog. The Database(s) field is optional.

5. Click the Connect button. The connection details are saved, the software connects to the host and displays a browser window.

6. Click the plus sign beside the database you wish to work with in the list of databases on the left side of the window. The list of tables in that database is revealed (**Figure 15**).

7. To see posts on your blog right-click on the table whose name contains 'posts' and choose View Data from the contextual menu. For example, unless you changed the table prefix in the wp-config file when you installed WordPress, the posts table should be named wp_posts.

8. The Table Data pane displays information about the fields within the wp_posts table (**Figure 16**). Scroll as needed to locate the cell you wish to edit.

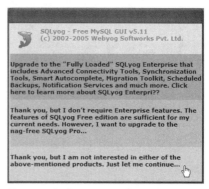

Figure 11 The free version of SQLyog includes a nagware screen, inviting you to upgrade to a paid version.

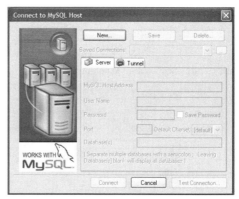

Figure 12 The Connection window in SQLyog if you have no saved connections.

Figure 13 Name this connection.

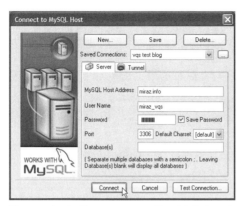

Figure 14 I enter the same connection details I used in the wp-config file when I installed my blog.

Figure 15
The tables belonging to the miraz_vqs database are listed in SQLyog.

9. Click once on the cell you wish to edit (**Figure 17**). For example, if I wanted to edit the body of my first post I would click the cell where the row whose ID is 1 intersects with the post_content column. The field opens into an editing window (**Figure 18**).

10. Make changes as required, click the OK button then click another cell. The changed information is sent to the server.

✔ Tips

■ The contents of any edited cells are not updated in the database on the server until you take an action such as selecting a different cell or refreshing the browser display.

■ The real power of a stand-alone client is to be able to search the database and use MySQL queries to carry out operations on large numbers of posts. Such techniques are beyond the scope of this book.

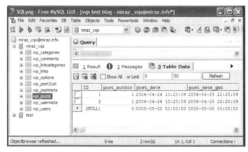

Figure 16 The fields for wp_posts are displayed in SQLyog.

Figure 17 Click once on a cell...

Figure 18 ...and it opens into an editing window.

EDITING POSTS WITH SQLYOG

To edit a post with CocoaMySQL-SBG

1. Enable access to the database, as explained in the previous instructions.

2. Open CocoaMySQL-SBG. The New Connection sheet appears.

3. Enter the Host, User, and Password details to connect to your blog. The information required here is the same as you entered in the wp-config file when you installed your blog (**Figure 19**). The Option settings section is optional.

4. Click the Connect button. The software connects to the host and displays a browser window.

5. From the Databases pop-up on the left choose the database for your blog (**Figure 20**). The client connects to the database and displays a list of tables.

6. To see posts on your blog click on the table whose name contains 'posts' (**Figure 21**). For example, unless you changed the table prefix in the wp-config file when you installed WordPress, the posts table should be named wp_posts. The right-hand pane changes to display information about the fields within the wp_posts table.

7. Click on the Content button from the buttons across the top of the right-hand pane (**Figure 22**). A list of posts is displayed.

8. Scroll as needed to locate the cell you wish to edit.

Figure 19
Enter the same connection details as in the wp-config file.

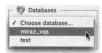

Figure 20
Choose a database to display from the pop-up list of databases.

Figure 21
Select a table to display from the list of tables.

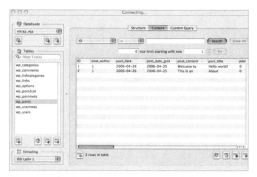

Figure 22 The fields for wp_posts are displayed in CocoaMySQL-SBG.

Figure 23 Edit text in the Text tab of the editing window. Then click the OK button.

9. Double-click any cell to edit it. For example, if I wanted to edit the body of my first post I would click the cell where the row whose ID is 1 intersects with the post_content column.

10. The cell opens into an editing window. Click the Text tab to view text fields.

11. Make changes as required and click the OK button (**Figure 23**). The editing window closes.

12. Click another cell in the browser window. The changed information is sent to the server.

✔ Tips

■ The contents of any edited cells are not updated in the database on the server until you take an action such as selecting a different cell or refreshing the browser display.

■ The real power of a stand-alone client is to be able to search the database and use MySQL queries to carry out operations on large numbers of posts. Such techniques are beyond the scope of this book.

Importing from Other Blogs

Whether you just want to test out WordPress to compare it with other blogging and Content Management tools or have decided to switch away from another blogging system you may find yourself wanting to move existing content into a WordPress blog.

While it is always tricky to move content between widely differing systems, WordPress has several tools to help you with the process. Some are available through WordPress' adminstration panels (**Figures** 24 and 25).

The overall principle is straightforward: use the existing blogging system to export a file containing your posts and maybe comments, then use the WordPress tools to import that file into WordPress. This can save you hours of copying and pasting.

The work doesn't end there though. WordPress may be able to import posts and comments, but it is unlikely to be able to import lists of links or other content from the original site. You may need to upload images and files to your new site and check the file path for each image or file. You should begin this checking well in advance of deleting your old blog on the other system so that links to images and files don't fail before you've had a chance to check and update them.

WordPress.com blogs include tools to import posts and comments from Movable Type / TypePad and Blogger, while WordPress installed on your own server can import from half a dozen systems with scripts installed by default. You may also be able to import from other systems, using additional scripts. Check codex.wordpress.org/Importing_ Content for full details on importing content into WordPress.

Although server-installed WordPress blogs are capable of importing from many different

Figures 24 & 25 You can import from other blogs systems to both WordPress.com blogs (top) and WordPress blogs (bottom) installed on your own server. Server-installed blogs can import from a wider range of systems, including some not listed on the Import panel.

Figure 26 Miraz's Oddity 59 blog at TypePad has 1179 posts. To export it as a file we click on the Import/Export link.

Export Posts

To export your Posts, click on the Export Posts from your TypePad Weblog link below. To save the exported data to a file, you can right-click the link and choose Target As... to choose a location. On the Macintosh, hold down the option key while clicking on the link.

Export Posts from your TypePad Weblog: Oddity 59

Figure 27 The TypePad Export Posts section has instructions and a link to download posts and comments.

Figure 28 The 1.3Mb file exported from TypePad contained more than 1100 posts—almost 33,000 lines of text.

systems, we provide instructions below for Movable Type / TypePad and Blogger as they are options common to both WordPress.com and server-installed blogs. We also provide instructions for importing from an RSS feed, as systems of many types offer feeds.

If you are adding content to an existing WordPress blog be sure to make a backup before you start. **Chapter 7** shows you how to back up a blog installed on your own server.

✔ Tip

■ The WordPress import scripts ease the process of moving posts and perhaps comments from one system to another, but don't cover images, files, separate pages, or other content.

To export posts from TypePad

1. Log in to your TypePad Control Panel.

2. Click on the Weblogs tab in the top row of buttons. Your Weblogs are listed.

3. Click on the link for the Weblog whose content you wish to export. The Manage tab becomes active (**Figure 26**).

4. Click on the Import/Export button in the Manage tab. The Import/Export Posts panel is displayed.

5. Scroll down to the Export Posts section (**Figure 27**).

6. Follow the instructions in that section to export your posts, using the link provided. Your posts are exported to a file named post.htm on your computer (**Figure 28**).

✔ Tip

■ A blog with a lot of content will create a large file that may take some time to download.

To import TypePad posts to WordPress

1. Log in to your WordPress Dashboard.

2. Click on the Import button in the top row of buttons. The Import panel opens.

3. Click on the link to import posts and comments from a Movable Type / Type-Pad account (**Figure 29**). The Import Movable Type wizard opens.

4. Click the Browse button. Use the dialog box that opens to navigate your hard drive and locate the file you created in step 6 of the previous section.

5. Click the Import button (**Figure 30**). WordPress uploads the file and applies the correct import script.

6. WordPress provides options for you to change the Authors on the posts it is importing (**Figure 31**). Choose names as you wish from the menu or enter names in the text boxes, then click the Submit button.

7. As it imports the posts and comments WordPress adds a confirmation to a results page. Once it's finished it displays an 'All done' note (**Figure 32**). WordPress removes the file it previously uploaded to the Uploads directory.

8. View your blog to see that WordPress has imported archives, categories, posts, and comments. It has not imported any lists of links. It has not imported associated files and images. WordPress has not edited your content or changed any links. If you delete your TypePad blog many items on the WordPress site are likely to function incorrectly.

9. Check each post on your blog for problems, as explained later in this chapter.

Figure 29 Choose the Movable Type import option for a TypePad file.

Figure 30 Select the post.htm file previously downloaded from TypePad and click the Import button.

Figure 31 I don't have an author named Miraz on my WordPress blog so I enter that name in the text box.

Figure 32 WordPress has imported all 1179 entries and confirms that for me.

✔ Tip

■ WordPress needs to upload your exported TypePad file to work with it. Make sure your Uploads directory is writable. **Chapter 6** explains how to make a directory writable.

Import Blogger

Howdy! This importer allows you to import posts and comments from your Blogger account into your WordPress blog.

Log in to Blogger

The script will log into your Blogger account, change some settings so it can read your blog, and restore the original settings when it's done. Here's what you do:

1. Back up your Blogger template.
2. Back up any other Blogger settings you might need later.
3. Log out of Blogger
4. Log in *here* with your Blogger username and password.
5. On the next screen, click one of your Blogger blogs.
6. Do not close this window or navigate away until the process is complete.

Username:
Password: Start

Figure 33 The Import Blogger screen explains the steps for importing from a Blogger account.

Import Blogger

Howdy! This importer allows you to import posts and comments from your Blogger account into your WordPress blog.

Selecting a Blog

• CommunityNet Kiwi 0%

Figure 34 I have only one Blogger blog I could import from. If I had others they would appear in a list here.

Import Blogger

Howdy! This importer allows you to import posts and comments from your Blogger account into your WordPress blog.

Congratulations!

Now that you have imported your Blogger blog into WordPress, what are you going to do? Here are some suggestions:

• That was hard work! Take a break.
• Go to Authors & Users, where you can modify the new user(s) or delete them. If you want to make all of the imported posts yours, you will be given that option when you delete the new authors.
• For security, click the link below to reset this importer. That will clear your Blogger credentials and options from the database.

Reset this importer

Figure 35 The Blogger posts and comments have been imported into my WordPress blog. Now I should click the link to Reset the importer. This clears my username and password from the WordPress system.

To import from Blogger to WordPress

1. Log in to your WordPress Dashboard.

2. Click on the Import button in the top row of buttons. The Import panel opens.

3. Click on the link to import posts and comments from a Blogger account. The Blogger import wizard opens (**Figure 33**).

4. Enter your Blogger username and your Blogger password in the Blogger login form in the Import panel and click the Start button.

5. WordPress logs in to your Blogger account and displays a list of your Blogger blogs (**Figure 34**).

6. Click on the link for the blog you wish to import.

7. WordPress imports the posts and comments from your Blogger blog and provides a confirmation.

8. Click the link at the bottom of the confirmation page to Reset the importer (**Figure 35**). This clears the Blogger username and password from the WordPress system and returns you to the Log in to Blogger page.

9. View your blog to see that WordPress has imported archives, posts, and comments. It has not imported any lists of links. It has not imported associated files and images. WordPress has not edited your content or changed any links. If you delete your Blogger blog many items on the WordPress site are likely to function incorrectly.

10. Check each post on your blog for problems, as explained later in this chapter.

To determine the address for an RSS feed

1. Use your Web browser to visit the blog whose entries you wish to import.

2. View the source of the page. Most browsers allow you to do this with a menu item under the View menu.

3. Look in the head of the page for a line which resembles this: `<link rel="alternate" type="application/rss+xml" title="WordPress Blog RSS Feed" href="http://www.example.com/blog/?feed=rss2" />`.

4. Copy the feed address listed at the end of that line. Example: `http://www.example.com/blog/?feed=rss2`.

5. Use your old blog's settings to temporarily set the number of items that should appear in a feed to be greater than the number of posts in that blog.

✔ Tips

■ If your previous blog has a feed link or icon visible on the page then hover over the link or icon and right-click or Control click to brings up a contextual menu. Choose from that menu the option to copy the address (**Figures 36a** and **36b**). You may need to remove any characters before the `http` portion.

■ Remember to go back and reset the number of items in your old blog's feed to its original number, or those who read the feed may get a very unpleasant surprise when every item from the blog shows up.

Figures 36a & 36b Right-click on Windows (top) or Control click on a Macintosh (bottom) on an RSS feed link to choose to copy the link address from the contextual menu.

Figure 37 The RSS Feed displays as an XML file in your Web browser. Here we are using Firefox.

To create the RSS feed file

1. Use your Web browser to visit the address you copied in step 4 on the previous page. The blog's contents are displayed as an XML file (**Figure 37**).

2. Wait until the whole page has loaded, then select and copy the contents.

3. Create an empty text document and paste in the text you copied in step 2 above.

4. Save the file to your computer.

✔ Tips

- If you have another application, such as a desktop aggregator or a Web browser, set to automatically handle feed addresses you may need to temporarily disable that setting.

- You may find your usual commands to Select All do not work. In that case, click before the first character of the file, use the scrollbars to scroll to the end of the file, hold down Shift and click after the last character of the file. The whole page is selected.

CREATING THE RSS FEED FILE

To import an RSS Feed to a WordPress blog

1. Log in to your WordPress Dashboard.

2. Click on the Import button in the top row of buttons. The Import panel opens.

3. Click on the link to import posts from an RSS feed (**Figure 38**). The RSS Feed import wizard opens.

4. Click the Browse button and choose the file you previously saved to your computer from the dialog box that appears.

5. Click the Import button (**Figure 39**). The import process begins.

6. Wait while WordPress imports the entire file. WordPress displays a message for each entry and then displays an 'All done' notice (**Figure 40**).

7. View your blog to see that WordPress has imported archives, categories, and posts. It has not imported any lists of links. It has not imported associated files and images. WordPress has not edited your content or changed any links. If you delete your previous blog many items on the WordPress site are likely to function incorrectly.

8. Check each post on your blog for problems, as explained later in this chapter.

✔ Tips

- WordPress.com blogs do not offer this option.

- RSS feeds vary in what information they include. Exactly what is imported depends on the content of the RSS feed.

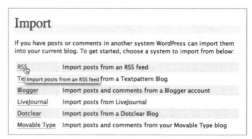

Figure 38 Click the RSS import link to start importing from an RSS feed.

Figure 39 Select the RSS file and click the Import button.

```
533. Importing post...Done !
534. Importing post...Done !
535. Importing post...Done !
536. Importing post...Done !
537. Importing post...Done !
538. Importing post...Done !

All done. Have fun!
```

Figure 40 WordPress confirms the RSS file has been imported.

In the Style window that appears select MyCode from the list of Styles at the left, then click the Modify? button. The Modify Style window appears, with a pop-up button at bottom left which will show the word Format. Click the Format pop-up and choose Shortcut key?. The Customize Keyboard window appears.

In the Style window that appears select MyCode from the list of Styles at the left, then click the Modify◆ button. The Modify Style window appears, with a pop-up button at bottom left which will show the word Format. Click the Format pop-up and choose Shortcut key◆. The Customize Keyboard window appears.

Figures 41 & 42 This post originally included ellipses. The import process has not handled these characters well. Firefox (top) simply displays them as easy to overlook normal question marks, but Safari (bottom) is displaying obviously strange characters.

> WEDNESDAY, NOVEMBER 16, 2005
>
> Arthritis New Zealand is the national voluntary organisation in New Zealand which represents the interests of those with arthritis. The website contains news, information and links about the various forms of arthritis, treatment and support available.
>
> POSTED BY MIRAZ JORDAN AT 10:55 AM   0 COMMENTS ✉ ✏

> 113209173751385192
> November 16th, 2005
>
> Arthritis New Zealand is the national voluntary organisation in New Zealand which represents the interests of those with arthritis. The website contains news, information and links about the various forms of arthritis, treatment and support available.
>
> Posted in Uncategorized | Edit | No Comments »

Figures 43 & 44 The importer hasn't done such a good job. It created a string of digits (bottom) to replace a missing title (top).

Figure 45 On TypePad this thumbnail image of my cat Ares was linked to a larger version that opened in a popup window. This link has not been changed, as we can see by the address in the browser's Status Bar. If I delete my TypePad blog both versions of the image will be deleted and the image in this post will be broken.

□ job opportunitya	203.97.79.10	Exciting blog. Your site was amazing and will be back again! I never get tired of looking for blogs just like this ...
□ job opportunitya	203.97.79.10	Super blog. I web surf when I have the time for blogs like this one. Your site was nice and will be visited ...
□ job opportunitya	203.97.79.10	Cool blog. I dig your site outline and I plan on returning again! I just love finding blogs like this when I ...
□ job opportunitya	203.97.79.10	Incredible blog. I admired your site and I will be back once again to view it! I use much of my ...
□ job opportunitya	203.97.79.10	Charming blog. Your site was off the chain and I will return! When I get the time I look for blog ...
□ job opportunitya	203.97.79.10	I look for blogs as great as your work. Fine blog. I found your site suitable for another visit! Look who checking ...

Figure 46 Importing from another system brought a lot of comment spam into WordPress. The IP number in this screenshot is not that of the spammer, but was added at import time.

To check an import for problems

Check each post on your blog for problems:

◆ **Posts**: do your posts look correct or do they contain strange characters (**Figures 41** and **42**)? Systems differ in how they handle certain characters such as curly quotes or ellipses. You may need to manually edit some posts to correct such problems.

◆ **Post headers and content**: are they correct? The conversion to WordPress may introduce unexpected text (**Figures 43** and **44**).

◆ **Image thumbnails**: are images still on the original site (**Figure 45**)? Are they linked to larger versions on the original site? You need to upload images to your WordPress site and update the coding for each one.

◆ **Files**: Did you have sound, movie or other files on your original site? You need to upload them to your WordPress site and update the coding for each file.

◆ Did you moderate comments on your original blog? If not, you may find spam comments on your new WordPress blog (**Figure 46**).

✔ Tips

■ If you have imported large numbers of spam comments install the Spam Karma plugin and moderate all comments. **Chapter 7** has more information on installing and using plugins.

■ If you can access the WordPress database directly and have a good knowledge of MySQL you may be able to write queries to update file paths for images and files in bulk. You could at least find all the posts that contain file paths that need updating.

Podcasting

Podcasting is a way to distribute content such as sound files, movies, or even applications by means of an RSS feed. Subscribers add the feed address to an aggregator such as NetNewsWire on the Macintosh or Feed-Demon on Windows, or perhaps iTunes (**Figure 47**). That application then checks the feed at regular intervals and downloads the latest entry, complete with its audio or other attached file, to the user's computer. It may also go one step further and add audio or movie files to a portable player such as an iPod.

Since WordPress automatically creates an RSS feed for posts, it's a very useful tool for creating podcasts. Once you have created the media files you upload them to your blog, and publish a post containing links to the files. If you create a separate category for your podcast, it makes it easier for your site's visitors to choose exactly the content they want to subscribe to.

You may find that you need to make some changes to the Web server to ensure it delivers your files with the correct file type. This is particularly the case for newer formats such as .m4v video files.

After some checking, the final step is to give your visitors links for the podcast feed (**Figure 48**).

Figure 47 Revival Rollcast at www.rollingrevival.com uses WordPress to supply both audio and video content about skating in a podcast feed available in iTunes and through other podcasting channels.

Figure 48 Revival Rollcast (www.rollingrevival.com) uses PodPress to help create its podcast. PodPress adds buttons to the post for various podcast aggregators, as well as a Listen Now button and other helpful links. Listeners can easily choose how to receive this podcast.

✔ Tips

■ When you insert a file using the instructions that follow, the Web browser should insert the full path to the file. If the browser you use inserts only a partial path, then try another browser or manually add the correct full path. At the time of writing Safari did not reliably insert the full path.

■ How to create the multimedia files is beyond the scope of this book.

■ See **Chapter 3** for detailed information on creating posts and uploading files.

■ You cannot create a podcast from files in Pages; only Posts are included in any RSS feed.

Figure 49 The File Browser displays files I can add to my post. I've clicked on the first file to display the file's options.

To create a podcast stream

1. Create your audio, video or other files in a suitable format.

2. Create a post, assign any categories and upload the media file.

3. Scroll to the Upload section of the Write Post page and click the Browse All tab. The file browser displays files available to add to your post.

4. Click the link for the file you wish to use. A menu of options appears over the link (**Figure 49**).

5. To choose which type of link to use, click the first option to toggle settings:

   ▲ **Linked to Page**: A link to a page containing a link to the file is inserted into the post. When a visitor to your blog clicks the link in the post a separate page opens, containing a link to the file and an icon representing the file type. The file plays when the visitor clicks the icon.

   ▲ **Linked to File**: the file is inserted into the post as an enclosure. When a visitor to your blog clicks the link, the file plays. An aggregator downloads the file, if set up to do so. This is the correct choice for a podcast.

6. To choose the link text, click the second option to toggle settings:

   ▲ **Using Filename**: the link will use the file name, including the extension.

   ▲ **Using Icon**: the link will be a blue rectangular audio file icon.

   ▲ **Using Title**: the link will be on the text you entered in the Title field when you uploaded the file.

Continued on next page...

CREATING PODCAST STREAMS

Continued from previous page.

7. To insert the file with the settings from steps 5 and 6 at the insertion point in the Post content box (**Figure 50**), click Send to editor. The file appears in the editing box (**Figure 51**).

8. Publish the post. Depending which option you chose in step 5 the post contains a link to a page linking to the file or the audio file is embedded in the RSS feed as an enclosure (**Figure 52**) and linked directly from the Web page.

✔ Tips

- WordPress.com is not intended to operate as a full hosting site. It may not allow certain file types and there may be limits on file sizes.

- We recommend the PodPress plugin, available from: www.mightyseek.com/podpress. It provides comprehensive tools for easily creating a podcast.

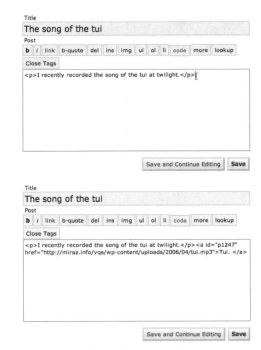

Figures 50 & 51 My post is ready (top). I add the media file as a link. The full path is used in the link to the file (bottom).

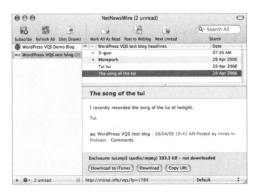

Figure 52 The NetNewsWire Pro desktop aggregator displays the file as an enclosure, ready for download.

To provide a Podcast feed

1. Assign any podcast posts to a podcast category.

2. Add /tag/ and the podcast category name to the address of your WordPress.com blog. Example: http://wpvqs.wordpress.com/tag/podcast/.

   or

   Add &category_name= and the podcast category name to the feed address of your server-installed blog. Example: http://miraz.info/vqs/?feed=rss2&category_name=podcast.

3. Add a link on your blog to the podcast feed address (**Figure 48**).

4. Validate the podcast feed, using the instructions later in this chapter.

✔ Tips

- The podcast category does not need to be named podcast.

- Find help and information about WordPress.com feeds at: faq.wordpress.com/tag/rss/.

- Find podcasting help for server-installed WordPress blogs at: codex.wordpress.org/Podcasting.

- For help with listing a podcast at iTunes visit www.apple.com/itunes/podcasts/techspecs.html.

To set server file types

1. Log in to your server's Control Panel.

2. Use the File Manager to navigate to the .htacccess file for your blog (**Figure 53**) and open it for editing.

3. Add rules to register file types as needed (**Figure 54**):

   AddType audio/mpeg .mp3

   AddType audio/x-m4a .m4a

   AddType audio/x-m4b .m4b

   AddType video/mp4 .mp4

   AddType video/x-m4v .m4v

4. Click the Save button at the bottom of the page to save your changes.

5. Test your podcast to ensure files are downloading correctly to feed aggregators.

✔ Tips

- Subscribe to your own podcast with an aggregator. This will help you quickly catch any problems that might discourage your audience from subscribing to your podcast.

- Working with a File Manager and with .htaccess files is beyond the scope of this book.

- If you do not have access to a Control Panel for your Website you may need to contact the Helpdesk and ask them to ensure that file types are set correctly on the server.

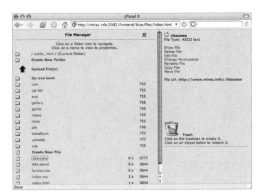

Figure 53 The File Manager available with my Control Panel gives me access to all folders and files within my website, including the .htaccess file.

Figure 54 I use the File Manager to open the .htaccess file, add the media file types, and save my changes.

Figure 55 Enter the address for your feed at the Feed Validator and click the Validate button.

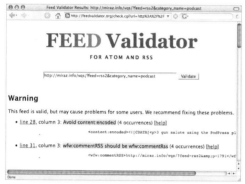

Figure 56 The Feed Validator has found potential problems in my podcast feed. These are only warnings: the feed is valid.

To validate a feed

1. Visit feedvalidator.org.

2. Enter the address for your feed in the address box (**Figure 55**).

3. Click the Validate button. Wait while the validator checks your feed.

4. The validator displays the results (**Figure 56**).

VALIDATING FEEDS

251

Reading Blog & Feed Stats

The Blog and Feed Stats sections of the WordPress.com Dashboard allow you to discover how many visitors have accessed your blog, how they reached your blog, which posts are most popular, and how well your RSS feed is used. The statistics don't include visits you make to your own blog while you're logged in.

You can find more information about Word-Press.com statistics at: faq.wordpress.com.

This panel is not available if you installed WordPress on your own server, but you can gather similar information by installing plugins or visiting the statistics section of your server's Control Panel, if you have one. We discuss plugins, including the WP-Short-stat plugin, in **Chapter 7**.

Once you know how many visitors you have, how they found you, and which posts are most popular you can use that data to improve your blog to better meet both your own objectives and the interests of your audience.

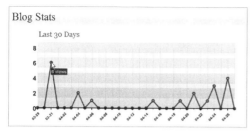

Figure 57 Our test blog at WordPress.com has not been very popular. There was an all-time high of 6 views about a month before viewing this chart.

Figure 58 & 59 Our secret test blog at WordPress.com has just been set up (top). No-one has visited so we have no Referrers, no Top Posts and no Search Engine Terms. Once word starts getting out (bottom) we have a Referrer and some Top Posts, but still no Search Engine Terms as yet.

To read Blog Stats

1. Log in to your WordPress.com Dashboard.

2. Click on Blog Stats in the second row of buttons. After a few moments the Blog Stats page is displayed (**Figures 57, 58** and **59**):

   ▲ **Last 30 days**: the line graph shows how many people visited your blog over the last 30 days. The y-axis shows the number of visitors. The dates for the last 30 days are displayed on the x-axis. You can quickly see which days your blog received most visits. Hover over the various points on the line to see a tooltip displaying the number of views that point represents.

   ▲ **Referrers**: visitors arrived at your blog by clicking links on these sites. Click the link on the word Referrers to see more detail for the last 7 days.

   ▲ **Top Posts**: this is a list of the most visited posts. Click the link on the phrase Top Posts to see more detail for the last 7 days.

   ▲ **Search Engine Terms**: Visitors arrived at your blog after searching on these terms. Click the link on the phrase Search Engine Terms to see more detail for the last 7 days.

✔ Tips

- The Stats pages require the Macromedia Flash Player plugin. If you do not have it already installed, your browser should prompt you to install it. For additional help visit www.macromedia.com/support/flashplayer.

- In the Top Posts detail page click the links for a summary of the last 7 days or the last 30 days to see a ranked listing of top posts for that period.

To read Feed Stats

1. Log in to your WordPress.com Dashboard.

2. Click on Feed Stats in the second row of buttons. After a few moments the Feed Stats page is displayed (**Figures 60** and **61**).

   ▲ **Last 30 days**: the line graph shows how many people accessed your blog's feed over the last 30 days. The y-axis shows the number of readers. The dates for the last 30 days are displayed on the x-axis. You can quickly see which days your feed had most readers. Hover over the various points on the line to see a tooltip displaying the number of readers that point represents.

   ▲ **Feed Readers**: the pie graph shows the feedreaders, also called aggregators, that accessed your feed in the previous day. Hover over the various slices of the pie to see a tooltip displaying the percentage numbers.

✔ Tips

■ The Stats pages require the Macromedia Flash Player plugin. If you do not have it already installed, your browser should prompt you to install it. For additional help visit www.macromedia.com/support/flashplayer.

■ Feed statistics are like magazine circulation numbers: one magazine does not necessarily equal one reader: magazines are often passed around or read by many people in waiting rooms. A feed may be read by one person using their own feed reader such as NetNewsWire or FeedDemon, or it may be acquired by an aggregator, such as Newsgator Online, and then read by dozens, hundreds, or thousands of people.

■ Web browsers have differing capabilities. The tooltips may not appear if your browser is unable to display them.

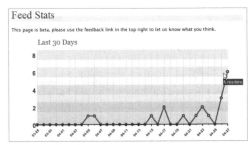

Figure 60 Our test blog at WordPress.com now has about 6 people subscribed to the RSS Feed.

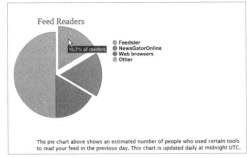

Figure 61 16.7% of our feed audience used Feedster to read the feed, while others used web browsers, NewsGatorOnline, and other methods.

READING FEED STATS

Setting Up Additional Sites

Perhaps you have a Website at www.example.com. You'd like to offer a blog for your business, but also another blog for your hobby, and you don't want the two mixed in together.

WordPress makes it easy to run more than one blog from one database by using different table prefixes. This would make it possible for you to have your business blog at www.example.com and your hobby blog at www.example.com/hobby. And if you were a real blog enthusiast you could just as easily have more blogs at www.example.com/family, www.example.com/friends, and so on.

To achieve this you create multiple directories containing the WordPress files on your server—one for each blog. The wp-config file in each directory uses a different table prefix. WordPress then stores the posts, links and all other content and configuration options for each blog in its own set of tables within the one database.

✔ Tip

- Another way to do this is to set up a separate MySQL database for each blog. This is how Maria manages multiple WordPress blogs on her server.

To set up additional sites

1. Use your FTP client or server Control Panel to create a separate directory for each blog (**Figure 62**) and upload the WordPress files into each directory.

2. Use the instructions below to edit the wp-config file for each blog to use a separate table prefix.

3. Complete the installation for each blog. WordPress creates separate sets of tables for each blog (**Figure 63**). Each blog operates independently of the others.

✔ Tip

- **Chapter 1** shows how to install Word-Press.

To edit wp-config

1. For each blog decide on a unique table prefix, for example: work_, hobby_, family_, friends_.

2. Open each wp-config file in turn. Locate the line that says $table_prefix = 'wp_'; and replace wp_with the table prefix you have selected for that blog (**Figure 64**).

3. Save each wp-config file in the directory for the blog it belongs to. When you complete the install, WordPress creates separate sets of tables for each blog within the one database. Each blog operates independently of the others.

✔ Tip

- **Chapter 1** explains how to create and set up a wp-config file.

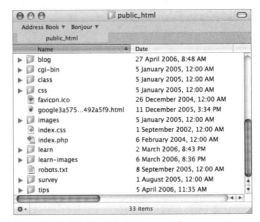

Figure 62 At MacTips.info Miraz runs three separate blogs from one database. The blogs are in separate directories: blog, learn, and tips. There are some other, unrelated, directories and files on the site too.

Figure 63 This database contains two separate sets of tables for two separate blogs. One blog uses the prefix vqs200406_ while the other uses the standard wp_.

Figure 64 For my test blog's wp-config file I've chosen the table prefix of vqs200406_.

SETTING UP ADDITIONAL SITES

Using Custom Fields

Custom fields, available only for WordPress server installations, give you some interesting possibilities for working with your posts. You might use one of the many plugins that require you to edit custom fields, such as those listed at codex.wordpress.org/Plugins/Meta. Or perhaps you sometimes like to add some extra information to your post, such as your mood, what music you're listening to, or a list of related links.

You add a *key* and then give the key a *value*. For example, if I wanted to add a line to my post telling my visitors what book I'm currently reading then my key may be: "Currently reading". The value would vary from post to post, and would be the title of whatever book it is I'm reading at that time.

To use custom fields you must both add the field key and value to your post and edit one or more theme files. We show you in detail how to edit theme files in **Chapter 6**.

If you add any custom fields WordPress treats them as an unordered list. It wraps the items in list tags when it generates the page, as you can see in this example:

```
<ul class='post-meta'>

<li><span class='post-meta-key'>Music:</span> Elena</li>

<li><span class='post-meta-key'>TV Show:</span> Futurama</li>

</ul>
```

This WordPress-generated coding creates what you see in **Figure 73**. The ul is given a class of post-meta, while the key is wrapped in a span of class post-meta-key. The key and value are both contained within an li tag. You can set up rules within the CSS file to control the appearance of the various items.

Continued on next page...

Continued from previous page.

If you have more than one custom field attached to a post, they are displayed sorted by alphabetical order of the Key field.

You can add custom fields through the Write Post or Write Page administration panel. If you use a stand-alone blogging tool, such as those we wrote about in **Chapter 9**, you may find you are unable to add any custom fields by that means.

Figure 65 I've added one custom field previously to this post and am now adding another.

To add a custom field to a post

1. Log in to the Dashboard.

2. Create a new post or edit an existing post in the usual way.

3. Scroll down to the Custom Fields area below the Uploads box.

4. If necessary, click the plus sign in the blue header area to reveal the Custom Fields area.

5. Add a Key and Value in the Add a new custom field form (**Figure 65**):

   ▲ **Select**: this pop-up contains any keys you have used previously. If you have already used "Coffee blend" as a key, for example, then that will be available under Select.

   ▲ **Key**: add the Key text here. Examples: Currently reading, Listening to, Menu of the day, Coffee blend.

   ▲ **Value**: this is a free-form field into which you can add text, HTML, and even the HTML code for an image.

6. To add further Custom Fields click the Add Custom Field button. Further blank fields become available.

7. Save or Publish your post when you are ready. Your custom field information is saved in the database with the post. The fields will not display until you edit the blog's theme, as explained at the end of this chapter.

To edit custom fields

1. Log in to the Dashboard.

2. Edit an existing post in the usual way.

3. Scroll down to the Custom Fields area below the Uploads box.

4. If necessary, click the plus sign in the blue header area to reveal the Custom Fields area (**Figure 65**).

5. Edit the contents of the Key and / or Value field.

6. Click the Update button. The Key and/or Value field changes are saved in the database.

To delete custom fields

1. Log in to the Dashboard.

2. Edit an existing post in the usual way.

3. Scroll down to the Custom Fields area below the Uploads box.

4. If necessary, click the plus sign in the blue header area to reveal the Custom Fields area (**Figure 65**).

5. Click the Delete button in the Action column beside the Key and Value pair you wish to delete. The Key and Value pair are removed from the post.

EDITING & DELETING CUSTOM FIELDS

To display custom fields

1. Open the theme file you wish to edit, for example: wp-content/themes/default/index.php.

2. Move the cursor to the point where you wish the custom fields to display, for example, above or below the postmetadata section below the body of the post (**Figure 66**).

3. Add in this code: `<?php the_meta(); ?>`.

4. Save the edited theme file to the server. Any custom fields will be displayed as list items below the post.

5. View a post with custom fields to confirm it is working as expected (**Figure 67**).

To style custom fields

1. Open the style sheet for the theme your blog uses, for example: wp-content/themes/default/style.css.

2. Add rules for .post-meta, .post-meta li and .post-meta-key (**Figure 68**).

3. Example:

   ```
   .post-meta { font-style: italic; }

   .post-meta li { list-style-image:
   url(images/asterisk_yellow.png); }

   .post-meta-key { font-style: normal; }
   ```

4. Save the style sheet to the server. Any custom fields will be styled according to the new rules.

5. View a post with custom fields to confirm it is working as expected (**Figure 69**).

✔ Tip

■ If you use an image as the list marker, as in the coding above, you need to make sure you have uploaded an image of the same name to the location defined in the style.

```
◀ ▶  index.php ▾

        <?php while (have_posts()) : the_post(); ?>
        <div class="post" id="post-<?php the_ID(); ?>">
            <h2><a href="<?php the_permalink() ?>" rel="bookmark"
title="Permanent Link to <?php the_title(); ?>"><?php the_title(); ?></a></h2>
            <small><?php the_time('F jS, Y') ?> <!-- by <?php the_author()
?> --></small>

            <div class="entry">
                <?php the_content('Read the rest of this entry &raquo;'); ?>
            </div>
            <?php the_meta(); ?>
```

Just another post

April 30th, 2006

I've been too busy writing a book to blog much lately.

- Music: Elena
- TV Show: Futurama

Posted in Uncategorized | Edit | No Comments »

Figures 66 & 67 Add the code to index.php to display the custom fields. Here I've added it just below the post entry (top). When I view the Home Page my custom fields are listed below the post in a very plain list (bottom).

```
/* End Various Tags & Classes*/

.post-meta { font-style: italic; }
.post-meta li { list-style-image: url(images/asterisk_yellow.png); }
.post-meta-key { font-style: normal; }

/* "Daisy, Daisy, give me your answer do. I'm half crazy all for the love of
you.
    It won't be a stylish marriage, I can't afford a carriage.
    But you'll look sweet upon the seat of a bicycle built for two." */
```

Figure 68 Add rules to the style sheet to style the display of the custom fields.

Just another post

April 30th, 2006

I've been too busy writing a book to blog much lately.

❋ Music: *Elena*
❋ TV Show: *Futurama*

Posted in Uncategorized | Edit | No Comments »

Figure 69 Adding styles for the custom fields makes them more attractive.

Online Resources

Online Resources

The following is a list of Web sites and pages mentioned throughout this book. Consult these resources for up-to-date information, software products, or examples of WordPress in action.

WordPress Information

WordPress information:
wordpress.org

WordPress.com:
wordpress.com

WordPress.com support:
faq.wordpress.com

WordPress Codex:
codex.wordpress.org

WordPress forums:
wordpress.org/support

Introduction to Blogging:
codex.wordpress.org/Introduction_to_
blogging

WordPress server requirements:
wordpress.org/about/requirements

WordPress compatible Web hosts:
wordpress.org/hosting

Words that commonly appear in spam comments:
codex.wordpress.org/Spam_Words

Using images:
codex.wordpress.org/Using_Images

Codex themes information:
codex.wordpress.org/Using_Themes

Featured themes, links to lists of themes:
wordpress.org/extend/themes

Templates information:
codex.wordpress.org/Templates

Codex template tags information:
codex.wordpress.org/Template_Tags

Template hierarchy:
codex.wordpress.org/Template_Hierarchy

Plugins information:
codex.wordpress.org/Plugins

Plugin directory:
wordpress.org/extend

Importing content into WordPress:
codex.wordpress.org/Importing_Content

Custom fields:
codex.wordpress.org/Plugins/Meta

Other Resources

Aggregators

FeedDemon:
feeddemon.com

iTunes:
apple.com/itunes

NetNewsWire:
ranchero.com/netnewswire

Newsgator Online:
newsgator.com

Wizz RSS News Reader extension for Firefox:
addons.mozilla.org/firefox/424

Blogging tools

BlogJet:
blogjet.com

Ecto:
ecto.kung-foo.tv

MarsEdit:
ranchero.com

w.bloggar:
wbloggar.com

Browsers

Firefox:
www.getfirefox.com

Web Colors

An online list of color codes:
www.december.com/html/spec/colorhslhex.html

Favicons

Create a favicon:
www.chami.com/html-kit/services/favicon

Google AdSense

Google AdSense:
www.google.com/adsense

Macromedia Flash

Macromedia Flash Player plugin:
www.macromedia.com/flashplayer

MySQL

CocoaMySQL-SBG client:
www.theonline.org/cocoamysql

MySQL & MySQL Administrator:
www.mysql.com

SQLyog client:
www.webyog.com/sqlyog/index_sqlyogfree.php

OPML

Outline Processor Markup Language (OPML):
www.opml.org

PHP

PHP:
www.php.net

Ping and other services

Learn more about Ping-o-Matic and other services:
codex.wordpress.org/Update_Services

Plugins

Adhesive:
redalt.com/wiki/adhesive

CG-Feedread:
www.chait.net/index.php?p=238

Customizable Post Listings:
www.coffee2code.com/
archives/2004/08/27/plugin-
customizable-post-listings

Duh Gallery:
blog.perfectspace.com/2006/03/28/
duh-gallery-the-simple-wordpress-
photo-gallery-plugin

Event Calendar:
blog.firetree.net/2005/07/18/
eventcalendar-30

Exec-PHP:
www.soeren-weber.net/post/2005/08/18/50

Jerome's Keywords Plugin:
vapourtrails.ca/wp-keywords

PodPress:
www.mightyseek.com/podpress

Random Header:
www.martinet.nl/wp-site/random-header-
plugin

Search Pages Plugin:
randomfrequency.net/wordpress/
search-pages

Spam Karma:
unknowngenius.com/blog/wordpress/
spam-karma

Static front page:
semiologic.com/software/static-front

Subscribe to comments:
txfx.net/code/wordpress/subscribe-
to-comments

WordPress Contact Form:
ryanduff.net/projects/wp-contactform

WP-Cron and WP-Cron-Mail plugins:
www.skippy.net/blog/category/wordpress/
plugins/wp-cron

WP-Shortstat:
jrm.cc/archives/blog/wp-shortstat

Robots.txt files

Learn about robots.txt files:
www.searchtools.com/robots/robots-txt.
html

RSS feeds

RSS feed icons:
www.feedicons.com

Validators

Validate CSS files:
jigsaw.w3.org/css-validator

Validate web pages:
validator.w3.org

Ben Hammersley's tool to validate RSS feeds:
www.benhammersley.com/tools/xhtml_
validator_to_rss.html

Web servers

Apache:
`httpd.apache.org`

Litespeed:
`litespeedtech.com`

XFN

XHTML Friends Network (**XFN**):
`gmpg.org/xfn`

Blogs

Maria Langer, the Official Web Site & WebLog
`marialanger.com`

wickenburg-az.com:
`wickenburg-az.com`

Miraz Jordan:
`mactips.info`

Camden Lady (new site):
`camdenkiwi.org`

Captain's Quarters:
`www.captainsquartersblog.com`

Daily Kos:
`www.dailykos.com`

Using FTP

Using FTP

Transferring files between your computer and the server is fundamental to installing and customizing a WordPress server installation. You transfer files with File Transfer Protocol (FTP) client software such as FileZilla or CuteFTP on Windows and Fetch or CuteFTP on Mac OS.

You use FTP client software to put or upload files from your local computer to a remote server. You also use it to get or download files on the remote server to your local computer. Much of the FTP terminology dates back to the days of command line interfaces; fortunately, there are several graphic user interface programs that make FTPing files easy.

In this appendix, we provide some basic information for using our preferred FTP client software applications. We explain how to copy files to and from a server and how to use FTP software to set file permissions, rename files, and delete files.

✔ Tips

■ To access your site with FTP client software you need three pieces of information you can get from your ISP or system administrator:

  ◆ The FTP address
  ◆ Your FTP user name or ID
  ◆ Your FTP password

■ For additional information about using specific software, consult its documentation.

■ Although this chapter only covers three popular programs, it should provide enough information to get you started if you choose a different FTP client.

FileZilla

FileZilla (**Figure 1**) is a simple and fast FTP client for Windows. Distributed as Open Source software, it can be downloaded from sourceforge.net/projects/filezilla.

To connect to a remote server

1. Start FileZilla.

2. If the Quick Connect bar is not visible choose View > Quick Connect Bar.

3. In the Quick Connect bar, enter your FTP login information (**Figure 2**):

   ▲ **Address** is the FTP server address.

   ▲ **User** is your user name or ID.

   ▲ **Password** is your password.

   ▲ **Port**, which is optional, is for entering a non-standard port. In most cases, you can leave this blank; FileZilla will fill it in automatically.

4. Click the Quickconnect button. FileZilla connects to the server and displays a list of files and folders in the Remote Site pane (**Figure 3**).

✔ Tips

■ If necessary, you can drag the divider bars between window panes to change your view of each pane's contents.

■ Use the down arrow beside the Quickconnect button to choose previously accessed servers. FileZilla remembers the details from previous connections.

Quick Connect bar

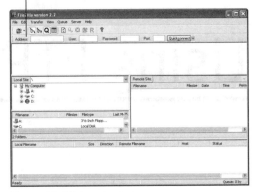

Figure 1 FileZilla's main window.

Figure 2 Enter your access information in the Quick Connect bar.

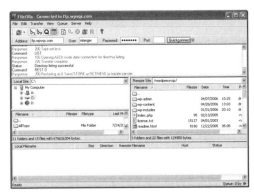

Figure 3 Once connected, the contents of the remote server's directory appear in the Remote Site pane.

USING FILEZILLA

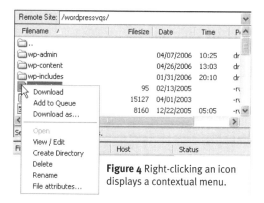

Figure 4 Right-clicking an icon displays a contextual menu.

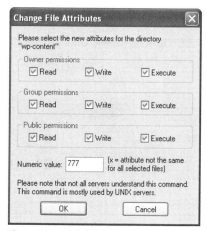

Figure 5 Use this dialog to set permissions with FileZilla.

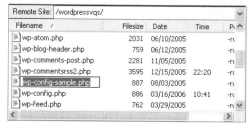

Figure 6 The Rename command puts an edit box around an item's name.

To navigate

Use the following techniques in the Local Site and/or Remote Site panes of the FileZilla window (**Figure 3**):

◆ To open a folder, double-click it.

◆ To back up to a previous folder in the Remote Site pane, double-click the folder with two dots beside it.

◆ To go to a specific folder, enter the path to the folder in the edit box at the top of the pane.

To change permissions

1. Display the contents of the folder in which the file or folder resides.

2. Right-click the file or folder for which you want to change permissions.

3. Choose File attributes from the contextual menu that appears (**Figure 4**).

4. In the Change File Attributes dialog (**Figure 5**), use the check boxes or Numeric value field to set permissions.

5. Click OK. The permissions are updated.

✔ Tip

■ We tell you more about permissions in **Chapter 6**.

To rename a file or folder

1. Display the contents of the folder in which the file or folder resides.

2. Right-click the file or folder for which you want to change the name.

3. Choose Rename from the contextual menu that appears (**Figure 4**). The file name is selected (**Figure 6**).

4. Enter a new name and press [Enter]. The name is changed.

To delete a file or folder

1. Display the contents of the folder in which the file or folder resides.

2. Right-click the file or folder you want to delete and choose Delete from the contextual menu (**Figure 4**). A confirmation dialog appears (**Figure 7**).

3. Click Yes to delete the item.

To transfer files or folders

1. In the Local Site and Remote Site panes, navigate to the folders in which you want to put or get files or folders.

2. To download files or folders, drag their icons from the Remote Site pane to the Local Site pane.

    or

    To upload files or folders, drag their icons from the Local Site pane to the Remote Site pane (**Figure 8**).

3. Wait while the transfer is conducted. When it's finished, the Status area near the top of the FileZilla window should display a *Transfer complete* message (**Figure 9**).

✔ Tips

- Dragging items on top of a folder in a window copies the files into that folder.

- If the file already exists in the destination location, a dialog like the one in **Figure 10** appears. Select the appropriate action option on the right side of the dialog and click OK to complete the transfer.

Figure 7 Click Yes in this dialog to delete the file.

Figure 8 Drag a file from one pane to the other.

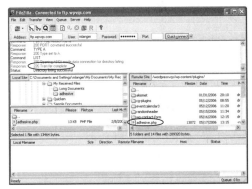

Figure 9 You'll see a Transfer complete message and the file you copied will appear in the destination pane.

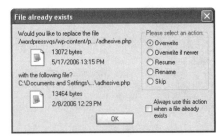

Figure 10 Use this dialog to tell FileZilla what to do if a file already exists.

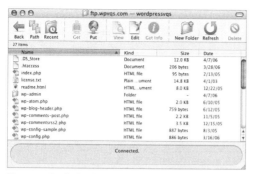

Figure 11 Fetch displays a remote folder's contents in a window like this one.

Figure 12 The New Connection dialog with options set for a connection.

Figure 13 Click the triangle to display additional options you might want to set, as shown here.

Using Fetch

Fetch (**Figure 11**) is an easy-to-use, affordable FTP client for Mac OS. Created and distributed by Fetch Softworks, you can download it from www.fetchsoftworks.com.

To connect to a remote server

1. Launch Fetch.

2. If necessary, choose File > New Connection or press ⌘N to display the New Connection dialog (**Figure 12**).

3. Enter your FTP login information:
   ▲ **Hostname** is the FTP server address.
   ▲ **Username** is your user name or ID.
   ▲ **Connect using** is the method of connection. Normally, this will be FTP.
   ▲ **Password** is your password. You can turn on the Add to keychain check box to add your FTP password for the site to your Mac OS Keychain.

4. To specify an initial folder and set other options, click the blue triangle to expand the dialog (**Figure 13**) and enter additional options:
   ▲ **Initial folder** is the remote folder you want to open when you first connect.
   ▲ **Port**, which is optional, is for entering a non-standard port.
   ▲ **Try to connect** *n* **times** specifies the number of connection attempts that should be made.

5. Click the Connect button. Fetch connects to the server and displays a list of files and folders (**Figure 11**).

USING FETCH

To navigate a remote server

In the Fetch file window (**Figure 11**), use the following navigation techniques:

◆ Double-click a folder to open it.

◆ To return to a recently visited directory choose a location from the Recent menu on the toolbar (**Figure 14**).

◆ To back up one folder, click the back button on the toolbar.

◆ To back up to another folder in the hierarchy, choose a location from the Path menu on the toolbar (**Figure 15**).

To add a shortcut

1. View the remote directory for which you want to create a shortcut.

2. Choose Shortcuts > New Shortcut to display the New Shortcut dialog (**Figure 16**).

3. Check, and if necessary, modify the settings in the New Shortcut dialog.

4. Click OK. The new shortcut is saved.

✔ Tip

■ Give the Shortcut a clear and memorable name.

To use a shortcut

Choose the shortcut name from the Shortcuts menu (**Figure 17**). The remote folder set in the shortcut opens.

Figure 14 Use the Recent menu to revisit a recently viewed folder.

Figure 15
Use the Path menu to back up to a previous folder.

Figure 16 Use this dialog to create a new shortcut.

Figure 17
To open a remote location quickly, choose it from the Shortcuts menu.

Figure 18 The Info window for a folder.

To change permissions

1. Display the contents of the folder in which the file or folder resides.

2. Select the file or folder for which you want to change permissions.

3. Choose Remote > Get Info or press ⌃ ⌘ I.

4. In the Info window that appears, if necessary, click the disclosure triangle to expand the Ownership and Permissions area (**Figure 18**).

5. Use the check boxes or UNIX equivalent edit box to set permissions as desired.

6. Click Apply. The permissions are updated.

7. Close the Info window.

To rename a file or folder

1. Display the contents of the folder in which the file or folder resides.

2. Select the file or folder for which you want to change the name.

3. Choose Remote > Get Info.

4. In the Info window that appears, if necessary, click the disclosure triangle to expand the Name and Extension area (**Figure 18**).

5. Change the name in the Name and Extension text box.

6. Click Apply. The name is updated.

7. Close the Info window.

USING FETCH

To delete a file or folder

1. Display the contents of the folder in which the file or folder resides.

2. Select the file or folder you want to delete.

3. Click the Delete button on the toolbar. A confirmation dialog appears (**Figure 19**).

4. Click Delete to delete the selected item.

To transfer files or folders

1. In the Fetch window, navigate to the folder in which you want to put or get files or folders.

2. In the Finder, navigate to the folder in which you want to put or get files or folders.

3. To download files or folders, drag their icons from the Fetch window to the Finder window or Desktop.

   or

   To upload files or folders, drag their icons from the Finder window to the Fetch window (**Figure 20**).

4. Wait while the transfer is conducted. When it's finished, the status area at the bottom of the Fetch window should display a *Transfer complete* message (**Figure 21**).

✔ Tip

■ Dragging items on top of a folder in a window copies the files into that folder.

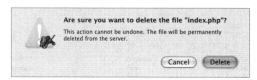

Figure 19 Click Delete in this dialog to confirm the deletion of a file.

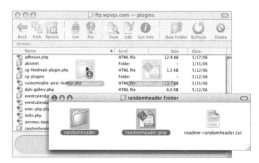

Figure 20 Drag files from a Finder window to a Fetch transfer window to upload them.

Figure 21 When the transfer is complete, Fetch tells you.

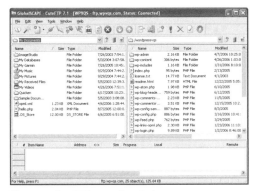

Figure 22 CuteFTP's transfer window.

Figure 23 The Site Manager window in Windows before adding any sites.

Figure 24 Connection details for a site appear on the right side of the Site Manager window when the site is selected.

CuteFTP

CuteFTP (**Figure 22**) is an FTP client with versions for Windows and Mac OS. There are two levels of CuteFTP: Home and Pro. For Windows, the Home version offers enough features to work with WordPress successfully. For Mac OS, you need the Pro version to change file permissions. Distributed by GlobalSCAPE, CuteFTP can be downloaded from www.globalscape.com.

To create a new site in the Site Manager

1. Start or launch CuteFTP.

2. If the Site Manager window (**Figure 23**) is not showing, choose Tools > Site Manager > Display Site Manager (Windows) or File > Site Manager (Mac OS).

3. In Windows, click the New button and choose FTP Site from the pop-up menu that appears.

   or

   In Mac OS, click the New Site button.

4. In the form on the right side of the window, enter your FTP login information (**Figure 24**):

   ▲ **Label** is a name for the remote site connection.

   ▲ **Host address** (Windows) or **Host name** (Mac OS) is the FTP server address.

   ▲ **Username** (Windows) or **User name** (Mac OS) is your user name or ID.

   ▲ **Password** is your password.

   ▲ **Port** (Mac OS only) is the FTP connection port. This is usually 21.

   ▲ **Login method** (Windows) or **Login type** (Mac OS) is the type of connection. Choose Normal.

✔ Tip

■ You only have to go through this process once for each site you connect to. CuteFTP saves your settings.

273

To connect to a remote site

1. In the Site Manager window, select the name of the site to which you want to connect (**Figure 25**).

2. Click Connect.

   The Site manager window disappears and the CuteFTP window appears. It displays the local computer's contents on the left and the remote computer's contents on the right (**Figure 22** or **26**).

To navigate

Use the following techniques in the two panes of the CuteFTP window (**Figure 22** or **26**):

◆ To open a folder, double-click it.

◆ To back up to a previous folder, choose a folder from the drop-down list (Windows) or pop-up menu (Mac OS; **Figure 27**) at the top of the file list.

◆ In Windows, to go to a specific folder, enter the path to the folder in the box at the top of the file list.

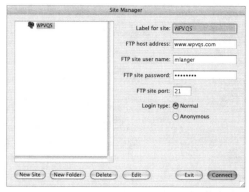

Figure 25 The Site Manager window in Mac OS with one site added.

Figure 26 CuteFTP's file transfer window on Mac OS.

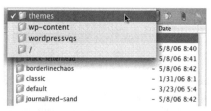

Figure 27 Choose a previous folder from the pop-up menu.

Figures 28a & 28b You can use the Properties dialog in Windows (top) or the Permissions info window in Mac OS (bottom) to change an item's permissions.

To change permissions

1. Display the contents of the folder in which the file or folder resides.

2. Select the file or folder for which you want to change permissions.

3. In Windows, choose File > Properties to display the Properties dialog (**Figure 28a**).

   or

   On Mac OS, choose File > Get Info to display the Info window for the item. Then click the Permissions button to display the item's permissions (**Figure 28b**).

4. Use the check boxes or text box to set permissions.

5. In Windows, click OK.

   or

   On Mac OS, click Set. Then close the window.

   The permissions are updated.

✔ Tips

- We tell you more about permissions in **Chapter 6**.

- Remember, if you're a Mac user, you must have the Pro version of CuteFTP, which is illustrated here, to change permissions.

To rename a file or folder

1. Display the contents of the folder in which the file or folder resides.

2. Select the file or folder for which you want to change the name.

3. Click the Rename button in the toolbar

   In Windows, an edit box appears around the name, which becomes selected (**Figure 29a**).

   or

   On Mac OS, a dialog like the one in **Figure 29b** appears.

4. Enter a new name for the item and press [Enter] (Windows) or click OK (Mac OS). The name is changed.

To delete a file or folder

1. Display the contents of the folder in which the file or folder resides.

2. Select the file or folder you want to delete.

3. Click the Delete button in the toolbar. A confirmation dialog appears (**Figure 30**).

4. Click Yes to delete the item.

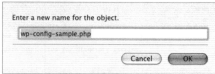

Figures 29a & 29b The Rename button puts an edit box around the file name in Windows (top) and displays a dialog for renaming the file in Mac OS (bottom).

Figure 30 You must click Yes in a confirmation dialog like this one to delete a file.

Figure 31 Drag the items from one pane to the other to copy them.

Figure 32 CuteFTP tells you when the transfer is complete.

To transfer files or folders

1. In the local and remote panes, navigate to the folders in which you want to put or get files or folders.

2. To download files or folders, drag their icons from the remote pane to the local pane.

   or

   To upload files or folders, drag their icons from the local pane to the remote pane (**Figure 31**).

3. Wait while the transfer is conducted. When it's finished, the status area near the top of the CuteFTP window should display a *Transfer complete* message (**Figure 32**).

✔ Tip

- Dragging items on top of a folder in a window copies the files into that folder.

Using Text Editors

Text Editors

Throughout this book, we provide instructions for customizing your blog by modifying theme files. Although WordPress's built-in theme editor enables you to edit files via a WordPress administration panel interface, using a text editor on your computer offers a great deal more flexibility and power.

There are two ways to modify your blog's theme files with a text editor:

- ◆ Use FTP software to download the file to your computer, edit the file and save changes with a text editor, and upload it to the server via FTP, thus overwriting the original file. **Appendix B** explains how to use FTP.

- ◆ Use a text editor with built-in FTP capabilities to open the file directly from the server, edit it, and save changes directly to the server. This technique makes editing a file on the server as easy as working with a file on your own computer.

In this appendix, we provide basic instructions for setting up and using two popular text editor programs, each of which includes built-in FTP capabilities: Chami.com's HTML-Kit for Windows and Bare Bones Software's TextWrangler for Mac OS.

✔ Tips

- ■ It's a good idea to back up a file before editing it. Then, if your edits mess up the file, you can simply replace the bad file with a known working copy.

- ■ Do *not* use a word processing application such as Microsoft Word to edit theme files. Doing so may introduce additional characters that could cause errors in your edited files.

Text Editor Settings

Most text editors offer options or preferences for how text is displayed. We suggest enabling the following options:

◆ **Line numbers** can help you find specific lines in a theme file. This is often helpful when instructions for a plugin refer to a specific line code that requires editing.

◆ **Invisible** or **non-printing characters** make it possible to clearly see spaces, tabs, and other characters that may or may not need to be present.

◆ **Syntax coloring** displays code and other content in a variety of colors, making it easier to distinguish various file content. Syntax coloring can also help you identify "broken" PHP or HTML coding.

◆ **Wrap text to window** prevents you from having to scroll horizontally to edit text on a long line.

In this Appendix, we explain how to enable these features in both HTML-Kit and Text-Wrangler. If you use a different text editor, use the Options or Preferences command or consult the software's documentation to learn how to enable these features.

✔ Tip

■ With syntax coloring enabled, when editing a file, watch for any text which seems to be in the "wrong" color. This usually indicates that you have an unclosed or invalid HTML tag or PHP command.

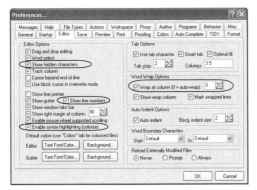

Figure 1 The Editor tab of HTML-Kit's Preferences dialog.

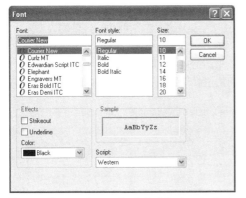

Figure 2 You can change the default font and color in the Font dialog.

HTML-Kit

Chami.com's HTML-Kit is a popular text editing program for Windows users. It can be used to edit text files on your computer or on a server.

In the following instructions, we introduce HTML-Kit. We explain how to configure it for working with WordPress theme files, as discussed on the previous page, how to set it up to access a server via built-in FTP, and how to open and save files.

To learn more about HTML-Kit and download a copy, visit www.chami.com/html-kit/.

To configure HTML-Kit

1. Start HTML-Kit.

2. Click the Cancel button in the Open file Wizard to dismiss the dialog.

3. Choose Edit > Preferences.

4. In the Preferences window that appears, click the Editor tab to display its options (**Figure 1**).

5. Turn on check boxes for the following options:

   ▲ Show hidden characters

   ▲ Show line numbers

   ▲ Enable syntax highlighting (colorize)

6. Under Word Wrap Options, turn on the Wrap at column check box and enter 0 in the text box beside it.

7. Click OK. The settings are saved and the Preferences window closes.

✔ Tip

■ To change text colors, click the Text Font/Color button beside Editor at the bottom or the Preferences dialog (**Figure 1**), set options in the Font dialog that appears (**Figure 2**), and click OK.

To add an FTP server

1. In HTML-Kit, choose Workspace > Add Folder / FTP Server > Add FTP Server. The Add FTP Server dialog appears.

2. If necessary, click the FTP Properties tab to display its options (**Figure 3**).

3. Enter the FTP server login information provided by your ISP or system administrator. At a minimum, you need the following information (**Figure 4**):
   ▲ Server address
   ▲ Login user name
   ▲ Password

4. Click OK. The server is added to the list of files in the Workspace pane on the right side of the window (**Figure 5**).

To open a file on a server

1. In HTML-Kit, if necessary, choose View > Workspace to view the Workspace pane's file list (**Figure 5**).

2. Click the + button beside the server for which you want to view files. The directory expands to list the files and folders it contains (**Figure 6**).

3. Click the + buttons beside folders to navigate through the hierarchy of files and locate the file you want to edit.

4. Double-click the name of the file you want to edit. It opens in an editing window (**Figure 7**).

✔ Tip

■ To create a larger working space within the Editor window, maximize the HTML-Kit window.

Figure 3 Use this dialog to add details for accessing your blog's files via FTP.

Figure 4 Here's an example of the required settings.

Figure 5 The Workspace pane with an FTP server added.

Figure 6 Opening an FTP server displays its files.

ADDING FTP SERVERS, OPENING SERVER FILES

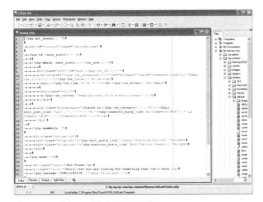

Figure 7 Editing a file in HTML-Kit.

To make changes to a file

1. If necessary, click the Editor tab at the bottom of the file's window to display file contents (**Figure 7**).

2. Make changes to the file's contents using standard text editing techniques.

To save a file

Choose File > Save, or press Ctrl S. One of two things happens:

◆ If you opened the file from the server, HTML-Kit copies the edited file back to the server, replacing the previous version.

◆ If you opened a file from your hard drive HTML-Kit saves the file to your hard drive, replacing the previous version.

✔ Tip

■ Be careful about saving to a live site—saved changes take effect immediately. If the saved file includes unfinished changes, your blog may be temporarily broken.

TextWrangler

Bare Bones Software's TextWrangler is a popular text editing application for Mac OS users. It can be used to edit text files on your computer or on a server.

In the following instructions, we introduce TextWrangler. We explain how to configure it for working with WordPress theme files, as discussed earlier in this chapter, how to set it up to access a server via built-in FTP, and how to open and save files.

To learn more about TextWrangler and download a copy, visit www.barebones.com/products/textwrangler/.

To configure TextWrangler

1. Launch TextWrangler.

2. Choose TextWrangler > Preferences to display the TextWrangler Preferences window.

3. In the list on the left side of the window, click Editor Defaults to display its options (**Figure 8**).

4. Turn on the check boxes for the following options:
   - ▲ Show Invisibles
   - ▲ Show Spaces
   - ▲ Syntax Coloring

5. Turn on the check box for Soft Wrap Text. Then select the Window Width radio button.

6. In the list on the left side of the window, click Text Status Display to display its options (**Figure 9**).

7. Turn on the check box for Show Line Numbers.

8. Close the TextWrangler Preferences window. Your changes are saved.

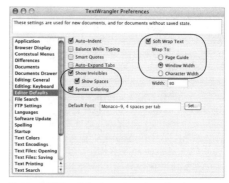

Figure 8 Editor defaults set options for the text editing window.

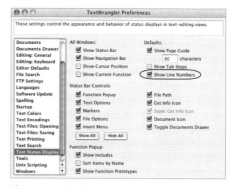

Figure 9 Enable line number display in the Text Status Display preferences.

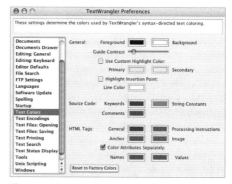

Figure 10 You can change text coloring options in Text Colors preferences.

✔ Tip

- ■ To change the colors used for Syntax Coloring, set options in Text Colors preferences (**Figure 10**).

Figure 11 The Open from FTP/SFTP Server dialog.

Figure 12 TextWrangler connects to the server and displays the contents of the remote directory.

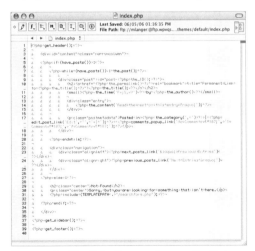

Figure 13 Double-click a file name to open the file in TextWrangler for editing.

Figure 14 Enter a name for a bookmark.

To open a file on a server

1. In TextWrangler, choose File > Open from FTP/SFTP Server to display the Open From FTP/SFTP Server dialog (**Figure 11**).

2. Enter the FTP server login information provided by your ISP or system administrator. At a minimum, you need the following information:
   - ▲ Server
   - ▲ User name
   - ▲ Password

3. Click Connect. The navigation panel displays a list of files and folders on the server (**Figure 12**).

4. Use standard Open dialog navigation techniques to locate and open the folder containing the document you want to edit.

5. Double-click the name of the file you want to edit. The file opens in a Text-Wrangler editing window (**Figure 13**).

✔ Tips

- After step 4, to quickly access the same directory again, choose Add Bookmark from the Bookmarks pop-up menu in the dialog. In the Bookmark Name dialog that appears (**Figure 14**), enter a name for the bookmark—perhaps the name of the directory—and click Add. From then on, you can quickly open that directory by choosing its bookmark from the Bookmarks pop-up menu.

- If you turn on the Remember Password and Auto-Connect check boxes, the next time you use the Open from FTP/SFTP server command, you'll automatically open the last accessed server directory. This also enables you to open recently used files from the Open Recent submenu under the File menu.

To make changes to a file

In the TextWrangler editing window (**Figure 13**), use standard text editing techniques to make changes to the file.

To save a file

Choose File > Save, or press ⌃⌘S. One of two things happens:

◆ If you opened the file from the server, TextWrangler copies the edited file back to the server, replacing the previous version.

◆ If you opened a file from your hard drive TextWrangler saves the file to your hard disk, replacing the previous version.

✔ Tip

■ Be careful about saving to a live site—saved changes take effect immediately. If the saved file includes unfinished changes, your blog may be temporarily broken.

EDITING & SAVING FILES

Index

INDEX